Making Amends

Making Amends

LINDA RADZIK

Atonement in Morality, Law, and Politics

OXFORD
UNIVERSITY PRESS

Oxford University Press, Inc., publishes works that further
Oxford University's objective of excellence
in research, scholarship, and education.

Oxford   New York
Auckland   Cape Town   Dar es Salaam   Hong Kong   Karachi
Kuala Lumpur   Madrid   Melbourne   Mexico City   Nairobi
New Delhi   Shanghai   Taipei   Toronto

With offices in
Argentina   Austria   Brazil   Chile   Czech Republic   France   Greece
Guatemala   Hungary   Italy   Japan   Poland   Portugal   Singapore
South Korea   Switzerland   Thailand   Turkey   Ukraine   Vietnam

Published by Oxford University Press, Inc.
198 Madison Avenue, New York, New York 10016

www.oup.com

Oxford is a registered trademark of Oxford University Press

Library of Congress Cataloging-in-Publication Data

Radzik, Linda, 1970–
Making amends : atonement in morality, law, and politics / Linda Radzik.
    p. cm.
Includes bibliographical references.
ISBN 978-0-19-537366-0 (hardcover)
ISBN 978-0-19-976725-0 (pbk)
1. Responsibility. 2. Atonement. 3. Reparation (Criminal justice) 4. Restitution.
5. Reconciliation. 6. Restorative justice. 7. penance. I. Title.
BJ1451.R33 2009
170—dc22   2008029039

Printed in the United States of America
on acid-free paper

For my parents, Leo and Margie Radzik

ACKNOWLEDGMENTS

I N 2004–2005 I was the fortunate recipient of a fellowship from the Alexander von Humboldt Foundation, which supported this work. At a conference of Humboldt fellows held in June, 2005, I learned that the foundation itself and its support for international cooperation among scholars is meant to be a form of amends for the perversion of science and scholarship that took place under the Nazi regime. I hope that this work honors the spirit of that project.

I owe many thanks to Professor Otfried Höffe at the Eberhard Karls Universität in Tübingen, Germany, for his hospitality, wisdom, and encouragement during my fellowship year. A faculty development leave from Texas A&M University enabled me to accept the fellowship. The Glasscock Center for Humanities Research at Texas A&M also provided financial support and lively audiences for this work. I was a visiting faculty member at the University of Minnesota when I first conceived this project, and I benefited greatly from my interactions with the students and faculty, especially the 3M reading group. Colleen Murphy and Christopher Bennett both commented on significant portions of the manuscript, and I am very grateful for their help. For their input, support, and encouragement over the life of this project I also offer sincere thanks to Ashley Currier, Norman Dahl, Susan Egenolf, Marian Eide, Elisabeth Ellis, Daniel E. Farnham, Theodore George, Heather J. Gert, Richard J. Golsan, Michael Hand, Thomas E. Hill Jr., Gerry Johnstone, Jacquelyn Ann Kegley, Katherine Kelly, Pamela E. Klassen, Avery Kolers, Michael LeBuffe, Shaun Longstreet, John W. Marshall, John J. McDermott, Geoffrey Sayre McCord, Prudence Rose, Roger Sansom, David Schmidtz, Robin Smith, Daniel Van Ness, Gary Varner, and Joan Wolf.

Special thanks and love go to Robert R. Shandley, my partner in all of life's adventures, philosophy included. He discussed every aspect of this project with me over and over again, at all hours and through every wild change in my mood. His patience and good sense were invaluable. Our daughter, Mary Shandley, shared her keen sense of fairness with me and kept me from making at least one major mistake. I look forward to even more help from her as she enters second grade. This book is dedicated to my parents, Leo and Margie Radzik, who gave me the opportunity to be a student and the confidence to be a teacher.

Some of the material in the book is drawn from essays I have published previously. Parts of chapters 2 and 4 appeared in "Making Amends," *American Philosophical Quarterly* 41, no. 2 (2004): 141–54. Portions of chapter 5 are drawn from "Do Wrongdoers Have a Right to Make Amends?" *Social Theory and Practice* 29, no. 2 (2003): 325–41. Most of chapter 6 and part of chapter 1 appeared as "Offenders, the Making of Amends, and the State," in Gerry Johnstone and Daniel W. Van Ness, eds., *The Handbook of Restorative Justice* (Portland, Ore.: Willan, 2007), 192–207. I thank the publishers for their permission to use this work.

CONTENTS

Making Amends

CHAPTER ONE | An Ethic for Wrongdoers

1.1   Introduction

Our moral theories should tell us not just what is right and what is wrong but also how to deal with wrongdoing once it occurs. Wrongdoing does not remain isolated in time. The effects and significance of a wrongful act often continue to upset the lives of those involved by causing resentment or guilt, injury or self-hatred, a desire for revenge, or an impulse to rationalize. Moreover, past violations lead to future transgressions both in private life and in the history of peoples. But the painful and dangerous legacy of wrongdoing can be rectified. As Herbert Morris notes, "wrongdoing arises in a world in which there is a conception of righting the wrong. It arises in a world in which persons possess a conception not just of separation from others but [also] of coming together again with them."[1] The goal of this book is to present a systematic examination and defense of the claims that wrongs can be righted and that amends must be made.

My hope is that this work will complement other philosophical research on the moral issues that arise in the wake of wrongdoing: work on forgiveness, mercy, moral emotions, punishment, reparations for historical injustice, and transitional justice in societies emerging from periods of repression or conflict. However, this project is distinct from the vast majority of the literature on the aftermath of wrongdoing in that it focuses on the wrongdoer. While philosophers usually ask what other people should do with wrongdoers, I ask what morality demands of the wrongdoers themselves. The benefits of this approach, I believe, are not just theoretical but ethical as well. By almost always taking the point of view of either a judge or a victim, the philosophical literature risks treating wrongdoers as people who must be handled in some way rather than as moral agents who are capable of appropriate and meaningful responses.

The lack of philosophical attention to the concept of making amends—or what one might call "atonement"—surely has many explanations. Chief among these, I suspect, is skepticism about whether wrongdoers are capable of doing anything that can be characterized as righting their wrongs. Moral change is possible. We can become better people in the future, but can we ever make up for the past? Literary and filmic treatments of atonement often leave one feeling skeptical. In these stories, attempts to atone are frequently represented as either doomed (*The Mayor of Casterbridge*),[2] tragic (*The Virginian*),[3] unhealthy (*Sex, Lies, and Videotape*),[4] absurd (television's *My Name Is Earl*),[5] or wildly implausible by requiring wrongdoers to perform heroic tasks. My favorite example of this last type is the Douglas Sirk melodrama *Magnificent Obsession*.[6] In the story, millionaire playboy Bob Merrick (played by Rock Hudson) is partially responsible both for the death of Helen Phillips's husband and the loss of Helen's sight through a "brain fracture." Bob manages to redeem himself and win Helen's heart by becoming a world-renowned and uniquely skilled brain surgeon (apparently within the space of five years) and repairing Helen's damaged brain just hours before the fracture would have caused her death.

Despite the lack of credibility that atonement may be given in philosophy and art, however, I believe it is part of our ordinary moral experience. Victims and communities frequently demand atoning actions, and wrongdoers often perform them with apparent success. We manage to put our pasts behind us through apologies, gestures of respect, and acts of self-sacrifice. The challenge is to develop a philosophical account that identifies, explains, and justifies such interactions and that helps us to explore the possibilities and limits of atonement in human relationships.

In this chapter I introduce the concept of making amends by considering the language we use in talking about wrongdoers' responses to their misdeeds. I also examine several different sources of skepticism about the possibility and advisability of developing a moral theory of atonement. Some of these doubts will be fully answered only when we have developed a satisfactory theory of what it takes to right a wrong. The arguments provided in this chapter, however, should motivate the search for such a theory.

In following chapters I formulate and evaluate a number of distinct theories of atonement, frequently drawing inspiration from both theological accounts of atonement to God and treatments of criminal punishment in the philosophy of law. I explore the connections among agents' attempts to right their wrongful acts and victims' and communities' responses to wrongdoing, such as forgiveness and criminal sanctions. The book discusses the proper role of atonement in a broad spectrum of contexts—from cases of relatively minor wrongs in personal relationships to crimes and the historical injustices of our political and religious communities. In all of these contexts, I argue, a proper understanding of the correction of wrongdoing requires a proper understanding of wrongdoing, one that includes a comprehensive view of its nature, consequences, and symbolic power.

1.2 The Concept of Making Amends

The core moral idea under consideration, put most simply, is this: One who has morally wronged another person must do something about it. Some sort of response—some action or reaction, perhaps internal, perhaps external—is required. The sorts of responses that come to mind include feelings of guilt, remorse, or shame; resolutions to behave better in the future; acknowledgments of wrongdoing and blameworthiness; apologies; self-improvement; acts of restitution or reparation; the performance of good deeds that would otherwise be deemed supererogatory; self-punishment; and voluntary submission to punishment at the hands of an authority. Which particular responses are appropriate in which circumstances are sometimes matters of heated debate, but the basic idea is familiar. When one person wrongs another, the transgressor incurs a moral obligation to respond.[7]

However, even familiar moral claims can be difficult to justify. For example, although most people agree that crimes ought to be punished, there is no consensus as to why this is the case. Indeed, when we consider the language with which we talk about the moral obligations of wrongdoers, these obligations become quite puzzling. We say that wrongdoers must "right the wrong." However, upon reflection, it seems that wrongful acts, once committed, are timelessly wrong. How could an unjust action be transformed into a just deed? Wrongdoers must "clean the slate" by "paying their debts." The term 'amends' comes from an old French word for "pecuniary fines."[8] Yet, the past cannot be erased like accounting records written in chalk upon a slate, nor do most wrongful actions consist of literal debts that admit of literal repayment.

'Expiation' is another term associated with the idea that wrongdoers must respond to their wrongful actions. It is usually defined as a kind of cleansing or purification, a removal of guilt from one's soul. The representation of guilt as pollution that might be washed away is surely (and perhaps has always been) metaphorical, but it is a metaphor with surprising psychological power. In 2006 the journal *Science* published the results of a study that found that people who felt morally compromised were twice as likely to express a desire to wash their hands.[9] The researchers call this the "Macbeth effect" (as in "Out, damned spot!"). Unfortunately, the Macbeth effect might be a bit too effective. Of those subjects who felt morally stained, those who were allowed to clean themselves physically were only about half as likely to volunteer to help a fellow student in need, which would presumably have been a morally better outlet for their guilt.[10]

Another member of this family of concepts is 'atonement,' which has two sets of connotations that are in tension with one another. The *Oxford English Dictionary* defines 'atonement' as "The action of setting at one, or condition of being set at one, after discord or strife."[11] This suggests that the reconciliation of relationships should be the wrongdoer's main goal. The etymology of 'atonement' is 'at-one-ment.'[12] However, when I first happened upon this fact, I did not believe it. For many speakers of English, the word has come to be strongly associated with images of suffering. To atone is to undergo some kind of pain or sacrifice for wrongful acts. A demand for atonement is usually perceived as threatening—a demand for punishment—rather than a call to the resumption of friendly relations. The explanation for this dual set of associations is that suffering has often been demanded as a precondition for reconciliation. Over time, the end and the means have become disassociated.

Talk of "repairing" and "restoring" is commonplace in discussions of the aftermath of wrongdoing. The phrase "to right a wrong" is available to such an interpretation. Perhaps wrongs are "righted" in the sense that ships are "righted." To right a ship is to restore its balance. To right a wrong might be to restore interpersonal balance or to bring a relationship or a community back into harmony. These images of repairing, restoring, balancing, and harmonizing also bring to mind the therapeutic images that we so often use to discuss cases of wrongdoing: We talk of a need for "healing," and wrongs are to be "remedied."

In redressing a wrong, it is often said, the offender hopes for redemption. The term 'redemption' is itself rich in meaning. Its major connotations are religious and usually imply salvation (specifically, from the terrible consequences of sin), liberation (from the bondage of either the devil or one's own sinful nature), ransoming (liberation through purchase), or reconciliation (with God).[13] In more secular contexts, we tend to use the term to suggest a restoration of status, standing, or value. To return one's deposit bottles for money is to "redeem" them. When we speak of "redeeming oneself" after a failure or misstep, we usually have in mind the regaining of one's place in a community. Redemption involves some significant kind of improvement in the deserved evaluation of the wrongdoer. In theological contexts, the term 'redemption' implies the permanent assurance of an ultimate standing. But in secular contexts we can speak of someone as having redeemed himself at one point in time and then having failed again later on or as having redeemed himself in one aspect of his life (say, his profession) while continuing to deserve criticism in another aspect (perhaps in his role as father). In questioning what redemption is and what could earn or merit redemption, we are led to think about the criteria of success for atonement.

This brief examination of the language of making amends foreshadows some of the differences that will surface when we begin to formulate various accounts of and justifications for the moral obligations of wrongdoers. Some accounts will be punitive in character, while others will be more therapeutic or conciliatory. Some will be oriented toward eliminating past wrongs, while others will focus on future good consequences. To discuss these contrasting views, it would be helpful to have some neutral means of talking about wrongdoers' moral obligations that does not favor one interpretation over another. Unfortunately, English does not provide this. For stylistic purposes I have chosen to favor a couple of terms: 'making amends' and 'atonement.' I use both simply to stand for whatever wrongdoers must do in order to respond in a morally proper way to their wrongful acts.

The role of the wrongdoer distinguishes the moral issue of atonement from standard discussions of punishment. Atonement is an action the wrongdoer carries out, whereas punishment is generally something that another person imposes upon the wrongdoer. However, we will give serious attention to the possibility that atonement either is equivalent to or includes *self*-punishment. Submission to punishment might also count as an atoning act insofar as it is a voluntary action of the wrongdoer. So, in theory atonement and punishment are distinct, although in practice it is often difficult to tell them apart. An employee whose boss demands she deliver a humbling apology to a client is one such example. Depending on the details of the case, including the threatened penalty for refusal, the employee's attitude, and the available options, this case might best be described as atonement, punishment, or a bit of both.

In characterizing atonement as a voluntary action of the wrongdoer, I may appear to be begging some substantive questions. Prominent theological accounts of atonement allow for atoning actions to be carried out by someone other than the wrongdoer. Christians believe that Jesus atoned for human sin. Josiah Royce's Christian-inspired theory of interpersonal atonement suggests that only someone other than the wrongdoer can make amends for cases of serious wrongdoing.[14] According to Royce, treason against one's own ideals (a kind of wrongdoing that encompasses many other subcategories of transgression) admits of correction only by another member of the moral community, a "suffering servant," who in a grand creative act responds to the misdeed in such a way that the world is actually better off for its having taken place. In Royce's view, the traitor is so deeply trapped in "the hell of the irrevocable" as to be personally incapable of such a creative act.

Although Royce's view offers much that is interesting and valuable (see chapter 3), it does not count as a theory of atonement as I am using the term. Instead, it suggests that atonement for serious wrongdoing is impossible. Although Royce provides a model of how *wrongs* can be repaired, he does not show how *wrongdoers* might be redeemed—how they might come to merit a better moral evaluation. However, most Christian accounts of Jesus's sacrifice for human sin (known as "the Atonement" with a capital *A*) count as theories of atonement in this sense. Although wrongdoers receive a crucial form of aid from Jesus, they are still required to contribute their own efforts in the form of repentance, faith, and (sometimes) their own suffering. So the Christian view of atonement need not, like Royce's account, suggest that someone other than the wrongdoer can fully atone for a wrong. Instead, it claims that others can help wrongdoers in the work of atonement. While the details of this process are complicated and highly controversial even among Christian theologians, the view shares the basic idea that wrongdoers are obliged to atone.

There is yet another way in which we might think of atonement as something other than a wrongdoer's action or response. Sometimes the making of amends is represented as an inherently interactive phenomenon, which is suggested by expressions such as "*They* have made amends" or "You should make amends *with* him." This language suggests that atonement requires the cooperation of both the wrongdoer and the person wronged. The wrongdoer may *offer* amends, but it is up to the victim to accept that offer and thereby complete the act.[15] This view highlights the conception of atonement as "at-one-ment," a form of reconciliation, and therefore something that wrongdoers and victims do together. However, it rings false to say that victims "atone," or even "atone with" wrongdoers. Such formulations might also prejudice us in favor of the reconciliation view of atonement. Thus, I use both 'atonement' and 'making amends' to refer to wrongdoers' actions.

However, this linguistic choice leaves us free to raise a substantive issue: Are wrongdoers' efforts ever sufficient to earn redemption, or will they also need the victims' or the community's forgiveness or reconciliation? This is a particularly delicate issue. If redemption depends on other people, then the wrongdoer's moral standing lies out of that person's control. On the other hand, to say that atoning wrongdoers can earn redemption through their own efforts is to imply the controversial view that victims may have a duty to forgive the people who have wronged them. This issue is more fully addressed in chapter 5, which explores the connection between redemption and forgiveness. In the meantime, I use the term 'atonement' to refer to wrongdoers' attempts to respond in a morally appropriate way to their wrongful actions. I describe the wrongdoer as attempting to *merit* redemption and leave for chapter 5 the question of whether those meritorious responses suffice for redemption and place victims under a duty to forgive.

1.3   Resistance to an Ethic of Atonement

Since coming upon the topic of making amends, I have often wondered why there is so little discussion of the concept in secular moral theory. After all, there are large and highly sophisticated literatures on what I take to be closely related topics—punishment and forgiveness. Recent discussions of alternative criminal sanctions and political reconciliation call for the making of amends as if this were a well-established moral concept, familiar in daily life but neglected in legal and political contexts. Yet when we look to moral theory, accounts of atonement are hard to find.

As I suggested earlier, such neglect by moral theorists might be rooted in skepticism about a wrongdoer's ability to right a wrong. Perhaps punishment and forgiveness are the only real options for resolving wrongdoing. The only way to address such doubts is to examine and evaluate various theories of atonement, which is the project of the book as a whole. However, in this section I discuss three other sources of resistance to a moral theory of atonement. The first argues that atonement is a specifically theological concept and thus is inappropriate as a topic for secular moral philosophy. A second set of objections charges that a philosophical theory of the making of amends is possible but of no practical value. The third warns that the concept of atonement has oppressive tendencies and suggests that we are better off without it. In illustration of this third charge, I consider the case of the Magdalen asylums of Ireland and the system of atonement they instituted. This case will then serve as a cautionary tale against which I judge the theories of atonement presented later in the book.

1.3.1   THEOLOGICAL OBJECTIONS

The fact that a large and ancient literature exists on the concept of a sinner's atonement to God gives theologians some ownership of this topic. Although today's language and conceptions of atonement descend from religious contexts, there must be room for a secular conception of atonement as well. In addressing atonement to God, theological discussions focus on sin (wrongs that human beings commit against God) or sinfulness (not particular wrongful acts but deeper tendencies or features that are wrongful) and how humans might make amends to God. A secular theory of atonement, on the other hand, focuses on interpersonal wrongs. Its topic is the moral violations that we human beings commit against one another and the responses we make to our victims, our communities, and ourselves in light of those transgressions.[16]

However, some have argued that something about the concept of atonement itself disqualifies it as a topic for discussion in secular philosophy. Michael Wyschogrod offers three different reasons that "philosophical ethics almost never deals with the possibility of correcting wrongdoing."[17] First, he points to

> the philosopher's realization that there is not and cannot be any method for erasing wrongdoing ... what is done is done, and the past cannot be changed. The past can be learned from and the repetition of the mistake can be avoided, but the past mistake cannot be erased. And because this is so, there is no place for a doctrine of atonement in autonomous human ethics.[18]

Royce's description of "the hell of the irrevocable" in "Time and Guilt" seems to support Wyschogrod's claim:

> If I ever say, "I have undone that deed," I shall be both a fool and a liar. Counsel me, if you will, to forget that deed. Counsel me to do good deeds without number to set over against that treason. Counsel me to be cheerful ... Counsel me to plunge into Lethe. All such counsel may be, in its way and time, good. Only do not counsel me "to get rid of" just that sin. That, so far as the real facts are concerned, cannot be done. For I am, and to the end of endless time shall remain, the doer of that wilfully [sic] traitorous deed. Whatever other value I may get, that value I retain forever. My guilt is as enduring as time.[19]

Many of the images that we associate with atonement—erasing the past, becoming a new person, washing away guilt—seem rather magical. As Wyschogrod suggests, there may be hope of making sense of them in a theological frame of reference, but secular philosophy should have no truck with such ideas. Secular philosophers can tell wrongdoers what would count as better future behavior, but only God can "convert the sins into acts of virtue."[20]

For the moment it suffices to say that our evaluation of Wyschogrod's claim should await further inquiry. The seemingly supernatural elements of our common ways of describing atonement may rest on mistakes and thus deserve no place in our moral theory. Alternatively, these elements may admit of redescription in ordinary terms.

Wyschogrod also argues that atonement is no proper topic for secular moral philosophy, whose work is to present rational ideals for behavior. Wrongdoing, since it is both nonideal and (sometimes by definition) irrational, is something about which philosophers have nothing to say.[21] Precedent for this argument appears in the writings of Hermann Cohen.[22] However, this argument is easily rejected. After all, philosophers think about the nonideal and the irrational when they offer theories that justify criminal punishment or discuss phenomena such as weakness of the will. Furthermore, to offer a theory of atonement can be seen as offering a theory of the ideal, rational response to one's own past acts of wrongdoing. Thus, it fits even within Wyschogrod's own narrow picture of moral philosophy.

Wyschogrod's third argument contends that specifically Kantian moral theories (with which I have sympathy) cannot support a theory of atonement: "In [Kantian] ethics it is the moral law itself which makes its demands on the subject. But because the moral law is not a person, it cannot forgive anything, just as mathematics cannot pardon those who add incorrectly or drop an integer in a subtraction."[23] The lawgiver is wronged when the law is broken. Because Wyschogrod sees forgiveness as a requirement of redemption, he refers to "the personal relationship with the lawgiver" as "an essential precondition for atonement."[24] In the absence of a lawgiver, both forgiveness and redemption are precluded.

Let us assume for the moment that Wyschogrod is right to see forgiveness as a requirement of redemption. Even without a lawgiver to confer it, forgiveness would still be a possible response to the wrongdoer's efforts in a range of interesting cases. Most instances of wrongdoing involve a victim and therefore someone with the proper standing to forgive. Furthermore, it is simply not true that Kantian ethics does not involve a personal lawgiver. Kant tells us that we, as rational individuals, give the moral law to ourselves.[25] Moreover, if sense can be made of the concept of self-forgiveness, a Kantian can have a theory of atonement and redemption in this way as well.[26]

Although the theological literature will prove to be very helpful to our discussion, I believe that we can pursue a theory of interpersonal atonement that is independent of the details of atonement to God (should such a being exist). A comparison with theories of criminal punishment might help clarify this. Many theists interpret God's justice retributively. They believe that

God justly punishes sinners simply because sin deserves suffering. No further goal need be cited in defense of God's punishment. However, a subset of these people would argue that, although retribution may be just for God, it should play no role in human beings' relations with one another. One argument for this view is that, while an omniscient and perfectly good God is capable of accurately determining a sinner's moral desert, our epistemic and moral limitations prevent us from properly making such judgments.[27]

Similarly, we might find the best theories of theological and interpersonal atonement to be quite different. Such dissimilarity would follow from the differences between the agent's relationship to God and her relationship to other human beings, as well as the sorts of harms one could inflict upon God and other people. God, we are told, is an immaterial, eternal, all-loving, all-knowing, and all-powerful being. Our fellow humans are embodied, mortal, imperfectly benevolent, epistemically limited, and vulnerable to a multitude of harms. So, what may suffice to achieve redemption in God's eyes may be insufficient to satisfy the legitimate claims of one's victim or community. Given the problems that tend to arise when interpersonal wrongs and resentments are not resolved, we have reason to find interpersonal atonement independently valuable. For these reasons, the secular theory of atonement I pursue in this book will, I hope, be of interest to both theists and nontheists.

1.3.2 PRACTICAL OBJECTIONS

Another source of resistance to a theory of interpersonal atonement does not rest on the idea that such a theory is impossible but rather holds that it is of no practical value. One version of this objection questions the motivation to atone. Do we really think that wrongdoers would repair their misdeeds voluntarily? After all, they are wrongdoers. Jacob Adler observes that philosophers today tend to "ignore or ridicule" the question of whether criminal wrongdoers should submit to punishment, a topic he has treated at length.[28]

I believe this reaction displays a disturbing tendency to see the wrongdoer as the "other," as a distinct kind of being who is different from ourselves, whom we presume to be perfectly responsive to the call of morality. It takes only a moment's reflection to notice that this presumption is not just false but also dangerous. All of us are guilty of wrongdoing from time to time, even if these misdeeds are not terribly severe. Many of our failings in everyday life permit us to put things right so easily that we often do not think of our actions in these terms. Still, we must admit that we are often wrongdoers and that the call to make amends applies even to us. The tendency to "other" those people who are guilty of severe wrongs, such as serious crimes, is no more defensible. As Adler argues, our ideal of a legitimate state

> requires seeing our fellow citizen as a moral subject, and there is a tendency to see the criminal only as a moral object. To put it another way, legitimacy requires us to ask, "How should we behave toward our fellow citizens, and how should they behave toward us?" but when it comes to dealing with criminals, we often are tempted to drop the second half of the question. We ask only, "What can we do with them?" or "... to them?" as if they were things to be manipulated.[29]

When we stop thinking of wrongdoing as something "someone else" does, we are forced to reconsider not only our responses to our own moral failings but also our reactions to those who have wronged us.

Furthermore, we have good reason to think that wrongdoers have an interest in making amends. Atonement promises to be a means by which wrongdoers can be freed from the continued resentment and suspicion of their victims and communities. Broken relationships may be restored, and the wrongdoer's former social position and reputation may be regained. In making amends, the wrongdoer can ease the burden of guilt and rebuild his image of himself as a good person.

A second practical objection to the project at hand suggests that a moral theory of atonement will be of little use because redemption is not something one can earn by consciously aiming at it. Jon Elster appears to take this position in a discussion of attempts to make amends by those who had collaborated with the Germans in occupied France and Norway.[30] As Elster reports, when it became increasingly clear that Germany would lose the war, those French and Norwegian citizens who had been working with the occupation governments sometimes engaged in acts of resistance, actions that either undermined the Germans' work or aided the organized resistance movements. As it did with many postwar legal tribunals, the timing of these acts leads Elster to discount their redemptive value because they were performed *for the purpose of achieving redemption*:[31]

> An argument why such strategic behavior is incompatible with genuine redemption relies on an analogy to religious salvation. The religions that hold that good works may lead to salvation usually stipulate that the works have to be performed "for love and fear of God" and not for the sake of salvation.... Redemption, like salvation, is essentially a by-product. You can be redeemed or saved by your good actions, provided they were not undertaken with that goal in mind.[32]

If redemption is the sort of thing that one can achieve only when one does not consciously pursue it, then my proposal to argue for a moral obligation to atone will be of questionable value. After all, to identify an obligation is to prescribe a course of action.

Even if Elster were right in his claim that redemption is the sort of thing that one cannot rationally pursue, a moral theory that explains exactly why that is the case would still be worth having. There would still be a point to the project of exploring various theories of atonement and redemption. However, I believe that Elster is mistaken.

For at least the beginning of an argument for this claim, let me highlight the fact that Elster's article uses 'redemption' in a couple of different ways. Sometimes (especially when he describes the collaborators as having a strategic interest in redeeming themselves), redemption is equivalent to the avoidance of punishment. And indeed this conception of redemption appears in the theological literature. A related sense of redemption is the regaining of social status (something that the collaborators also consciously pursued). However, a third conception of redemption has it that one is truly redeemed only when one has transformed one's deserved moral evaluation. The first two kinds of redemption may come without the third having been achieved, a point Elster recognizes when he notes that, "unlike God, courts can be fooled."[33]

Indeed, it seems that, although Elster uses the word 'redemption' in various ways, his own, normative conception of redemption hinges on moral reformation and not the mere avoidance of punishment or return of social status: "Only redemptive acts carried out from a conviction of their intrinsic rightness should have the power to redeem," presumably because only these acts signify the requisite kind of moral improvement.[34] If we say, then, that redemption requires something like moral reformation or a change in the deserved moral evaluation of the wrongdoer, then I see no reason that one cannot consciously pursue redemption. It will involve a deliberate effort to fulfill one's duties and become a better person. In that case, an account of the moral obligation to make amends will be both coherent and useful.

1.3.3   POLITICAL OBJECTIONS: THE CASE OF THE MAGDALEN ASYLUMS

Discussion of a moral obligation to atone sometimes raises a very different kind of objection, one much more sympathetic to the plight of wrongdoers. Some observers, I have found, view an ethic of atonement as a form of social control that tends toward the oppression of particular groups of people, often those who are already marginalized in existing power structures. Even a cursory study of the history of systems of atonement reveals disturbing abuses. Although in theory, systems of atonement have been intended to help wrongdoers improve their moral situation, in practice, penitence has often left one at the mercy of the worst impulses of one's neighbors. It has marked the offender as a legitimate target of aggression, discrimination, or plain *Schadenfreude*. In my opinion, this is the most troubling objection to my project of reviving the moral concept of atonement. I would like to examine it at length by considering a historical case study that illustrates how norms of atonement can be oppressive: the case of the Magdalen asylums of Ireland.[35] The influence of moral theory upon practice reveals aspects of the former that we might otherwise miss. For this reason I return to the Magdalen case throughout the book.

The Magdalen asylums of Ireland were institutions that housed "fallen women" throughout the nineteenth and twentieth centuries.[36] The asylums were originally designed to offer former prostitutes a safe place to live and an opportunity to learn a trade as a transition to a new and better life. However, a main emphasis of this movement was that the transition period should be one of repentance and penance. The "penitents," as they were called, should spend their time in prayer, silence, and taxing labor and live in hard circumstances as atonement for their past sins.[37] The name "Magdalen asylum" is a direct reference to the Christian figure of Mary Magdalene, a prostitute who is said to have repented and become one of Jesus's early followers.

In Ireland, these asylums came to be most commonly housed on the grounds of Catholic convents, where the penitents lived and worked under the nuns' constant supervision. Laundries were operated both to financially support the convent and to provide job training for the penitents.[38] Other institutions such as schools and prisons, as well as families in the neighborhood, were encouraged to send their laundry to the asylums to help the women "wash away" their sins.[39]

However we may judge the original ideals that were meant to guide the Magdalen asylums, the reality fell wide of the mark. Though the shelters were first organized to house former prostitutes, such women in fact made up only a fraction of their populations. Instead, many of the women and girls were unwed mothers who had been forced to give up their children or were simply believed to have engaged in nonmarital sexual relations. A few young women and girls simply considered to be too bold or too pretty were sent to the asylums as punishment or warning.[40] Some were (and were known to be) victims of incest or other forms of sexual assault. This group included girls as young as 12 and 13.[41] Another category of "penitents" included women or girls who had a mental disability and had no one else able and willing care for them.[42] All of these types of women and girls were interned in an institution that was closely associated by their society with prostitution.

In Frances Finnegan's study of nineteenth-century asylums, approximately 40 percent of inmates were registered as having entered the institutions voluntarily.[43] Many were listed as having been "brought" by priests or family members.[44] Some of the prostitutes went there as an alternative to incarceration in either the jails or the "lock hospitals" of the day.[45] Except for minors or those sent by court order, the inmates were legally entitled to leave the asylums at will, but there is reason to believe that many (if not most) of the inmates were unaware of this fact.[46] Doors were kept locked and windows were barred. Walls topped with glass shards or barbed wire surrounded the convents.[47] Those who expressed a desire to leave were either punished or strongly pressured to remain by the nuns and priests, who would emphasize the gravity of the women's sins and the threat of hellfire should they fall prey to the temptations of the outside world.[48] In practice, the most reliable methods for exiting a Magdalen asylum were to be expelled for outrageous behavior[49] or to be released to a family member. Since their families frequently wanted nothing more to do with these girls and women and since the nuns restricted and closely supervised correspondence, inmates could do little to secure this latter means of escape.[50]

While the asylums represented themselves as training the penitents for domestic service, it seems that such placements were exceedingly rare.[51] In part, the potential employers' prejudices against "fallen women" were to blame. However, there is also little evidence that the nuns made much effort to find placements for the penitents. Instead, many advocated that the penitents remain permanently in the asylums, where they would be "safe from sin."[52] They would also provide the experienced labor required to run the laundries, which soon became financially necessary for the support of the sisters, as well as the penitents. In the end, an estimated thirty thousand Irish women and girls, some for years and some for lifetimes, were interned behind stone walls and barred windows, under enforced silence and relentless supervision, where they labored for long, exhausting hours *without pay*, surrounded by the constant rhetoric of sin, remorse, and penance.[53]

One might claim that the case of the Magdalen asylums can be dismissed from the point of view of the ethics of atonement. In my approach, atonement consists in an agent's own voluntary responses to wrongdoing. Most contemporary readers are unlikely to classify the behaviors that generally led these women and girls to be placed in the Magdalen asylums as morally wrongful. While 40 percent of the inmates covered by Finnegan's study were described as entering the asylums on their own volition and many seemed to have agreed to remain there for years, given the limited options open to and the psychological pressures imposed on these women and girls, such decisions clearly stretch the meaning of "voluntary" to the breaking point. The Magdalen asylums institutionalized punishment, not atonement, one might argue.

However, I believe the Magdalen case has quite a bit to teach us about the dangers associated with an ethic of atonement. Although we can draw an important theoretical distinction between punishment and atonement, in practice these concepts can be hard to disentangle. Atonement must be undertaken by the individual, but calls for atonement often issue from the community, and there are penalties for ignoring such calls. Furthermore, when community moral standards are combined with established norms of atonement, the system of atonement itself becomes a means of enforcing that moral code. For these reasons, individuals feel compelled to atone for actions the community defines as wrong, even when they have good reason to disagree with the moral claims being made. Of course, taking this point too far would lead to a paralyzing moral skepticism, and the project of developing a full-fledged theory of right and wrong lies beyond the scope of this project. Still, it is important to keep the coercive potential of a system of atonement in mind as we continue to articulate what morality requires of wrongdoers.

Another point to notice about the Magdalen case is that atonement systems can be applied in discriminatory ways. When we compare the fates of the prostitutes and their clients, the young women and men who engaged in nonmarital sex, and the wealthy versus the poor "fallen" women, the differences are extreme. In general, society's more vulnerable groups are likely to suffer disproportionately under atonement systems. Interestingly, there are numerous historical examples of atonement norms unfairly burdening the most privileged classes as well. Public calls for atonement are sometimes more strongly motivated by political than moral reasons. The case of Bill Clinton's affair with Monica Lewinsky is the first that comes to mind. But historian Sarah Hamilton claims that public calls for penance have been used in political power games at least as far back as the seventh century.[54]

The Magdalen asylum case highlights the way in which some members of society profit by enforcing strict standards of atonement upon others. As noted earlier, the nuns who ran the Magdalen asylums earned their keep from the penitents' toil. Even when we assume that the nuns sincerely believed they were helping the asylum inmates, the very structure of the system invited abuses. The need for the penitents' labor created perverse incentives for the nuns to accept women and girls who were not appropriate candidates for the asylums, to pressure unfairly those who wanted to leave, and to encourage a lifetime of penance even for minor violations of sexual norms. However, the intangible benefits the nuns and other supporters of the system received from the penitents may have been even more responsible for the resulting abuses. In a world where sexual misconduct was represented as a sin deserving of imprisonment, hard labor, and unrelenting remorse, the virginal nuns gained a saintlike status.[55] Generally speaking, when atonement systems degrade wrongdoers, the status of nonoffenders is enhanced as a result.

Hardy's *The Mayor of Casterbridge* provides another such example. As a young and discouraged journeyman in the throes of a drunken rage, Michael Henchard sells his wife and daughter at a county fair. He later tries in vain to find them, foreswears drink as both a gesture of his remorse and an effort at rehabilitation, and builds himself into a man of influence in a new town. When the wife and daughter turn up on his doorstep years later, Henchard attempts to put things right by marrying the woman again and treating her and the girl decently. When the secret becomes public, however, the community so enjoys the scandalous nature of the wrongful act and the opportunity to see a big man fall that no thought is given to Henchard's twenty years of atonement. Henchard is financially and socially ruined, falls into despair and drink, and dies.

Elster notes another means by which people prey on the guilt of wrongdoers under the guise of an interest in atonement. In his discussion of both the trials of collaborators in postwar France and the anticommunist backlash in Eastern Europe in the early 1990s, Elster reports that those who failed to resist criminal regimes were often the most demanding of those wrongdoers seeking redemption.[56] Those hiding their own guilt acted "as if posttransition aggression toward the wrongdoers could magically undo pretransition passivity."[57]

The history of atonement is in large part a history of degradation. From the West to the East, the prayers of penitents often contain extreme exaggerations of personal sinfulness and extraordinary expressions of self-deprecation. In the early days of the Eastern Christian church, penitents were physically marked by their proximity to the altar.[58] The worst sinners were required to stand outside the building altogether. In other places, bishops would literally walk over the backs of prostrate penitents on the way to mass.[59] Penitents in the Magdalen asylums were always referred to as "children" and the nuns as "mothers," even when the penitent was fifty years older than the nun.[60] The whole Magdalen system was designed to eliminate the penitent's power of choice, which is the mark of both adulthood and moral agency. Whether defended in terms of retribution, rehabilitation, or reconciliation, the idea that humiliation is the path to redemption is ubiquitous in the literature on atonement.

However, in the Magdalen laundries and in many other cases as well, the promise of regaining one's place in the moral community through degradation and suffering was simply a lie. Although the girls and women were promised the possibility of a respectable new life through good behavior in the asylum, this rarely occurred. According to Finnegan,

> regardless of why they entered the institution in the first place, the stigma of having been in a Magdalen Home (whose very name denoted its purpose) dogged most women leaving. Former inmates were shunned by respectable society and considered "fair game" by those inclined to vice. By all who knew their past they were regarded with suspicion and seen as a source of cheap, exploited labour, or worse.[61]

Perhaps the Magdalen women found their redemption in Heaven, but in their earthly communities, despite the alleged connection between atonement and forgiveness, penitence was an enduring stigma. The case reminds me of the rhetoric surrounding criminal punishment in the United States, where convicts are told that they must go to prison to "pay their debts" to society. However, they emerge from prison only to find that the community refuses to treat them as if the accounts have been settled. They are not reintegrated as regular members of society. Instead, they are "ex-cons" for the rest of their lives.[62] I imagine this tendency to refuse social redemption to the penitent or the punished is related to the point noted earlier. People enjoy an elevated status when someone else is marked as a wrongdoer.

Joanne Carlson Brown and Rebecca Parker offer another reason for being suspicious of the doctrine that suffering is redemptive.[63] They argue that when suffering is glorified, people (and especially the least powerful members of society) learn to be submissive to abuse. *Any* cause of pain or loss may be interpreted as atonement for wrongdoing and thus accepted and even welcomed rather than questioned and fought. In this way, an ethic of atonement can become a barrier toward the development of more just societies. Part of the challenge of developing a normative account of atonement is to find a way to acknowledge fault while continuing to see others and ourselves as intrinsically valuable beings.

The close connections between atonement and suffering present a daunting obstacle to my project of developing a moral theory of atonement. Hair shirts and self-flagellation live on in our cultural memory of atonement, even though they have become rare in Western practice.[64] Beyond such historical associations, however, almost all modes of atonement involve some sort of emotional, physical, or material suffering, some sort of pain, loss, or sacrifice. Guilt and remorse are painful. Acknowledging wrongdoing and offering an apology can be humiliating. For many, the very painfulness of these responses to wrongdoing gives them meaning and weight.

These associations between atonement and suffering raise legitimate concerns about abuse. However, they also indicate the depth of longing for redemption and moral renewal that makes atonement valuable. To be a morally perceptive person is to suffer over one's misdeeds. I will feel the pain of guilt "unless I call treason my good, and moral suicide my life."[65] If we are to escape the hell of the irrevocable while remaining morally alive, we must find a way to put the past behind us while also accepting the reality and significance of that past.

The proper response to histories like that of the Magdalen asylums is not to abandon the concept of atonement altogether but to ask the following: How *should* we think of atonement? What *should* we count as grounds for redemption? How can we prevent our norms for atonement from becoming degrading and oppressive? We all have had positive experiences of the making of amends that may be contrasted with the horrors of the Magdalen asylums. Heartfelt apologies are made and accepted every day. A well-chosen gift can dissolve resentment. Acts of voluntary community service, especially when they are closely connected to the offending act, can transform the reputations of even serious offenders.[66] Truth telling, the acknowledgment of wrongdoing, and apology are coming to be political tools of significance and promise. When performed well and received in the right spirit, acts of atonement serve the ends of justice and peace, leaving both wrongdoers and victims feeling whole again. Despite the bad reputation of the concept of atonement and its abusive history and potential to become oppressive, atonement is a concept worthy of redemption.

1.4   Outline of the Book

My goal is to develop an account of wrongdoers' moral obligations to respond to their misdeeds that is specific enough to guide us in acting but general enough to shed light on a wide variety of cases of wrongdoing. In order to do this, I discuss the main goal that wrongdoers should pursue in responding to their wrongful act. Then I ask what this goal suggests in terms of particular types of actions or reactions (e.g., apology, payment of reparations, experience of guilt).

I found it unworkable, in writing this book, to defend both a specific criterion for right and wrong and a theory of righting wrongs. However, it is also impossible to talk about the correction of wrongdoing without making assumptions about which actions are wrong and why. I subscribe to a broadly Kantian approach to moral theory, and in chapters 4 and 5 especially this commitment plays an important role. However, I hope that the issues I raise and the intuitions I appeal to will resonate with adherents of a variety of theoretical perspectives.

Because the literature in moral theory rarely addresses the topic of making amends, I often turn to discussions of the correction of wrongdoing in theology and law. Neither of these literatures directly focuses on the problem that motivates this book, which is moral (rather than legal) wrongdoing committed by an individual or a group against another individual or group, and the question of how the wrongdoers must respond. However, many of the values and interests expressed in theology and law clearly generalize. The three most common conceptions of the making of amends that I have encountered are atonement as the repayment of a moral debt, atonement as moral transformation, and atonement as the reconciliation of a relationship. I defend the third approach.

Chapter 2 focuses on atonement as the repayment of a moral debt. The image of repayment is traditionally developed in two ways. First, retributive theories of atonement suggest that wrongdoing can be repaid only through suffering. The theological position known as "satisfaction theory" provides the most dramatic exposition of this view. The claim that wrongdoing intrinsically deserves suffering is heard in popular and scholarly debates about criminal punishment as well. The moral duty to atone, it would follow, is a moral duty to impose suffering upon oneself. The second way in which the metaphor of moral debt and repayment is interpreted focuses not on a loss or harm for the wrongdoer but on compensation for the victim. I label these "restitutive" theories of atonement. Although retributive and restitutive theories share a conception of wrongdoing, they make opposing mistakes. Retributive theories elide the moral significance of victims. Restitutive theories, on the other hand, fail to recognize the significance of the wrongdoer in that they are unable to justify the intuition that it is the transgressor who must make the reparative response.

In chapter 3 I examine the view that atonement consists in a moral transformation of either the wrongdoer or the wrongful action. The interest in transformation is most commonly expressed in a demand for repentance, a regretful turning away from the wrongful path, and a recommitment to the right and the good. Repentance is identified as a necessary (and sometimes sufficient) condition for atonement to God within the Jewish, Islamic, and Christian traditions. Ideals of moral transformation appear in rehabilitation and moral education theories of criminal punishment as well. Repentant wrongdoers are sometimes described as undergoing a change of identity that frees them from their guilt. At other times, repentance and other forms of atonement are described as changing the meaning of the past, whereby an act once deemed wrongful is recast as something positive in light of the wrongdoer's later responses. The value of repentance and moral reformation in the aftermath of wrongdoing are relatively uncontroversial. However, I argue that these responses are insufficient because they fail to address properly the social nature of wrongdoing. While repentance may satisfy an all-powerful and invulnerable God who can infallibly read the hearts of offenders, human victims and communities deserve a form of atonement that respects their needs and limitations.

Chapter 4 is dedicated to exploring the third moral ideal often connected to atonement: reconciliation. Theological and legal approaches to atonement often identify retribution and repentance as preconditions for reconciliation with God or the state. However, I believe that the ideal of reconciliation introduces a new value that takes us beyond the views discussed in the preceding two chapters. Because reconciliation is a matter of repairing relationships, a secular theory of atonement built on this ideal better attends to all of the parties who are negatively affected by wrongdoing: victims, communities, and wrongdoers themselves. Furthermore, by highlighting an interest in the damage done to relationships, we are encouraged to notice the varied kinds of harms that wrongdoing creates—from material harms, to sullied reputations, to the creation of fear and self-hatred—and to consider what can heal those wounds. In this chapter I defend a particular version of a reconciliation theory of atonement. The remaining chapters of the book test the theory by seeing whether it coheres well with our moral views about forgiveness and self-forgiveness, state sanctions for crime, and the resolution of group wrongdoing and historical injustice.

Chapter 5 takes up the topic of forgiveness and its connection to the moral redemption of the wrongdoer. In my view, the wrongdoers' proper aim in atoning is a distinctively moral reconciliation with themselves, their victims, and their social circles. This sort of reconciliation involves a normalization of their standing in the moral community. Nonetheless, if something like this sort of restoration of standing is indeed the aim of atonement, then it seems that wrongdoers cannot redeem *themselves* at all. They need others to forgive or to reconcile with them. This account can help explain the commonly held (but rarely defended) view that victims have a prerogative to forgive. The idea of such a prerogative suggests not only that victims alone have the standing to forgive wrongdoers but also that other people's relations with the wrongdoer should be guided to some extent by the victim's decision to forgive or to withhold forgiveness. However, the claim that victims have a prerogative to forgive threatens to leave wrongdoers, their moral standing, and their ability to forgive themselves at the mercy of their victims. I argue that the reconciliation theory of atonement provides grounds for granting but also restricts the victim's prerogative to forgive.

Our attention turns from moral to criminal wrongdoing in chapter 6. Known as "restorative justice," a growing movement of scholars, legal practitioners, and activists argues that the restoration of relationships among offenders, victims, and communities is the proper goal of a criminal justice system. On the basis of this claim, restorative justice theorists argue for significant procedural reforms, including a diminished role for legal professionals, intense moral discussions between offenders and victims, and restitution rather than punitive sanctions. In this chapter I ask whether the moral theory I defend in the first part of the book is acceptable as a theory of criminal justice. My response is mixed. One major objection to restorative justice is that it is illiberal in the sense that a state guided by restorative justice would fail to be neutral among competing conceptions of the good. However compelling an ethic of atonement might be, it is not the sort of thing that the state should enforce. I examine this objection in depth and conclude that it can be answered satisfactorily. However, I take exception to the tendency in restorative justice theory to undervalue the distinction between moral and criminal wrongdoing. This problem threatens the procedural reforms associated with the restorative justice movement because those reforms de-emphasize the state's legitimate claims.

Chapter 7 concludes the book by asking whether the reconciliation theory of atonement can be applied to cases of group wrongdoing, including examples of wrongdoing in the distant past. Reconciliation is surely a moral value that we should pursue in such situations. Communities that have been ripped apart by ethnic violence, scandals, or political oppression need healing and a restoration of trust. But does atonement have anything to do with this? To require atonement, it seems, is to attribute culpability for wrongdoing. However, can a group be held culpably responsible even for wrongs committed by earlier generations of that group? In this chapter I argue that the reconciliation theory of atonement coheres with attributions of collective responsibility in a way that lends credibility to both views. While I believe that states are the sorts of groups that can have obligations to atone, I focus on an instance of group wrongdoing that is political in a more extended sense of the term. I return to the case of the Magdalen asylums and view it as a social injustice for which group atonement by the Catholic Church is required. The contrast between the kind of atonement that I advocate and that which was imposed upon the inmates of the asylums supports my claim that an ethic of making amends is not inherently oppressive or dangerous but something that can play a positive, constructive role in our personal and social lives.

CHAPTER TWO | # Repaying Moral Debts
Self-Punishment and Restitution

2.1 Introduction

Our modest, starting hypothesis is that, when one has wronged another person, one must respond in some way. But why exactly is this so? Why must we respond to wrongdoing rather than simply move on as if the wrongful action had never happened? We would usually prefer to forget our past mistakes rather than address them. In this chapter we begin the search for a moral theory that can both characterize in general terms what a response to wrongdoing should achieve and provide a compelling justification for requiring such a response.

The specific features of a proper response to a particular wrongful action (i.e., the precise actions or reactions that an offender ought to take in order to correct his action) surely vary from case to case, depending on the severity of the wrong, as well as other circumstances. The atonement for mildly insulting a coworker should differ in many respects from that for betraying a dear friend or robbing a stranger. However, what we are searching for here and in the following chapters is the guiding principle or principles for atoning responses. Which values or goals should a transgressor pursue in the aftermath of wrongdoing? Once we have an understanding of the goal of atonement, we should be in a better position to identify appropriate acts of atonement.

The views of atonement that are explored in this chapter are all rooted in a familiar idea: To wrong another person is to incur a moral debt, and so the way to correct wrongdoing is to repay that debt. As we will see, different theories of atonement use this economic language more or less strictly. For some, debt and repayment are simply metaphors that soon give way to other moral ideas. Others take quite seriously the suggestion that wrongdoing and atonement are matters of transferring proportional and fungible burdens and benefits among persons.

Why must moral debts be repaid? One might answer this question in a generally consequentialist manner, emphasizing the benefits that usually proceed from paying off such debts and the problems that persist when debts go unpaid. However, the theories of atonement that interest me in this chapter take a decidedly nonconsequentialist approach. They hold that repayment is an intrinsically appropriate response to debt. Like a financial debt, a moral debt must be repaid even when the debtor and the third parties are made worse off by the repayment and the creditor will only put it to ill use. The repayment is required by the fact of the debt, not by the consequences of repayment. At this point, however, two different views arise among the nonconsequentialists. Some say that debts must be repaid because the debtor deserves to incur a loss. Others emphasize the idea that the creditor deserves to receive compensation. These two ideas develop into distinct, though frequently combined or confused, principles for the correction of wrongdoing: retribution and restitution.[1]

Retributive theories say that wrongdoers deserve to suffer some sort of loss or penalty because of their wrongful actions. This principle is frequently defended in both popular and scholarly debates about criminal punishment. Those guilty of criminal wrongdoing are said to deserve punishment simply because of their wrongful actions and not because punishment may achieve a net increase of good consequences (such as deterrence or rehabilitation). The imposition of a loss or penalty proportional to the offense is held to be an intrinsically just response to crime. Given our focus on the wrongdoers' own responses to their moral misdeeds, the application of the retributive principle is straightforward. In order to atone for moral wrongdoing, the agents must impose a proportional punishment upon themselves.

Those theorists who believe that the crucial value of debt repayment is the return of a good to the creditor rather than the loss of a good by the debtor commit themselves to a principle of restitution rather than retribution. While not as popular, restitutive defenses of criminal sanctions appear in the legal literature as well. The idea here is that the state is permitted to fine, imprison, or otherwise compel responses from criminals in order to compensate their victims. As a principle of atonement for moral wrongdoing, restitution requires wrongdoers to present their victims with a form of compensation that is proportional to the harm or wrong.

In examining the possible justifications of retribution and restitution as principles of atonement, I draw heavily on the discussions of their counterparts in the criminal justice literature. First, however, I present a related, theological account of atonement that is rooted in the writings of Anselm of Canterbury and known as "satisfaction theory."[2] This theory incorporates elements of both retribution and restitution by requiring that humanity's debt to God be repaid with suffering, a form of moral currency conceived in such thoroughly economic terms that it can be not just measured but also saved in advance, pooled among allies, and redistributed. Satisfaction theory is both a historically significant predecessor to our current legal and moral conceptions and a formidable player in continuing debates among Christians about the nature of atonement to God.

The examination of satisfaction theory raises a number of objections, particularly to its characteristically economic defense of retribution. In an effort to avoid those objections, I turn in section 2.3 to alternative, secular defenses of the basic retributive principle that wrongdoing deserves suffering. Section 2.4 focuses on contemporary restitutive theories of criminal punishment and the theories of atonement they seem to recommend. Under this heading, I consider a version of restitution theory that will bring us full circle to the themes of satisfaction theory by arguing that restitution for wrongdoing can be made only through the suffering of the wrongdoer. Both retributive and restitutive principles for the correction of wrongdoing contain disturbing features, and neither can suffice for a general principle of atonement. However, the views examined here highlight a number of values and concerns that should influence our final theory of atonement.

2.2   Satisfaction Theology

To sin, according to Anselm, "is nothing other than not to give God what is owed to him."[3] The representation of human sin as creating a debt to God is joined with the insistence that God is to be repaid in full. "As long as [the sinner] does not repay what he has taken away, he remains in a state of guilt. And it is not sufficient merely to repay what has been taken away: rather, he ought to pay back more than he took, in proportion to the insult which he has inflicted."[4] Atonement requires the payment of "satisfaction" to God.

But how is God to be compensated? Surely not simply through obedience to God's laws since such obedience is already obligatory.[5] Obedience and the fulfillment of duty cannot make up for past sins; they can only be the means of avoiding future sin. Instead, the sinner must turn to one of two options: merit or punishment. "Merit" is defined in this context as good works performed over and above one's duties.[6] In carrying out meritorious acts, one offers a good to God in order to counterbalance evil. Anselm explains how punishment also helps cancel out moral debt: "Just as a man by sinning seizes what belongs to God, likewise God, by punishing him, takes away what belongs to man."[7] However, simply suffering punishment (and all earthly suffering will be interpreted by some as God's punishment for sin) is not quite enough. Suffering must also be combined with the sinner's faith and repentance for sin in order properly to address the affront to God's honor.[8] In these ways, either by suffering or good works, joined with faith and repentance, one makes restitution to God for one's sin. The penitential system of the Middle Ages instituted specific norms for such repayment.

Yet, a problem remains. Because human beings are so sinful and because sinning against God creates an enormous debt, they appear to have no hope of ever repaying the entirety of their debt to God.[9] They simply cannot be good enough or suffer enough in this life to make full compensation. At this point in the debate, many religious thinkers appeal to God's love and benevolence to solve the problem. Since human beings cannot repay their debt to God, they argue, God mercifully forgives the debt.[10] However, this move conflicts with Anselm's conception of God's dignity and sense of justice.[11] As Gustaf Aulén characterizes Anselm's view, God's forgiveness of sinners who have not atoned through suffering or good works "would mean that sin is not treated seriously and so would amount to a toleration of laxity."[12]

How, then, can human beings settle their debt to God? Anselm's solution to this problem turns on two key claims. The first is that an overabundance of merit can be transferred from one being to another.[13] The second is that Jesus Christ, who is himself sinless, earns an extraordinary amount of merit that he shares with humanity.[14] Jesus, in short, makes satisfaction for humanity's debt to God.[15] In this way, Anselm provides a theory of atonement that remains true to the central Christian tenet that it is Jesus who secures atonement for human sin.

So formulated, satisfaction theory follows a strict, pecuniary logic of restitution. The crucial thing is that God be compensated for sin, whether by the sinner or by Jesus. However, punitive elements are present as well insofar as imposed and self-induced suffering are valued as forms of compensation. In the centuries following Anselm, the punitive features of satisfaction theory received greater emphasis, such that Aulén characterizes satisfaction theory as it was formulated in the sixteenth century and thereafter as a form of retributive justice.[16] Timothy Gorringe, examining the influence of satisfaction theory on eighteenth- and nineteenth-century Britain, characterizes it as the view that "Suffering is the alchemy which brings good out of evil."[17] Good deeds come to be valued insofar as they are costly, difficult, or painful to perform rather than for the positive good they bring about.[18] Yet, this defense of punishment differs importantly from contemporary retributivism in that it allows for the punishment of one person to satisfy moral claims against another.[19]

This doctrine is known as "penal substitution" or "vicarious punishment." It is without doubt the most controversial aspect of satisfaction theory among contemporary theologians. Interestingly for our purposes, proponents of satisfaction theory generally do not answer the objection by defending vicarious punishment or penal substitution across the board. They grant, for example, that the criminal justice system should not allow a criminal's best friend to serve the specified term in prison for the criminal. The case of Jesus's atonement for human sin is considered a special case of punishment, one that requires special treatment. Yet even if vicarious punishment is restricted to the case of Jesus, it retains its disturbing character specifically because of Jesus's innocence and the horrible nature of his death. As John Hick puts it, "God's insistence on the blood, sweat, pain, and anguish involved in the crucifixion of his innocent Son now seems to cast doubt—to say the least—on the moral character of the Deity."[20] This line of objection dates back to Anselm's contemporary, Abelard, who wrote the following:

> How cruel and wicked it seems that anyone should demand the blood
> of an innocent person as the price for anything, or that it should in any
> way please him that an innocent man should be slain—still less that
> God should consider the death of his Son so agreeable that by it he
> should be reconciled to the whole world![21]

Any theory that permits or endorses a role for suffering in atonement faces a demand for justification. How can present suffering correct past wrongdoing? Satisfaction theory portrays suffering as a form of compensation, as a good that is commensurable to a good lost or damaged through wrongdoing and that can be offered in place of the original good. But this suggests that God values suffering—even the suffering of an innocent—as a good.[22]

From an explanatory point of view, the moral, atoning significance attributed to suffering throughout history is understandable.[23] Suffering is inevitable in life, and, until very recently, human success in controlling suffering has been extremely limited. Pain is easier to bear when it can be made sense of and justified in some way, whether as an intrinsically warranted punishment for one's own sinfulness or as an appeasement to a god. However, our project here is not to explain the significance traditionally attributed to suffering.

It is instead to ask whether we are justified in continuing to endorse the self-infliction of suffering in response to wrongdoing. The suggestion that suffering is an intrinsic good that may be offered by way of compensation is too bloody minded to be acceptable.

For an additional objection to satisfaction theory, we may note that the Magdalen asylum system developed and flourished in a religious context influenced by that view of atonement.[24] When suffering is seen as the currency God demands in repayment of an enormous moral debt and especially when it does not matter whether that suffering originates from the sinner's own will or from the punishing actions of others so long as it is eventually combined with repentance, the excesses found in the Magdalen system are hardly surprising.[25]

In the next section of this chapter I turn to the idea that not just any suffering but the suffering *of the guilty* is intrinsically justified in such a way that self-punishment is morally required of wrongdoers. This is the core idea of the retributivist view of atonement, and I examine several different approaches to defending it. The claim I have found in satisfaction theory—that suffering is a form of compensation for the one wronged—reappears later in the discussion.

2.3   Retributive Self-Punishment

In order to continue exploring the intuition that wrongdoing morally requires punishment and that atonement is therefore a matter of self-punishment, I consider a number of defenses of retributivism drawn from the debates about criminal sanctions. Each version of retributivism will need to be adapted from its original context to the problem of atonement. Before launching into the details of these different accounts, it is worthwhile to pause for a moment and consider some of the differences between the debate about criminal punishment and that about atonement. I also respond to the objection that atonement cannot be retributive because "self-punishment" is an oxymoron. Self-punishment, I argue, is a coherent sort of action one might take in response to wrongdoing.

2.3.1   SELF-PUNISHMENT

Debates about the state's punishment of criminals usually proceed under the assumption that such punishment is justified. People generally agree that the punishment of lawbreakers is a necessary part of social life. The controversy centers instead on the justification for punishment, and retribution is typically a prominently offered rationale. However, no such consensus exists on the necessity of self-punishment. Most contemporary writers on criminal justice dismiss out of hand the idea that criminal offenders will participate in their own punishment, and these writers make no effort to justify any obligation to submit to state punishment.[26] Self-punishment is as likely to be viewed as irrational or pathological as it is to be endorsed as a part of moral life. In this way, defending the moral necessity of self-punishment, whether on retributive or other grounds, appears to be a more difficult task than defending the punishment of other people.

In other respects, however, defending self-punishment looks comparatively easy. In the criminal justice context, the state forcibly imposes a penalty on an offender against his will. Issues arise about the authority to punish and the reliability of attributions of guilt that are more manageable in the context of self-punishment. It is odd to say that wrongdoers could violate their own rights through misguided self-punishment since wrongdoers generally have very good, though not infallible, epistemic access to their own actions and motives.

However, the Magdalen case should convince us not to take the issue of self-punishment too lightly. Although most of the asylum inmates were subjected to coercion, others seem to have submitted themselves relatively voluntarily to years of incarceration and drudgery in the laundries merely for engaging in nonmarital sexual intercourse. Here we have evidence that people do sometimes punish themselves too harshly, whether or not we wish to characterize such actions as rights violations. Furthermore, regardless of whether we classify these women as having wronged themselves by submitting to the Magdalen system, we can criticize the social groups that defined and promulgated such norms of atonement. Even when coercion is not part of the story, to endorse the suffering of any human being is a matter of the utmost moral seriousness.

This observation provides a response to the objection that the concept of self-punishment is incoherent. If one stipulates that punishment is the imposition of suffering on a guilty person by another party, then self-punishment is defined out of possibility.[27] Yet we know that people sometimes seek out or submit to suffering because they believe themselves to be guilty or full of vice, and the Magdalen case prompts us to see that such actions can be morally problematic in many of the same ways as standard cases of punishment. "Self-punishment" is a useful and informative label for a real phenomenon, one that raises moral questions.

Nor must we point to extreme cases such as the Magdalen laundries, outdated images of hair shirts, or disturbingly contemporary images of self-loathing teens cutting themselves in order to find examples of self-punishment. Many familiar and intuitively acceptable practices can be interpreted as self-punishment. Giving a gift to the person one has wronged can be a form of penance if the gift requires significant effort or sacrifice from the wrongdoer and is presented for that reason.[28] In other cases, wrongdoers perform services for those they have wronged as a means of self-punishment. After a quarrel with his mother, a son may dedicate his weekend to cleaning her garage. Others perform service to the larger community. In Ian McEwan's novel titled *Atonement*, the main character punishes herself for ruining the lives of two people by foregoing her opportunity to go to college and instead working as a nurse in a wartime hospital. Penance through community service is especially powerful when it is closely connected to the wrongful act, as when someone who has injured another person while driving drunk works to educate others about the dangers of drinking and driving. Penance also comes in the form of voluntary acceptance of punishment at the hands of the state, whether through surrendering when one is unlikely to be caught, freely confessing one's guilt, not opposing one's sentence, or perhaps simply endorsing one's sentence as deserved. A retributive justification of self-punishment will defend actions such as these.

The painful emotions of guilt, remorse, and shame are also sometimes characterized as forms of self-punishment. I suspect that the intuition that one should "suffer" such emotions lends much credibility to retributive theories of atonement. But should we classify these emotions as forms of self-punishment? The question pushes us to better define what counts as punishment. It is commonplace in defining punishment to draw a distinction between forms of suffering or loss that are imposed intentionally upon alleged wrongdoers (by themselves or others) and those forms of suffering or loss that occur as "natural consequences" or side effects of a wrongful act.[29] The pain of a hangover is a natural consequence of excessive drinking, not a punishment for it.[30] Given this distinction, we have grounds to dismiss the classification of the painful experience of guilt as a form of punishment. Punishment is limited to intentional actions, but one cannot simply choose to feel guilt, remorse, or shame. Thus, the negative emotions of self-appraisal are something other than self-punishment. There are borderline cases here, including actions like deliberately brooding over wrongdoing and nursing feelings of guilt. However, in what follows I accept the distinction between self-punishment and the experience of painful emotions.

Drawing this distinction does not preclude the possibility that self-punishment and emotions such as guilt share a deeper justification and that a retributive theory of atonement should demand both. After all, guilt, remorse, and shame are sometimes labeled "retributive emotions."[31] In the next section I consider an argument for retributivism that turns on the commonalities between guilt and punishment.

2.3.2   MOORE ON GUILT AND RETRIBUTION

Michael S. Moore's article titled "The Moral Worth of Retribution" is interesting in many ways, given our project, because Moore is one of the few contemporary writers who attempt to justify practices of criminal punishment by appealing to intuitions about atonement.[32] Specifically, Moore claims that our own feelings of guilt show that we accept the retributivist principle that wrongdoing deserves suffering.[33]

Moore asks us to imagine "the feelings of guilt we would have if we did the kinds of acts that fill the criminal appellate reports of any state."[34] To aid in this imaginative exercise, Moore refers to the case of a young man who was convicted of the manslaughter of his ex-girlfriend:

> Then ask yourself: What would you feel like if it was you who had intentionally smashed open the skull of a 23-year-old woman with a claw hammer while she was asleep, a woman whose fatal defect was a desire to free herself from your too clinging embrace? My own response, I hope, would be that I would feel guilty unto death. I couldn't imagine any suffering that could be imposed upon me that would be unfair because it exceeded what I deserved.[35]

We should not feel uneasy about our desire to punish this man, Moore argues, since if we were in his shoes we would recognize that we deserved to suffer. Implicit in the emotion of guilt, Moore finds an acknowledgment of desert of suffering.

One might well accept Moore's reading of guilt yet be cautious about using it to defend criminal punishment as he does.[36] I do not pursue those issues here. Instead, the point of interest is Moore's claim that feelings of guilt reveal a commitment to the principle of retribution. In feeling guilty and accepting those feelings as legitimate, Moore argues, I am acknowledging the appropriateness of my suffering:

> We need to be clear just what judgments it is that our guilt feelings validate in this way. First and foremost, to *feel* guilty causes the judgment that we *are* guilty, in the sense that we are morally culpable. Second, such guilt feelings typically engender the judgment that we deserve punishment. I mean this not only in the weak sense of desert—that it would not be unfair to be punished—but also and more important in the strong sense that we *ought* to be punished.[37]

To recognize the justification of guilt is to concede the legitimacy of retribution, he argues.

But let us consider this argument. If a wrongdoer does not suffer guilt, what has gone wrong? What is missing? Is it the suffering, the pain itself? Or is the absence of suffering simply evidence that something else is missing?

Rüdiger Bittner titles one of his articles "Is It Reasonable to Regret Things One Did?" and answers "no."[38] According to Bittner, if one has committed a morally wrongful action, then one ought to acknowledge the wrong, make reparations, and act better in the future. However, suffering regret or remorse, he argues, adds nothing. It is pointless suffering, and pointless suffering should not be endorsed. Moore and I both disagree with Bittner and find his unremorseful wrongdoer morally lacking. Still, what precisely is wrong with this character? And how should his moral failure be remedied?

The retributivist might argue that Bittner's wrongdoer, who has all of the right beliefs and intentions but does not suffer, has thereby not satisfied the claims of morality. Because the suffering is missing, the response to wrongdoing is incomplete. Suffering in response to wrongdoing has an intrinsic value, and its absence in this case prevents the wrongdoer from satisfying his obligation to atone. If this is correct, then Bittner's unremorseful wrongdoer can rectify the situation by creating suffering where it is missing. He can impose some other form of suffering on himself, such as a fast or a burdensome service project, in order to complete his atonement. (Should he refuse, others might fill the gap by forcing suffering upon him.) If the moral worth of retribution explains the moral worth of the emotion of guilt, then this should provide a happy ending to the tale of the unremorseful wrongdoer. However, note that, although Bittner's wrongdoer has now suffered, he has not suffered *guilt* or *remorse*. He suffers, but he does not *suffer over* the wrongness of his action. For this reason, he still deserves criticism. Something important is still missing. Other forms of pain are not complete substitutes for guilt and remorse, so the value of these emotions must lie in something more than (or other than) their painfulness.

I favor an alternative response to Bittner's critique of guilt and remorse as pointless suffering. Bittner asks us to imagine a wrongdoer who holds all of the proper judgments about his past act and forms all of the right intentions about the future but who does not suffer over the past. I reject this psychology as unrealistic. If one acknowledges one's wrongful act and maintains a commitment to morality, then (as long as one is functioning normally) one will suffer. The absence of remorse in Bittner's wrongdoer is evidence that either he has not really come to terms with the nature of his action or he has not truly committed himself to morality. We cannot make everything right in such a case simply by punishing the morally insensitive wrongdoer or insisting that he punish himself. Supplying suffering does not necessarily fix the problem with wrongdoer's moral attitudes.[39] This indicates, contra Moore, that guilt and remorse are not valuable for their painful nature per se but as indicators that the wrongdoer has the proper attitudes about morality and his relation to it. In defending guilt, we need not subscribe to retributivism.

Let us develop this nonretributive defense of guilt in more detail. Earlier I endorsed a distinction between punishment, which is intentionally imposed in response to wrongdoing, and forms of suffering that are natural consequences or side effects of a wrongful act. Guilt falls in this latter category. It is a kind of moral hangover. Put so simply, the claim that guilt is a natural consequence of wrongdoing is clearly false. Not all of those who are in fact guilty of wrongdoing—even knowingly and according to their own standards—suffer the pangs of guilt. Sometimes we are left cold by our misdeeds. At other times, we feel defiant, satisfied, or even exhilarated by our wrongful actions. The emotion of guilt is not a psychological consequence of wrongdoing as such. However, it might well be a psychological consequence of the following complex of beliefs and attitudes: belief that one has done something wrong according to a particular norm, acknowledgment of the legitimate authority of that norm, personal commitment to that norm such that one cares whether it is respected or violated, and acknowledgment that one has violated the norm under conditions that neither justify nor fully excuse its violation.

If an agent is in all of these states, then a painful feeling such as guilt or remorse will be a natural consequence for at least a period of time. The painfulness is accounted for by the nature of genuine commitment to a norm or value. As Jeffrie Murphy puts it, "Morality is not simply something to be believed in; it is something to be *cared* about."[40] Commitment is the aspect of our moral psychology that Bittner misreads in his dismissal of guilt.[41] If I perform a wrongful action but feel no guilt, then this is reason for suspecting that either I am not in one of the mental states mentioned (I do not know that I have violated the norm, or I believe myself to have an excuse; I do not accept that norm as authoritative, or I do not care at the moment about the fact that it is authoritative for me) or my cognitive or emotional processes are functioning abnormally (as they might be if I am terribly depressed, operating under great fear or stress, or engaging in self-deception). As P. F. Strawson argues, guilt is a sign that we regard ourselves as agents who are responsible for our choices.[42] It is also a sign that this responsibility matters to us.

Claims of naturalness raise suspicion, and rightfully so. Those who are socialized in a culture different from our own might well conceive of their relationships to the standards that guide their behavior differently and react differently to violations of those standards. For example, they might be more likely to feel shame rather than guilt, an emotion that focuses on oneself rather than one's actions. Such emotional variations are neither surprising nor problematic. A more radical difference is harder to imagine (e.g., people who feel joy rather than a negative emotion at violating the norms they accept as authoritative). However, the important point is simply that any such radical emotional differences would come along with radical differences in conceptions of responsibility, freedom, and morality. Guilt, shame, and remorse are natural emotions for people who see the world in certain ways (though not for others). If we continue upon reflection to endorse these ways of seeing the world, then we defend the related emotions even if we have not shown them to be uniquely appropriate for all rational beings.

This interpretation of the sense in which a feeling of guilt is a natural consequence of wrongdoing provides a nonpunitive defense of the role of suffering in atonement. Those who have committed a wrongful action are morally compelled to suffer from guilt, shame, or remorse, so long as they are morally required to acknowledge themselves to have violated a moral norm, to acknowledge that norm as legitimately authoritative over their behavior, to be personally committed to that norm, and to acknowledge that their violation of it was neither justified nor excused. Wrongdoers are frequently required to fulfill these conditions, and so they are frequently morally bound to suffer guilt or other painful moral emotions. They are obliged to suffer guilt not because the guilt itself is morally required but because the guilt will be a side effect of other morally required responses.

Let us call this the "moral hangover" defense of guilt. Notice the way in which it defends the suffering of wrongdoers. Wrongdoers ought to suffer guilt but not because wrongdoing intrinsically deserves suffering. The focus of the argument does not present suffering as the key feature of a proper response to wrongdoing or as the coin that repays the moral debt or as the magic elixir that washes away sin. Instead, it emphasizes the importance of the wrongdoers' sharing a commitment to morality and acknowledging the facts about their own behavior. When the wrongdoers stand in the proper relation to the facts and values at hand, they will feel guilt or a similarly painful emotion. However, their suffering is a side effect, a consequence, of seeing themselves as having violated something they care about.[43] It is evidence that they stand in a proper relationship to morality. Their suffering is not the main point or the core of their obligation; their moral commitments and judgments are. This defense of suffering is not retributivist.[44]

Moore argued that, in accepting the legitimacy of the pains of guilt, we implicitly embrace the principle of retribution. I have resisted that argument in two ways. First, I have argued that, if the value of guilt lies in the suffering it brings, then guilt should be replaceable with other forms of suffering. This is not true, however. In the case of Bittner's wrongdoer, penance and punishment do not obviate the value of guilt. Second, I have provided a defense of the "retributive emotions" of guilt, shame, and remorse that is nonretributive. We can endorse these emotions without committing ourselves to retributivism.

While on the topic of guilt, I wish to note that people sometimes object that guilt and related emotions either are psychologically unhealthy or weaken one's character. Freud and Nietzsche are often interpreted, whether justifiably or not, as having held such views.[45] Therapists sometimes encourage their patients to refrain from morally judging their own actions. Would-be strong figures chant the mantra "no regrets." Sometimes such discussions assume that guilt is misguided in some way, perhaps issuing from commitment to an inappropriate set of norms. Yet surely there are norms that are appropriate and whose violation merits the judgments and attitudes that bring on the feeling of guilt. Sometimes guilt is portrayed as a weakness or malady by those who believe that there is no way for transgressors to correct wrongdoing and to resolve guilt. Guilt is then viewed as a profitless or debilitating emotion. I reject that assumption as well. If redemption is possible (and I argue it is), guilt can find a satisfactory resolution.

2.3.3   SELF-PUNISHING EXPRESSIONS OF GUILT

To review, we are searching for a retributive defense of self-punishment. I have argued that, although emotions such as guilt and remorse involve suffering and although wrongdoers are criticizable when they do not experience such emotions, these emotions are not forms of self-punishment and can be defended without attributing any intrinsic value to the suffering they bring. Thus, we can endorse guilt and remorse without committing ourselves to the retributivist claim that wrongdoing requires punishment.

At this point, the retributivist might try to defend practices of self-punishment by suggesting that they are natural expressions of the emotions of guilt and remorse. This method of justifying self-punishment parallels those defenses of criminal punishment that characterize it as a natural manifestation of the morally legitimate emotions of resentment and indignation that victims and society as a whole feel in reaction to crime.[46]

At best, however, such arguments could show that punishment and self-punishment are permissible reactions to wrongdoing, while the retributivist is committed to showing that they are morally required.[47] After all, though resentment, indignation, and guilt sometimes manifest themselves in aggressive behavior, there is no psychological inevitability here. These emotions might trigger the "flight" rather than the "fight" response.

Furthermore, a sense of guilt might just as well express itself in an apology or an offer of reparation rather than a drive to inflict suffering on oneself. Offering an apology or providing reparations might be painful or humiliating to some degree but need not be. Furthermore, when an element of suffering is present in such actions, it is far from obvious that this is the source of their value as a response to wrongdoing. In the aftermath of wrongdoing, there are usually many goods worth pursuing. The victim may have been harmed financially or physically as a result of one's misdeed and may continue to suffer from hurt pride, alienation, or self-doubt. In light of such problems, wrongdoers who express their sense of guilt through the single-minded pursuit of their own suffering appear shortsighted and self-absorbed.

2.3.4   KANTIAN RETRIBUTIVISM

This response applies as well to standard Kantian arguments for retribution. Kant is generally taken to argue that one must punish a criminal wrongdoer because not to do so would be to treat the criminal as something less than a responsible moral agent.[48] One would be acting as if the criminal were a child or an incompetent, someone not capable of making genuinely free choices in the way that the rest of us are. To take such an insulting stance toward the criminal is to wrong that person. We can transform this into an argument for self-punishment. Not to punish myself for my moral misdeeds would be to fail to acknowledge my own status as a responsible moral agent. Yet, as I have already suggested, there are a number of ways to acknowledge one's status as a morally responsible being that are not punitive. The emotions of guilt, remorse, and repentance and the moral attitudes that underlie them acknowledge responsibility for wrongdoing but are not instances of self-punishment. One may also own up to one's responsibility for wrongdoing through apology and reparation, whether or not these turn out to cause one suffering. We have yet to identify a special value that can be achieved only through self-punishment.

Furthermore, there are many different ways in which I can make myself suffer in retribution for wrongdoing. I can fast or forego something that I enjoy. I can fall into financial straits by offering a hefty restitution payment to my victim. I can volunteer for difficult charitable work or perform a humbling public apology. In cases of criminal punishment, Kant favors a version of *lex talonis*, or "an eye for an eye."[49] However, such a principle runs into obvious difficulties. In the realm of atonement, it would advocate the suicide of those who wrongfully cause another's death and the self-mutilation of those guilty of seriously injuring others. Such measures do not sit well with a Kantian moral theory, which holds that agents must respect their own dignity, as well as that of others, even though Kant himself notoriously defended the death penalty for murderers. As Hegel develops Kant's ideas of justice, the execution of murderers is justified because, in killing these people, we are simply insisting that they live under the law they have themselves chosen.[50] However, to apply that idea to atonement would be odd indeed inasmuch as it would amount to insisting that wrongdoers continue to abide by a morally problematic law rather than see the moral light and adopt a better law. Indeed, when Kant addresses the *theological* problem of atonement, he emphasizes the value of repentance—a change of heart.[51]

To many retributivists what seems to matter is not the particular form of response but its proportional degree of painfulness. Yet, intuitively, the particular act of atonement matters quite a bit. Imagine my friend has carelessly ruined my cashmere sweater and then punished herself for her wrongdoing by fasting for a day or by donating her own favorite sweater to charity. Perhaps I will be moved by her actions if I come to know about them,[52] but I am still out one cashmere sweater. We have here the basis of an argument for a principle of restitution as at least a supplement to retribution. However, the example also raises a more general objection. Retributivist theories require wrongdoers to respond to their offenses but not to their victims. Thereby, they elide the moral significance of the fact that the wrong has been committed against a particular person.

Two challenges face the retributivists at this point. They must argue that the wrongdoers' response to their sense of guilt not only *may* but also *must* have a punitive aspect. Retributivists must also answer the objection that a retributive theory of atonement has nothing to offer victims. In the next section I examine a theory of atonement that attempts to solve both of these problems by adapting yet another defense of retributive criminal punishment.

2.3.5 EXPRESSIVIST RETRIBUTIVISM

Expressivist versions of retributivist criminal punishment start once more with the idea that resentment and indignation are morally proper responses to criminal wrongdoing. Punishment, argues Joel Feinberg, is "the expression of attitudes of resentment...and of judgments of disapproval and reprobation."[53] Criminal wrongdoing deserves punishment because, in a just state, it deserves condemnation. Feinberg adds that the condemnation of criminal wrongdoing is necessary for the maintenance of the normative force of the law.[54] Law loses its authority and its ability to maintain social order when infractions of the law are not condemned. The importance of condemning criminal wrongdoing is strengthened when we consider the fact that failures to condemn are also expressive. When a state refuses to punish a criminal, it sends the message that the criminal's action was acceptable.[55] Jean Hampton reminds us that inegalitarian societies have often punished people differentially depending on their race, class, or gender and that these punishing practices have both expressed and socially reinforced the view that some people simply are not as valuable as others.[56] By failing to disavow the crime through some form of condemnation, the state becomes complicit in the crime.[57] The state, then, seems to have an obligation to condemn criminal wrongdoing.

Moral wrongdoers have a similar obligation to condemn their own wrongful actions. As I have argued, a proper commitment to morality and an honest and realistic appraisal of their relationship to it leads the wrongdoers to feel guilty. If the agents are to retain their commitment to morality at this point rather than rejecting morality in a misguided effort to defend themselves from their own negative judgment, they must condemn their own actions. Refusal to do so would itself be a form of wrongdoing, a denial of the authority of morality. Thus, moral wrongdoers are required to condemn their own wrongful actions.

Criminal wrongdoing deserves the condemnation of the state, and moral wrongdoing deserves the agent's own condemnation. But can we support the link between condemnation and punishment? Feinberg himself claims that the connection between condemnation and punishment is merely conventional.[58] Although the state currently expresses its disapproval of criminals through fines and incarceration, it could certainly do so in other ways. "One can imagine an elaborate public ritual, exploiting the most trustworthy devices of religion and mystery, music and drama, to express in the most solemn way the community's condemnation of a criminal for his dastardly deed."[59] "Perhaps this is only idle fantasy," Feinberg continues. "The only point I wish to make here is one about the nature of the question. The problem of justifying punishment, when it takes this form, may really be that of justifying our particular symbols of infamy."[60] This challenge to the punishment of criminals extends as well to the self-punishment of atoning wrongdoers. Why must self-punishment be the means by which we express condemnation of our own actions? Why do guilt, remorse, repentance, apologies, or restitution not suffice?

In a series of papers Hampton takes up Feinberg's challenge in the criminal context by arguing that punishment is a uniquely appropriate form of response to wrongdoing.[61] Since she focuses on the punishment of wrongdoers by others, we will need to ask later whether or how her arguments can be extended to self-punishment as well. Hampton begins her defense of expressivist retributivism by pointing out that wrongdoing too is an expressive act. To wrong another person is to express the view that the victim is less worthy than oneself.[62] To condemn wrongdoing is to express a rejection of the wrongdoer's claim to superiority and to reassert the moral truth that all people are of equal, immutable value.[63] However, we should not mistake wrongdoing and punishment for mere speech and counterspeech. There is more going on here than simple expression.

According to at least one interpretation of Hampton, wrongdoing does not simply express the view that the victim is inferior to the wrongdoer; it also provides *evidence* that the view is true.[64] Through the wrongful act, the offender has actually dominated his victim. In order effectively to counter the claim to superiority expressed by that domination, we must present a similarly strong form of *counterevidence* to it. This is what punishment can do that speeches, music, and drama cannot. By inflicting a proportional punishment on the wrongdoer, the state—acting in the name of the victim—dominates the wrongdoer in return. "Punishment undercuts the probative force of the evidence provided by the wrongdoer's action of [her] superiority."[65] The wrongful action cannot be taken "to have established or to have revealed her superiority if the victim is able to do to her what she did to him."[66] In this way, punishment is not merely a form of counterexpression to the wrongful action; it is counterevidence that establishes the equality of the victim in a manner as convincing and weighty as the original evidence for inequality. As such, punishment amounts to a vindication of the victim's moral worth, and in this way Hampton answers the question of what criminal punishment has to offer victims.

In much of her discussion of criminal punishment, it seems to be the fact that punishment is forced upon wrongdoers *against their will* that enables punishment to play the expressive and evidential role that Hampton assigns to it. "The retributive punisher uses the infliction of suffering to symbolize the subjugation of the subjugator, the domination of the one who dominated the victim. And the message carried in this subjugation is 'What you did to her, she can do to you. So you're equal.'"[67] The fact that the victims can also wield coercive power (through the state) allows them to counteract the wrongdoers' claim to superiority. This feature of Hampton's theory ill qualifies it as a defense of self-punishment. An atoning wrongdoer's imposition of pain on himself may not provide any evidence of the victim's power.

However, at other points, Hampton says that what is important is that the wrongdoer is "brought low."[68] The wrongful act brought the victim low and made the wrongdoer appear superior in contrast. The suffering of punishment brings the wrongdoer low to express the view that the wrongdoer and the victim are in fact morally equal. "The more severe the punishment, the more he is being brought low; and how low we want to bring a criminal depends on the extent to which his actions symbolize his superiority and lordship over the one he hurt."[69] This interpretation of how punishment expressively corrects wrongdoing lends itself to an account of atonement. Perhaps the wrongdoer can "bring himself low" through a self-inflicted punishment and thereby offer his own correction to his former, false claim to superiority. Insofar as either the victim or the victim's community is privy to this expression, the victim will be vindicated.

As I have argued at length elsewhere with my colleagues Heather J. Gert and Michael Hand, Hampton's defense of retributive punishment suffers from a fatal flaw.[70] It works only if we assume that domination and suffering are evidence of moral value. Wrongdoing, according to Hampton, provides evidence of the offender's superiority, but this evidence is misleading. We might expect Hampton to say that the evidence is misleading because neither the coercive power displayed by the wrongdoer nor the victim's suffering at the wrongdoer's hands are the sorts of thing that could ever count as evidence of their comparable moral value. After all, the weakest, most long-suffering person is morally equal to the strongest and most fortunate person. Nonetheless, Hampton, despite her interest in defending an egalitarian moral view, does not say this. Instead, she suggests that the evidence provided by the wrongful action is merely incomplete. In the case of atonement, the wrongdoer's self-imposed suffering counts as counterevidence to his previous claim to superiority only because that suffering "brings him low." It shows that his value is not as high as he claimed. However, suffering can serve this role only if we accept that it is evidentially connected to value in the first place. So, rather than rejecting the offensive premise that suffering is evidence of moral value, Hampton *depends upon* it to defend the appropriateness of punishment.

Might the self-punishing act, rather than *showing* that the wrongdoer's value is not as high as he originally claimed, instead merely *express his view* that this is the case? Might he not simply be communicating a withdrawal of his previous claim to superiority through punishment? Surely he might. Nevertheless, he could accomplish the same task with a well-stated apology. In order to defend retributivism through expressivism, an unavoidable connection must exist between the expressive task and the imposition of suffering. However, as our examination of Hampton's theory suggests, making that connection is not easy. Hampton's own appeal to suffering suggests a view of the connection between suffering and moral worth that threatens to degrade human value rather than defend it.

2.3.6 HEGELIAN RETRIBUTIVISM

On the other hand, Daniel Farnham argues that the preceding critique of Hampton's expressivist retributivism rests on a misinterpretation.[71] As Gert, Hand, and I have presented Hampton, punishment operates as an epistemic corrective, a form of counterevidence to the expressive content of the wrongful or criminal action. However, a more Hegelian reading of Hampton emphasizes the metaphysical import of both the offense and the act of punishment. What is wrong with wrongdoing is not merely that it expresses the view that the victim is of lesser value than the offender. The wrongful action also hampers the realization of the victim's value in the world, argues Farnham. While the rape victim and the rapist are indeed people of equal moral status, the rapist's action prevents the victim from living a life consistent with that status. In Hampton's version of expressivist retributivism, according to Farnham, "expression is not just *saying* something, it is *making something the case*."[72] In committing a wrong, the offender shapes the world in such a way that diminishes the victim's ability to exercise her rights. In punishing the wrongdoer, the state reestablishes equality. Farnham labels this version of Hampton's retributivism Hegelian "because it invokes Hegel's idea of the need to give our abstract ideas (such as autonomy or right) concrete expression through the use of social conventions that mediate our lives together."[73] Indeed, Hampton herself claims to be fleshing out Hegel's idea that wrongdoing must be annulled through punishment.[74]

Farnham's defense of a Hegelian version of retributivism is compelling in many ways. We can adapt it to the topic of atonement by allowing that the wrongdoer's own attempts to "bring herself low" might remake the world so as to restore equality. However, the central question remains. How is it that the imposition of suffering brings about a restoration of equality and value rather than making it the case that both offender and victim are now degraded and that both are now less able to realize their value in the world? Farnham allows that it may be merely a matter of convention that, at least in a just state, the punishment of an offender reestablishes her equality with the victim. However, he insists, given that social conventions inevitably play a role in determining whether and how our values affect our existence, this is not worrisome.

My concern, however, is not that convention plays a role in our methods for correcting wrongdoing. It is instead that our punitive conventions do not actually carry the egalitarian social meaning that Hampton and Farnham hope to find in them. If the punishment of criminal offenders does not degrade those offenders and if it merely establishes that they are our equals and not our superiors, then why are the American people so supremely unconcerned about violence in our prisons? If our punishing actions express our commitment to universal human dignity, why is the high rate of rape in prison a frequent topic of jokes rather than a cause for moral outrage?[75]

Turning from criminal punishment to atonement, I find that it becomes even less plausible to maintain that wrongdoers must resort to punitive means in order to abandon their previous claims to superiority and help restore a social world in which their victims' value is realized. An apology, a payment of restitution, an expression of caring, or a helping hand can achieve the same ends and is usually more effective than the pursuit of suffering per se. Once again we have failed to find sufficient reason to require wrongdoers to impose a painful penalty upon themselves and have instead found value in alternative, nonpunitive forms of atonement.

2.3.7 NONRETRIBUTIVE SELF-CONDEMNATION

I reject both the evidential and the Hegelian versions of expressivist arguments for the necessity of punishment. However, I agree with the emphasis these arguments place on the condemnation of wrongful actions and the goal of reestablishing the moral equality of victims and wrongdoers. Wrongful actions must be condemned not simply because of the benefits that follow from condemning wrongdoing but also because repudiating immoral action is constitutive of a commitment to morality. Indeed, failing to condemn wrongdoing is frequently equivalent to condoning it. Certainly, at times other people's wrongful actions are simply none of our business, and we should keep our disapproval to ourselves. But when one stands in particular, close relations to the wrongful act—as is true of the victim, the parent of an underage wrongdoer, and the state in cases involving legal wrongs—to fail to condemn the wrongful action is to send the message that one condones it.[76] When wrongdoers fail to condemn their own misdeeds, they express the idea that they continue to endorse their claim to superiority. They fail to acknowledge their accountability for the damage they have done to the realization of the victims' value in the world. Thereby, they continue to wrong their victims. For these reasons, self-condemnation is morally required of wrongdoers.

Have I now conceded the main idea of retributivism? Is there something inherently retributive in the very notion of condemnation?[77] "Condemn" is etymologically related to "damage" and "hurt."[78] We might substitute the words "blame" or "repudiate" for "condemn" here, but that would merely paper over the fact that the self-critical attitudes that I am endorsing as part of the project of atonement encompass something painful. However, while self-condemnation is unpleasant, we need not see the unpleasantness as the source of justification for the condemnation. Self-condemnation is both morally required and painful. However, it is not morally required because it is painful. Furthermore, in accepting the legitimacy of this form of pain-inducing response to wrongdoing we do not license the infliction of other forms of pain.

The self-condemning agent suffers because she recognizes what she has done yet retains or renews her commitment to morality. As Brown and Parker have put it, "At issue is not what we choose to endure or accept but what we refuse to relinquish. Redemption happens when people refuse to relinquish respect and concern for others, when people refuse to relinquish fulness of feeling, when people refuse to give up seeing, experiencing, and being connected and affected by all of life."[79] When one is alive to value, to other people, and to one's own wrongful past, then one is vulnerable to suffering. However, this does not demonstrate that suffering is intrinsically valuable. It does not support the view that atonement requires the intentional infliction of suffering as such upon oneself.

My goal has been to refute the retributivist claim that self-punishment is morally required by the fact of wrongdoing. I have not argued that self-punishment is impermissible, although I have raised worries about the meanings expressed by punitive actions. I have also criticized those who would pursue self-punishment to the neglect of more victim-centered responses such as apology or restitution. Nonetheless, one could certainly combine such tasks with punitive measures or pursue costly or painful forms of apology and restitution. This obliges us to ask whether self-imposed suffering might yet add something of value to a wrongdoer's atonement, such as a deterrent to future wrongdoing or an especially compelling form of communication with victims. Might self-punishment play a positive role in moral education, rehabilitation, or the reconciliation of relationships? Should we recommend it as a powerful means to atonement even if we cannot identify retribution as a morally required goal of atonement? I return to these questions in chapter 4.

2.4 Restitution Theories of Atonement

As an alternative to retributively based theories of atonement, I now examine theories that focus on the idea of restitution.[80] That restitution should be included in our theory of atonement seems quite straightforward. If I have destroyed your sweater, then I ought to give a new one or its equivalent to you. However, the proposal that I now discuss is that restitution is not a part of atonement; rather, it is the whole of it. As we have already seen, especially in the case of satisfaction theory, some theories of retribution have restitutive ideas at their core. Indeed, the moral language of retribution and that of restitution are sometimes indistinguishable. The word 'retribution' itself is etymologically connected to the idea of repayment.[81] Both retributive and restitutive theories often represent wrongdoing as debt and atonement as repayment. Nonetheless, while the core retributive idea is that wrongdoers deserve to suffer a loss of some kind, restitutive theories argue that victims deserve to be compensated.[82] In this section I discuss two different versions of restitutive theory: pure restitution theory, which does not include any special interest in the suffering of wrongdoers as such, and punitive restitution theory, which maintains that the suffering of wrongdoers is an important and sometimes uniquely appropriate *means* of paying restitution to the victim.[83]

The first thing we should note about restitution theories generally is that they are nonconsequentialist. While it is true that many good consequences usually ensue when victims receive restitution for the wrongs they have suffered, these increases in utility as such are not included in the justification. Rather, restitutive theories of atonement appeal to a basic, deontic moral intuition. When a person is harmed at the hands of another person, the injured party deserves to have that harm made good again. When a person's property is taken without permission, the person's right to that object remains, and the person deserves to have it returned. When the possession has been damaged beyond repair, the owner deserves to receive something of equivalent value. The principle of restitution looks backward to the rights held at the moment of the wrongful action in order to justify the wrongdoer's obligation to make restitution to the victim.

2.4.1   PURE RESTITUTION

Let us examine first the pure restitution model of atonement. This version of the theory is "pure" in the sense that it is purely restitutive and not a mixture of restitutive and retributive theories. The theory foreswears any claim that wrongdoers deserve to suffer as such in hopes of avoiding the objections that plague retributive theory.[84] As we have seen, the retributivists' insistence on suffering leaves them vulnerable to charges of bloodthirstiness in the case of criminal punishment and masochistic self-absorption in the case of self-punishment. The restitutive theorist looks not for suffering from wrongdoers but fair compensation for victims. We have also seen how the retributivists face the objection that they do not pay enough respectful attention to the victims of wrongdoing. In contrast, pure restitution theory is heavily victim centered, focusing as it does on the restoration of the victim's rightful holdings.

The principle that wrongdoers should pay restitution is familiar and compelling. It is part and parcel of a scheme of property rights. To have a right to property is to have a right to restitution for property that is taken or damaged. This right is a justified claim against the person responsible for damage or loss. The question is whether these principles of property rights are generalizable as a theory of atonement.

One objection to pure restitution theories of atonement is that, while restitution can be made to the victim by parties other than the wrongdoer, atonement cannot. If the main goal of justice in the aftermath of wrong-doing is that the victim receive compensation, then a just resolution need not involve the wrongdoer's participation at all. The wrongdoer's family or friends could compensate the victim just as effectively.[85] Restitution voluntarily offered by wrongdoers and restitution forcibly taken from them are also equivalent from the point of view of restitution theory. Yet restitution that is either compelled or paid by others provides no reason for considering the wrongdoers as having met their moral obligations or as redeemed. Victims and communities would be rather naïve to put the past behind them on such grounds since the wrongdoers have provided them with no reason to trust them not to repeat their misdeeds. If retributive theories sometimes elide the significance of the victim, restitutive theories seem to elide the significance of the wrongdoer. Perhaps the restitution theorist will say that, in order to count as *atonement*, reparations must be paid by the wrongdoers themselves. However, this move seems to be merely semantic. Why would atonement be in any way preferable to other forms of restitution if all that matters is the victim's compensation?

This lack of attention to the wrongdoer's particular relationship to the wrong is also evident when we think about the wrongdoer's state of mind. I might damage your car either negligently, recklessly, or intentionally. If the same amount of damage is created in these three cases, then I seem to owe the same amount of restitution. But the actions are wrongful in different degrees.[86]

Another problem with pure restitution theories of atonement is that the obligation to atone will lie much more lightly on wealthy wrongdoers than on poorer ones.[87] When wrongs are conceived as debts that can simply be paid off with material goods, then atonement comes to be seen as just another cost of getting what one wants. The wealthier one is, the more one can afford to act wrongly. I am reminded of a joke a stand-up comedian told several years back, when Montana had reduced the fine for speeding to five dollars. The comedian reported having been stopped for driving at a very high speed. "I gave the cop a fifty and said, 'Here, I'm going to speed through the whole damned state.'" I have long forgotten who told the joke. However, I am confident that the phrase "damned state" was part of it, and it is a telling part, indeed. When wrongdoing can be easily "paid off," respect for the one wronged will decline. This example is rather amusing. Nonetheless, we can easily come up with cases that are not funny at all. Imagine a fabulously wealthy movie star who feels he can have sex with whomever he wants and whenever he wants because, if he is accused of rape, he can afford to pay the restitution.

One very basic problem with restitutive theories is that what requires restitution is harm, but harms are not identical to wrongs. For this reason, pure restitutive theory is both too broad and too narrow to count as a theory of atonement. It is too broad because not all harms are also wrongs. To use a hackneyed example, if I break your favorite vase because I am struck by a violent epileptic fit, then I should pay restitution for the vase. However, I am certainly not guilty of any wrongdoing. More important for our topic, not all wrongs are also harms. Failed attempts at wrongdoing provide such examples. Imagine that I maliciously intend to break your favorite vase. When you step out of the room, I dash it to the ground. To my surprise, though, it is made of rubber and merely bounces. No harm was done—not even harm to our relationship if you never come to know of my failed attempt to hurt you—but I have certainly done something wrong. Some response is required from me, such as shame and a resolution to control my temper in the future, but not restitution.

Furthermore, certain types of harm do not admit of restitution. Imagine that you do witness my failed attempt to break your favorite vase. Now I have harmed our friendship. I have also hurt your feelings, damaged your sense of security, and undermined your confidence in your choice of friends.[88] The pure restitution theorist might well demand that I provide some sort of compensation for this less tangible sort of damage. For example, I might bring you a beautiful platter with a design and color scheme that complement the vase. This might in fact be just the sort of thing that could restore our relationship and soothe your feelings of hurt and bewilderment. However, does my offering to you achieve this end *because it is an act of restitution*?

Restitutive theories talk about such exchanges as the paying off of a debt. In fact, I can imagine offering the platter to you with the words "I really feel that I owe this to you for what I did." But what if I elaborate on this idea?

"I was going to buy you the soup tureen of the same design, which cost a hundred dollars. My mean-spirited attack on your vase was just a passing fit of anger, though. So it really struck me as more of a fifty-dollar sort of harm. Don't you agree?" Would you still forgive me after such a speech? Wouldn't you instead slam the door in my face?

As Hampton has pointed out, our responses to wrongdoing send messages. The expressive content of an act of restitution includes the message that the value of the harm done to the victim is commensurable with the value of the thing offered in return. If I present a material object with the suggestion that it is comparable in value to your friendship or your feelings, I do not repay my moral debt to you. Instead, I insult you. This insult, which seems clear in the case of a relatively minor act of wrongdoing like this dispute between friends, becomes even more egregious when we consider severe cases of wrongdoing such as rape or child abuse. To suggest that harms such as these could be "bought off" with money or other material goods, as our wealthy movie star from the earlier example believed he could do, is shocking.

In response, the pure restitution theorist will point out that at least restitution offers victims *something* of value. When wrongdoers are merely punished (either by themselves or by the state), the victims are left just as badly off as ever.[89] Even though a cash settlement cannot fully pay off the myriad sources of harm suffered by assault victims, it does improve their situation. If there is any doubt of this, the restitution theorist suggests that we ask such victims whether they would like to receive restitution and points to the popularity of monetary settlements for physical pain and suffering in tort law.[90] However, to say that victims would prefer restitution to punishment or to nothing at all is not yet to establish that restitution fits our ideals of atonement. We have still other options to consider.[91]

Let us return to the case of my failed attack on your favorite vase. Imagine again that I return the next day with the lovely platter that will set off the vase to its best advantage. If you perceive me as trying to buy back your friendship, the offering will fail. However, you might interpret my presentation of the platter differently. You might see it as a sign of my remorse. Its monetary value might be thought to symbolize the depth of my remorse. Just as importantly, the particular item offered has symbolic value. The fact that it is a platter that complements the vase shows that have been I thinking about the particular details of my offense. In response to an attempt to destroy something for which you had affection, I offer you something that seems likely to enhance your affection for that thing. My sensitivity to your taste, displayed in my ability to find a perfect companion piece for the vase, shows that I have been paying attention to who you are and what you care about. The time and creativity I clearly dedicated to finding just the right object are further evidence of both the seriousness with which I take my wrongdoing and the value I place on our relationship. I could not have communicated these ideas simply by giving you the fifty dollars I spent on the platter. My offering is most likely to succeed in winning your forgiveness when it is presented and received not as an act of restitution but as a gift that symbolizes my remorse for my action, my respect for you, and my appreciation of our friendship.

It may well be that voluntary acts of restitution, understood as such, often communicate remorse and respect. However, whether they do so often depends on how one makes the offer of restitution. Even in straightforward cases of wrongfully damaged property, compensation should be made with a show of remorse such as an apology and not as if it were merely a business transaction. Only when these clues about the wrongdoer's inner state are added to the compensation of harm will payments of restitution do their best work. In other cases, when what was harmed was something more intangible than property, say in a case of physical harm or personal betrayal, then the payment of material reparations can add to atonement only by serving as a symbol of something else, not as the literal repayment of a debt. For example, the wrongdoer might say, "I cannot make your body whole again. I have nothing to offer that can do that. However, I do have money, and I hope you will take it to make your life a little easier than it is now. And I hope you will accept the money as a sign of my regret for having caused those harms I can never repair." So, although material payments may well be an effective *means* of achieving redemption, restitution seems ill equipped to serve as our main conception of atonement.

2.4.2   PUNITIVE RESTITUTION

Whereas pure restitution theories of atonement aim to replace self-punishment with the compensation of the harms, punitive restitution theory combines these two measures. The punitive restitution theorists will agree with many of the critiques that we have leveled against pure restitution theory. They will agree that millionaires should not be less heavily burdened by wrongdoing than working-class folk and that there are debts that third parties cannot pay. They will insist that we attend to the fact that *this person* was the wrongdoer, and so *this person* must pay. They will agree that certain forms of harm cannot be compensated with material goods. Material harms should be repaid materially, they will argue, but nonmaterial and intangible harms must be paid back through the wrongdoer's suffering. The difference between this theory and traditional forms of retributivism is a difference in the core justification of suffering. The retributivist argues that the wrongdoer deserves to suffer, period. The punitive restitution theorist argues that the wrongdoer must suffer because the victim deserves to be compensated, and this is the only form of compensation that will do. As a theory of atonement, punitive restitution suggests that the wrongdoer pay whatever material compensation is fitting and then (at least in many cases) also perform some form of self-punishment.

While we can see that this theory is distinct from retributive theory, it is not at all clear that it is distinct in a helpful way. Why is suffering the uniquely appropriate coin to compensate for wrongdoing? What good does the wrongdoer's suffering do the victim? According to David Hershenov, victims receive a compensatory benefit insofar as they receive the pleasures of vengeance.[92] Notice the difference between Hershenov's view and the consequentialist claim that a desire for retribution is a natural emotion that must be allowed a legitimate outlet for expression if we are to avoid harmful cycles of revenge. Resentment and hatred are represented by the consequentialist argument as dangerous but natural forces that must be indulged in order to be controlled. However, Hershenov's theory treats vengeance as an intrinsically valuable form of compensation. The charge of bloodthirstiness therefore hits Hershenov's view with full force.

Herbert Morris's well-known defense of punishment as removing an unfair advantage might also be classed as a version of punitive restitution theory.[93] Morris brings to our attention the reciprocal respect for the system of rights that allows society to function. One person agrees implicitly to respect the rights of others in exchange for having others respect her own rights. To put it another way, she agrees to restrict her own activities and choices in certain ways in return for others doing the same. It is a system in which all benefit. While Morris is thinking primarily about the system of legal rights within a just state, we could also describe the rights and expectations that characterize the moral community in similar terms. When people violate a right, argues Morris, they are taking unfair advantage of the system. The wrongdoers claim more freedom than the others have allowed themselves. In this way, the wrongdoers have benefited unfairly by their wrongful actions. Punishment takes away this unfair advantage. When the state limits the liberty of criminals, it prevents them from enjoying the unfair surfeit of liberty they claimed in their wrongful actions. Perhaps the self-punishing wrongdoers can do the same thing by voluntarily forfeiting some form of liberty in order to compensate for the excess of liberty they enjoyed in acting wrongly.[94] Like restitution theories generally, this view emphasizes the necessity of compensation. The imbalance of liberty is unfair to the community, and so the community deserves to have equilibrium restored. The theory includes retributive elements insofar as it insists that the only form of compensation that will do is one that consists of a harm done to the wrongdoers—the limitation of their liberty.

My objections to the "unfair advantage" account as a theory of atonement parallel those that have been raised in the literature on criminal justice. First of all, not all wrongs or all crimes can be characterized as the taking of benefits. Failed attempts to commit wrongs are cases in which wrongdoers do not achieve an unfair advantage yet still owe some sort of response.[95] Worse yet, Morris's account suggests a disturbing view of what is wrong with cases of violent crimes. Hampton asks the following:

> Are we to understand that the reason we punish rapists is that we believe they derived a benefit from being able to rape (which is greater than that gained by those who merely steal cars or speed on the highway) that we wish *we* could have but which we prevent ourselves from enjoying because we believe such conduct, when performed on a widespread basis, is collectively disadvantageous?[96]

In this way, Morris's theory seems to commit him to an unacceptable theory of value.

Does the latter objection maintain its force when we turn from the state's punishment of criminals to the self-punishment of wrongdoers? Although the other members of the community (hopefully) do not count raping as an advantage to the rapist, the rapist himself seems to see things that way. Presumably rapists rape because they believe that it will somehow be satisfying. Perhaps, then, when the rapist decides to atone for his wrongdoing, he can negate the unfair advantage that he understands himself to have claimed through self-punishment.

However, this interpretation of the value of self-punishment continues to be disturbing. If in punishing himself the rapist is saying, "I enjoyed a benefit in violation of the rules that we all agreed to live by, and now I am paying back what I owe," then the rapist is continuing to conceive of rape as beneficial. However, the suggestion that he continues to hold this view undermines the claim that he is atoning. It is evidence that he continues to hold problematic moral beliefs. Instead, it seems to me that the rapist could be redeemed only if he comes to see his former action not as the unfair taking of a benefit but as a trauma he inflicted upon another person. As the expressivist view claims, self-punishment sends a message, and if self-punishment is to be justified, then the message must be morally acceptable. The message will not be morally acceptable if it shows disregard for the victim's point of view.

Respect for victims is undervalued in Morris's theory as a whole. In committing the wrongful act, the offender has taken a benefit denied to other participants in the overall scheme of rights and responsibilities. Compensation is then owed to the community as a whole. The rape victim is included in this compensatory scheme only insofar as she is a community member who has herself refrained from raping others. Her particular role as the victim has no special value. For the victim, the devastating nature of the violation plays no particular role in the justification of punishment or atonement. Of course, the theory recognizes that her right was violated, but the justification for the punishment of the offender is not the fact that he violated her fundamental rights. Rather, the justification is grounded in the unfair advantage the offender claimed viv-à-vis the group (whether the state or the moral community) by failing to restrain himself when others had accepted the burden of restraint. In this way, the theory fails to grant the victim the respect and status she deserves.

2.5   *Conclusions*

To sum up this evaluation of retributive and restitutive theories of atonement, we have found some compelling ideas and moral claims, but we have also discovered that both theories leave out much of what is important in the aftermath of wrongdoing. The expressive retributivists' demand for self-condemnation is compelling, as is their claim that the response to wrongdoing should remake the world in a way that will promote the realization of human value. However, their insistence that these values morally necessitate the self-punishment of wrongdoers was not borne out. If we accept that wrongdoing deserves self-condemnation and that self-condemnation is a painful experience, suffering will have worked its way into the account of atonement. On the other hand, to say that atonement appears to include an element of suffering is a far cry from a full-blown retributivist theory. Similarly, certain principles of restitution are equally hard to deny. If wrongdoers have created a material harm, they ought to offer restitution. But again, restitution cannot be a complete principle of atonement. Wrongdoers should do certain things besides paying restitution, and, in particular cases, offers of restitution are insulting.

Our discussion of retribution and restitution has also uncovered other moral concerns. Those retributive and restitutive theories of atonement that did not insist on the wrongdoer's sense of guilt or repentance were unacceptable on those grounds. We have had cause to inquire into the wrongdoers' moral improvement. What good, after all, is it for wrongdoers to "pay a price" for their offenses, either materially or through suffering, if they are just going to turn around and offend again? While retributivism focuses on the wrongdoer, we were also interested in victims and communities. While pure restitution theory ignores the distinction between harms and wrongs, we found both aspects to be important.

Both retributive and restitutive theories of atonement are enamored with economic images. Wrongdoing is conceived as the incursion of a debt, and atonement is described as a form of repayment. However, on closer examination, these metaphors lose their power. Debt and repayment are useful concepts when we are thinking about how goods may be transferred among persons. Nonetheless, the suffering of one person does not (or anyway *should not*) count as an intrinsic good to another person. Furthermore, many of the "goods" that may be damaged by wrongdoing are clearly not transferable. Trust, friendship, community, self-esteem, health, life, a sense of security, and a feeling of wholeness are all valuable things that, once damaged or destroyed, cannot simply be repaid or compensated. A response is called for from the wrongdoer, but the response will have to be of a different sort.

CHAPTER THREE

Changing One's Heart, Changing the Past

Repentance and Moral Transformation

3.1 *Introduction*

At least as common as the metaphors that represent atonement as the repayment of moral debt are the images of atonement as transformation. The transformation in question affects either the wrongdoer's self (she has a "change of heart" and "becomes a new person"), the course of her life (having "gone astray," she now "walks the straight and narrow"), or even the wrongful action itself (her atonement "changes the past"). These images of transformation or reorientation are, of course, familiar from religious discourses, but they also permeate secular sources and popular culture. In legal contexts, the transformation is frequently described as "reformation" or "rehabilitation," and emphasis is placed on changes in behavior that are consistent with a variety of internal motivations. In religious contexts, the key concept is repentance. Here, external change is rooted in an internal transformation.

The project for this chapter is to explore the suggestion that the proper goal of an atoning wrongdoer is transformation. In this exercise I ask what must be transformed. The role of repentance as a means of achieving the desired form of transformation is a secondary theme of the chapter. The words for repentance in Greek (*metanoia*), Hebrew (*teshuvah*), and Arabic (*tawbah*) are all associated with turning or returning. To repent is to reorient oneself with respect to the good through a transformation in one's emotions, attitudes, dispositions, and values. In repenting, one both accepts responsibility for the past action and repudiates that action as wrongful. One adopts the sincere intention to act better in the future if presented with similar choices. 'Repentance' also names a painful, remorseful emotion that is linked to judgments of moral wrongdoing and a process of moral change.[1] What counts as repentance is disputed. Some think of it as a purely internal state that one can achieve even upon one's deathbed. Others claim that internal change is genuine or complete only when it is expressed in external action, such as confession, apology, penance, or the successful resistance of temptation.[2] Once we have a clearer proposal as to what must be transformed, we will be better able to ask whether internal change, external action, or both are required for successful atonement.

This chapter examines various versions of the suggestion that atonement requires transformation, including those drawn from the writings of Kant, Josiah Royce, and Max Scheler. I consider, in turn, the goals of transforming the wrongdoer's identity, future behavior, and moral commitments, as well as the significance of the past. I conclude that none of these approaches to atonement gives a complete account of wrongdoers' moral obligations. This conclusion appears to be at odds with a popular way of thinking about atonement in the Christian tradition, which holds that repentance is sufficient for redemption. I argue that, when we look at this tradition more closely, it does not actually provide the ringing endorsement of the value of repentance one might expect. In fact, I argue that repentance is celebrated in Christian circles in answer to a question that is different from the one we are asking here.

3.2 Changing One's Identity

You have committed a wrong against another person. Something must change, but what? Perhaps the most extreme answer given in the literature is *you*. You must become not just a better version of yourself but a whole new person as well. You must undergo a change in your identity in order to free yourself from your status as wrongdoer. Kant proposes such a theory of atonement in *Religion within the Limits of Reason Alone*.

Much like the satisfaction theorists, Kant presents the problem of sin in terms of a debt that the sinner cannot pay off:

> Whatever a man may have done in the way of adopting a good disposition, and, indeed, however steadfastly he may have persevered in conduct conformable to such a disposition, *he nevertheless started from evil*, and

this debt he can by no possibility wipe out. For he cannot regard the fact that he incurs no new debts subsequent to his change of heart as equivalent to having discharged his old ones. Neither can he, through future good conduct, produce a surplus over and above what he is under obligation to perform at every instant, for it is always his duty to do all the good that lies in his power.[3]

Unlike the satisfaction theorists, Kant does not allow for such a thing as supererogatory merit that can make up for past wrongs. He also rejects their claim that a third party can pay a debt on the sinner's behalf.[4] He argues that the solution to the problem comes with the sinner's genuine and settled change of heart. Before this moral reformation, the wrongdoer deserves to suffer the consequences of his free actions and his poor disposition, namely punishment. Not even God could justify withholding punishment from such a person.[5] However, once the change is made, the debt is left behind:

> Can the moral consequence of his former disposition, the punishment (or in other words the effect upon the subject of God's displeasure), be visited upon his present state, with its bettered disposition, in which he is already an object of divine pleasure? ... *After* his change of heart ... the penalty cannot be considered appropriate to his new quality ..., for he is now leading a new life and is morally another person.[6]

Given the view that "the disposition is itself the only basis for moral self-identity,"[7] a genuine transformation of one's disposition qualifies as a change of identity. The new agent is no longer liable for the consequences of the past agent's moral failings.

However, Kant himself seems to point out the reasons for rejecting this account of a change in identity as a theory of interpersonal atonement. He emphasizes throughout book II of *Religion* that, while actions are merely the "appearance" of an agent's moral disposition—bits of evidence that are never complete or conclusive—they are all we have to go on. He repeatedly mocks the view that deathbed repentance is sufficient for salvation. His rejection of deathbed repentance does not stem from a claim that it is impossible for one's moral disposition to change suddenly at the end of life; instead, he rejects that view as incompatible with a moral theory that is fit for practical application.[8] Although the dying agent may believe himself to have undergone a moment of radical moral conversion, he has no way of knowing whether he really has. God can know, but the agent cannot. To give sinners the hope of achieving such a hasty transformation, Kant argues, is to make immoral behavior more likely.[9] However, we can turn this same point against Kant's own accounting of the power of a change of heart. We simply cannot tell whether we or others have undergone a moral transformation of a sort sufficient to secure a change in identity. Thus, his theory of atonement is of little use to a moral theory that proposes to guide human interactions.

In these same passages Kant also points out how poorly a theory of atonement based on personal moral transformation alone will serve the interests of victims. Arguing against those who would assure the sinner that deathbed repentance will bring salvation, Kant claims that we would serve the goals of morality better by emphasizing the significance of the wrongdoer's sins with the hope "of impelling him before his life ends to undo so far as possible what he has done, by reparation or compensation proportionate to his actions."[10] When a theory of atonement allows for redemption through "mere words," he adds, "the rights of humanity … are disregarded and no one gets back what belongs to him."[11] He continues, "This is a sequel so common to this form of expiation that an instance to the contrary is almost unheard of."[12] Unfortunately, Kant's own theory of atonement would have the same consequences were we to apply it in our interactions with one another. A change of identity would cut me off from any previous liability not only to God but to my victim as well.

Finally, we might ask why a change in one's moral disposition, however thoroughgoing that change might be, should count as a change in identity. Given how much we rely on the stability of identity for social and moral purposes, the decision to count someone as a genuinely new person should not be made lightly. Kant argues that God *allows* the change in disposition to count as a change of identity through an act of grace,[13] and that is a lucky thing indeed since Kant sees no other way out of the problem. He admits that to this status as a new person "we really have no legal claim."[14] The change of heart, then, despite initial appearances, does not *earn* the wrongdoer release from his guilt in Kant's theory of atonement. The wrongdoer requires God's mercy.

Putting all of these passages together, we find that, although "[Kant's] theology in general is the assertion of the priority of the apprehension of moral obligation over everything else,"[15] *Religion* offers little by way of an account of wrongdoers' moral obligations. We are told that we must develop a more perfect moral disposition, but when we inquire as to how that sort of improvement might free us from our guilt for the past, all we are told in the end is that we are permitted to hope for God's mercy. Kant gives us no reason to believe that such an improved moral disposition will satisfy either our own or other people's moral demands on us:

Although the man (regarded from the point of view of his empirical nature as a sentient being) is *physically* the self-same guilty person as before and *must be judged as such before a moral tribunal and hence by himself*; yet, because of his new disposition, he is (regarded as an intelligible being) *morally* another in the eyes of a divine judge for whom this disposition takes the place of action.[16]

Kant offers us no particular advice on how we are to redeem ourselves in one another's eyes other than his brief mention of reparation and compensation.[17]

I have not rejected the fundamental idea that a person might change so much in his psychological or moral makeup that it could make sense to speak of him as a "different person" from the one who committed the wrongful action. In cases of dramatic brain injury or disease, for instance, such judgments may be appropriate and lead us to conclude that the person before us is no longer morally bound by the misdeeds of the past.[18] Could dramatic moral conversions achieve the same result? We should be cautious about taking this view because of the important role that stable assignments of identity play in our interactions with one another. Granting a change of identity threatens to leave the victims carrying the burdens of the wrongs committed against them. Furthermore, while we sometimes describe a reformed wrongdoer as having become "a whole new person," such talk is reserved for cases of a dramatic moral improvement that follows upon either a severe wrong or a long-lasting pattern of wrongdoing that gave a marked shape to the offender's life. Surely these cases form only a subset of all of the cases of wrongdoing and repentance.

Most of the wrongs committed are the minor ones of everyday life. We break promises to one another out of negligence or fatigue. We hurt other people's feelings because we are frustrated, imperceptive, or self-absorbed. We avoid carrying our fair share of the burdens at home or at work. We tell petty lies to get benefits we do not deserve or avoid blame we do deserve. Such cases of wrongdoing call out for moral change on our part. We need to learn how to control our tempers, be more considerate and less self-centered, have more integrity, and be more honest. Yet, these improvements to our characters hardly constitute a change in personal identity. The changes they embody are neither that sharp nor that dramatic. Still, they are responses that we ought to make given our misdeeds and failings.[19] Significant and valuable changes can be made to the self without leading to a change of identity.

Meir Dan-Cohen develops this sort of account of atonement, according to which the wrongdoer leaves his guilt behind by altering the contours of his self rather than by becoming a different person altogether.[20] Dan-Cohen uses a metaphor of changing borders. A political state can move its borders in accord with certain reasonable political norms, such that a former part of its territory is no longer within the state and no longer its responsibility.

Similarly, "revisionary practices [which include repentance, forgiveness, and pardon] redraw the wrongdoer's boundary so as to leave the offense outside, thereby releasing the wrongdoer from responsibility and rendering any negative attitudes toward the wrongdoer based on the past misdeed no longer supportable."[21] The advantage to this view is that the "new" agent is numerically identical to the "old" one. At the same time, though, a change in the wrongdoer's self accounts for his freedom from continuing moral liability for the wrongful act. One does not become a completely new person through repentance, but one may become a sufficiently different person.

Unfortunately, Dan-Cohen does not offer us any particular view of how one manages to change the borders of one's self, opting instead for a pluralistic position. He allows that a number of equally legitimate sets of norms for reshaping identity may be held by different parties about one and the same subject.[22] The agent would continue to be responsible for the wrongful action according to some—but not other—normative points of view. There is no determinate fact of the matter as to whether the agent has successfully atoned or not. While there is much that is appealing about a pluralistic view such as this, it does not offer sufficient guidance to wrongdoers, victims, or communities who ask themselves what sorts of responses to wrongdoing they ought to count as achieving a change in borders. It also does not confront the fact that some widely held norms of atonement run into significant moral objections, which our inquiry has already shown.

3.3   Changing the Past

Despair over the possibility of atonement is frequently linked to the impossibility of changing the past. Josiah Royce writes, "That fact, that event, that deed, is irrevocable. The fact that I am the one who then did thus and so, not ignorantly, but knowingly,—that fact will outlast the ages. That fact is as endless as time."[23] Yet some writers on atonement, including Royce himself, suggest that the past can be changed in some sense after all: The *meaning* of the past is subject to revision.

Imagine two similar acts of robbery. In the first case, the thief remains unrepentant even though he never happens to repeat the action. In the second case, the thief does repent. She comes to be aware of how her crime has affected another person's life. She is shocked that she has become the type of person who could have made this choice. The wrongful act, through her repentant reaction, becomes for her a spur to a new life. The two robberies have different meanings because of the wrongdoers' differing responses. In the case of the unrepentant thief, the meaning of the robbery remains negative over time. It was a selfish violation of another person's rights. But to describe the second robbery in the same terms would be to ignore something important. Instead, we want to describe the second crime positively, as a turning point or a moment of epiphany.

Another Christian theory of the Atonement of Jesus provides a model for thinking about how the meaning of the past can change. Sometimes the claim that Jesus atoned for human sin is explained by narratively linking Jesus with Adam. Adam and Eve, said to be the first human beings, are also the first sinners, and their original sin is believed to have alienated humanity as a whole from God. Jesus, as a representative of humanity, later reconciles human beings with God through the goodness of his life and the sacrifice of his death. According to some interpretations, Jesus's sacrifice redeems Adam's sin insofar as the relationship between God and humans is actually better for this entire sequence of events having taken place than it would have been had Adam never sinned. The sin is "redeemed" in the sense that it is revalued. An action that looked at first to be a tragedy of human history is transformed into something of positive value in virtue of the role that it serves in the whole narrative of the human-divine relationship. It comes to be known as the felix culpa, or the "fortunate fall." Similarly, the repentant thief in our example might view her act of robbery as a fortunate fall in that it is a wrongful action that brings her to a new and morally better life.

Royce's theory of interpersonal atonement, in which a "suffering servant" reconciles the community to the traitorous deed of another by creatively using the wrong to rejuvenate the commitment of others to the cause, follows the same pattern.[24] Royce describes the work of the suffering servant as follows: "First, this creative work shall include a deed, or various deeds, for which only this treason furnishes the opportunity.... secondly, *The world as transformed by this creative deed, is better than it would have been had all else remained the same, but had that deed of treason not been done at all*."[25] The betrayal followed by the work of the suffering servant is more valuable than consistent loyalty would have been.[26] The past is not thereby erased, and the wrong remains a wrong, but the wrongdoer may now say to herself:

> Something in the nature of a genuinely reconciling element has been added, not only to my world and to my own life, but also to the inmost meaning even of my deed of treason itself.... [Something has occurred that] gives to my very treason itself a new value; so that I can say, not: "It is undone;" but "I am henceforth in some measure, in some genuine fashion, morally reconciled to the fact that I did this evil."[27]

The past has not changed, but the meaning or significance of the past has changed. In the remainder of this section I look at two different ways of envisioning how the meaning of the past can change. The first takes a consequentialist line on the transformative significance of good that is brought out of bad. The second explores the possibility that repentance and other acts of atonement change the meaning of the past by changing the context in which a past wrongful act ought to be narrated or interpreted.

3.3.1   CHANGING THE CAUSAL TRAJECTORY OF THE PAST

One way to defend the possibility of changing the meaning of a wrongful action is to appeal to an act consequentialist moral theory. According to the act consequentialists, whether an action is right or wrong depends on its consequences. A right action is an action that maximizes good consequences, such as happiness or well-being. A wrong action is an action that leads to an overbalance of bad consequences. If we appeal to this moral framework, then we might argue that an act that initially appears to be a wrongful action, such as the robbery committed by our soon-to-be repentant thief, actually comes to be (or is perhaps *revealed* to be) a right action after all. The robbery, which threatened to increase unhappiness on balance, turns out to maximize good consequences. To the thief it serves as such a dramatic representation of the terrible course her life is taking that it causes a deep and lasting change in her character. Were it not for that crime, she would have continued to get into petty forms of trouble and to live an uninspired and uninspiring life. Instead, the action sparked a repentance that has turned her toward a life filled with value. Our moral evaluation of the robbery is changed from what it would have been at the moment of the event because repentance changes the causal trajectory of the past. In this sense, the moral significance of the past action has changed.

My objections to this approach to atonement are rooted in standard objections to the act consequentialist moral theory that underlies it. An act consequentialist theory commits one to accepting that no matter how violent, harmful, or malicious a particular action might be, it could be justified by the consequences that unpredictably follow from it. Furthermore, by focusing solely on the consequences of action, one ignores the particularity of the victim. Notice that our repentant thief might achieve a surplus of good consequences over bad without ever addressing the victim directly. In fact, she is more likely to do so if she stays hidden from the victim, who might turn her over to authorities, who will imprison her and thereby prevent her from doing good works. The victim is left to deal with his feelings of anger and insecurity alone, and it seems only to add insult to injury to claim that the robbery was not actually a wrongful act after all.

The concentration on consequences also leads us to ignore the particularity of the wrongdoer. As the Jesus/Adam narrative and Royce's "suffering servant" already highlight, good could be brought out of bad by someone other than the thief herself. If her act of robbery causes her brother or her victim to enter into a life of charitable work, ought we to say that the act was not wrong after all? Morality places demands on the thief in virtue of her role as wrongdoer, no matter what her brother or her victim might do in response to her crime. The thief should herself repudiate the past, apologize, make restitution, and change her ways.

Finally, the consequentialist model for changing the significance of the past does not deal well with cases of minor wrongdoing. Consider a case in which someone is rudely short tempered with a friend, where this action is not part of a lasting pattern of behavior but instead occurs in a moment of weakness. In this instance, a brief feeling of repentance, a quick apology, and better future behavior seem to fulfill the wrongdoer's moral obligation. However, has he transformed the moral significance of his loss of temper? Has he, through his atonement, made the world better than it would have been had the wrong never taken place? The wrongdoer's response prevents any lasting harm from resulting from his bad behavior, but it need not be that he has made the world, himself, or this friendship better than it would have been had he restrained his temper in the first place.

3.3.2 CHANGING THE INTERPRETATION OF THE PAST

In "Repentance and Rebirth," Max Scheler considers the claim that "Repentance is the meaningless attempt to turn a past act into something which never happened."[28] This rejection of repentance, Scheler objects, rests on a mistaken view of time. Objective time—"a uniform one-dimensional and one-directional continuum" that is part of "the continuous flux of inanimate nature with its movements and changes"—is contrasted with time as we experience it.[29] "Every single one of these life-moments, corresponding with just one indivisible point of objective Time, contains within itself its three extensions: the experienced past, the present being experienced and the future, whose ingredients are constituted by awareness, immediate memory and immediate expectation."[30] The past, as we experience it, shapes our present and future. Nonetheless, the present as we experience it and the future that we anticipate also change our present experience of the past.

Put another way, the past has a meaning in virtue of being interpreted by a mind. How that mind interprets the past will depend on the context in which the past is being considered.[31] That context can change. One thing that changes the context of interpretation is repentance. In the case of the repentant thief, our understanding of the significance of the robbery is altered by the fact that the crime formed a turning point in the life of the actor that led to a better future. "As *past*," that is, as something interpreted and not just as an objective time-slice of the configuration of inanimate nature, "this time-content becomes 'ours'—is subordinated to the power of the *personal Self*. Therefore, the extent and nature of the effects that every part of our past may exercise upon the sense of our life lie still within our power at *every* moment of our life.... 'Historical reality' is incomplete and, so to speak, redeemable."[32] The significance of the past can always be changed. Atonement is always possible.

From this defense of the possibility of changing the meaning of the past, Scheler moves to a particular defense of the value of repentance as the means to change. Repentance "places the regretted conduct or attitude in a new relation within the totality of one's life, setting it to work in a new direction."[33] Only by both facing the past with an honest acknowledgment of its faults and committing oneself to a different and better set of values can one break free of the old patterns of life and have a better future. "You are now *free* from the floodtide of bygone guilt and wickedness that was sweeping you relentlessly away, *free* from that rigid chain of effect, such as subsisted before repentance, which produces ever new guilt from old so that the pressure grows like an avalanche."[34] By transforming the significance of the past and breaking its destructive hold on the future, repentance is the "neutralization,"[35] "the removal, the annihilation of guilt."[36]

Scheler's specific claim that repentance in and of itself can secure a change in the meaning of the past is worrisome. It suggests that the relevant or authoritative interpretation of the past is either the one that the wrongdoer holds herself, which raises the danger of bias and self-deception, or perhaps the interpretation that is held by an all-knowing God, which would have objective validity but is inaccessible to us. Furthermore, both of these positions on interpretative authority dismiss the relevance and the reasonableness of the victim's and the community's interpretations of the past.[37] When we consider this greater variety of interpretative perspectives on the past, we are forced to reconsider just what needs to change in the aftermath of wrongdoing.

Let us consider another example in which the wrongdoer changes the past through both repentance and the creation of a surplus of good consequences that a broad spectrum of society will value. A mother physically abuses her child. After the child has grown up and moved away, the mother comes to repent her actions and starts a twelve-step program for abusive parents. The mother's own experience as an abuser gives her an insight that psychologists and criminologists have generally lacked, and her methods prove to be effective. Groups based on her methods open around the country. Her efforts save thousands of children from the sorts of harms she inflicted on her own child.

There is certainly much that is good in this case. The community at large will almost certainly view the story as redemptive. But let us fill out a few more of the details. Let us suppose that the mother, from a mixture of fear and shame, has neither apologized directly to her son nor helped him in any way to heal from the harms she caused him. They no longer communicate at all. How might he view her social work? Will he interpret it as a sign of her remorse for what she did to him, as a humiliating revelation of his private affairs, or as an attempt by his mother to become successful and admired on the back of what was, for him, a devastating childhood? Were the public to learn that the son continues to be skeptical and resentful, their approval of the mother might wane (or they might criticize the son instead). Yet, I suspect that people would continue to see the mother as having redeemed the meaning of the past to a significant degree in virtue of her good works.

The example of the mother and son presses the question of whose interpretation of the past should carry the most weight. Perhaps it pushes us to Dan-Cohen's pluralistic position. On the other hand, I think it also shows that the meaning of the past can be changed, reasonably, significantly, and from a number of perspectives while still leaving much to be desired from the point of view of morality. Although the mother has changed her heart and is performing an invaluable service for others, she also owes something directly to her son. Scheler is concerned with the agent's conscience and relationship with God. As in most Christian discussions of repentance, the human victim of the wrongful action barely enters the discussion. Scheler makes only one oblique reference to "the urge to...repair the wrong."[38] Yet the victim surely deserves more consideration than this in an account of righting wrongs.

Focusing simply on the interpretation of the past or on creating good effects as a response to bad actions distracts us from the core relevance of the relationships among the parties directly involved in the wrongful action. I suspect that the account of atonement as changing the meaning of the past simply has things the wrong way around. Although the meaning of the past can be changed without proper atonement having been made, when proper atonement is made the meaning of the past will normally change.

3.4   Changing the Future

One might argue that the kind of transformation that is morally required of a wrongdoer is really much simpler than what we have considered so far. The past cannot be changed in the sense in which we want it to be changed. Wrongs, as opposed to mere harms, cannot truly be repaired. So, a realistic account of atonement will demand simply that the wrongdoer not repeat the offensive action. We want wrongdoers to change the course of their behavior. If particular means, such as repentance or self-punishment, will effectively motivate wrongdoers to better behavior, then they ought to take these steps. In support of this view, people often justify the claim that a former offender has redeemed himself by pointing to the fact that he has never repeated his misdeed. "He is no longer a thief," we say. "He has not stolen anything in twenty years." To distinguish cases of better behavior from cases of simple inability to repeat wrongdoing ("there's been nothing to steal, he's been stranded on a desert island for twenty years") we might define atonement in terms of active deterrence. To atone is successfully to deter oneself from reoffending.

In order for atonement to succeed fully, one cannot repeat the same sort of misdeed. However, the sole aim of deterrence makes for an anemic theory of atonement. We care about much more, from a moral point of view, than just better future behavior. Something is surely lacking morally if the harms to the victim are not repaired. Yet, wrongdoers may well be able to deter themselves from reoffending without making any form of reparation. Furthermore, we want the wrongdoers to deter themselves from wrongdoing for the right sorts of reasons.

Toying with the story in the film *Unforgiven*,[39] suppose the gunslinger begins walking the straight and narrow simply for the love of a good woman and not because that good woman has also convinced him that his past actions were wrong. This is not a redemptive narrative. We continue to blame him for his past and regard him with suspicion. In part, we may worry about the stability of any deterrent methods that do not include genuine repentance. Nonetheless, I would argue, repentance has a distinctive value that is independent of its role as a deterrent. In the actual plot of *Unforgiven*, the gunslinger shows a number of signs of repentance. However, when his beloved wife dies and he struggles to raise their children, he returns to his former career as a murderer for hire. The viewer is left to wonder whether this is a case of insincere repentance, weakness of will, or the irresistible logic of the Wild West. Still, it is clear that our moral evaluation of him turns on this point. He is a morally better person if his repentance is sincere, though flawed or defeated.

The images of turning or returning provide a clue to the value of repentance. Repentant persons reject their former actions, habits, thoughts, or character traits in favor of a new set of values, commitments, dispositions, and intentions. Repentance is not a mere change in one's future course. It is not like switching one's major in college or dropping one hobby for another. It is a repudiation of one's past as wrongful and as a mistake for which one acknowledges responsibility and blameworthiness. In this way, repentance includes what I have argued was the lesson of retributive theory—the idea that wrongdoing deserves condemnation. Repentant persons acknowledge that their former actions were wrong and neither excused nor justified by some other consideration. In repenting, one sometimes acknowledges that one's past values—the moral views to which one had dedicated oneself—were wrongful. At other times, one continues to endorse the old set of values but criticizes oneself as having fallen short in one's pursuit of them. Repentance is sometimes described as both accepting a wrong as one's own and rejecting it. One commits or recommits oneself to the right and the good.

This combination of a rejection of the past as wrongful and a commitment to better values makes the emotion of repentance a generally preferable response to wrongdoing than related emotions of self-assessment such as guilt, regret, remorse, or shame. In feeling guilt, one recognizes responsibility for wrongdoing but does not necessarily reject the past. To use Morris's example, a boy may see that he has wronged his father and feel the pain of guilt, yet defiantly refuse to wish the past any different.[40] He may value his mistreatment of his father as an assertion of his independence. The feelings of regret and remorse include a wish to change the past, but they are not necessarily moral emotions. I may regret delivering an insult against a coworker because it was not half as clever as another comment that occurs to me a few minutes later, or I may feel remorseful about it only because I have been punished and not because I have developed any regard for my coworker's feelings. Shame is an emotion that is often said to attach to a judgment of who I am rather than what I have done. Because shame can be created through an awareness of other people's evaluations of us, we sometimes feel shame even when we believe ourselves to be in the right.[41] Feelings of regret, remorse, and shame, then, may or may not signal recognition of moral wrongdoing. Most important, shame, guilt, regret, and remorse are all compatible with moral passivity.[42] They will not necessarily be combined with a disposition to improve oneself. To repent, however, is to recommit oneself to morality as one understands it.

Conceived of as a reorientation toward morality, the benefits of repentance are obvious. As noted earlier, repentance deters future wrongdoing. Truly repentant persons, in either changing their values or recommitting themselves to their existing values, adopt a disposition to act better in the future. But repentance is also intrinsically valuable, presuming, of course, that the agent's change of commitment is reasonable and that the agent is indeed embracing values or actions that are morally better rather than morally worse.

So far, this defense of the value of repentance supports the judgments and dispositional changes that are characteristic of repentance. However, it does not yet explain why wrongdoers must undergo the pain that is characteristic of repentance. Is it not enough that they acknowledge their mistakes and recommit themselves to a better path? Why must they also suffer for it?[43]

The answer to this question follows the pattern of the "moral hangover" defense of guilt defended in chapter 2. The pain of repentance is a natural consequence of wrongdoing for those who judge themselves to be guilty of wrongdoing and yet remain committed to moral norms. This commitment is an emotional, as well as an intellectual, attachment. When people are genuinely committed to norms for behavior and character, their adherence to those norms *matters* to them. Their well-being, as they themselves experience it, is affected by their beliefs about whether they have met those standards. To care about being a moral person is to open oneself up to the pain of repentance. However, the pain is not what gives repentance its value. The pain is instead a natural consequence of a requisite commitment to morality.

Under the moral hangover defense, it is a bit of awkward to say that wrongdoers "must" or "are required to" feel repentant or guilty. The moral emotions are not themselves morally required, but they are natural consequences of the attitudes that *are* morally required. Smoke is a natural consequence of fire, but it would be odd to describe someone who is required to start a fire (say, to keep us warm) as also required to make smoke. As convenient shorthand for the longer explanation provided by the moral hangover account, however, I sometimes talk about repentant or guilty feelings as required.

I have offered a justification of repentance, but how much does it accomplish? Repentance is a proper response to wrongdoing. Wrongdoers must repent. Nonetheless, repentance alone is not enough. If all we cared about in the aftermath of wrongdoing were the wrongdoer's character or future actions, repentance might suffice. But we want much more than this because wrongdoing is much more damaging and pernicious than either of these views acknowledges. By itself, repentance will not restore the damage that was done to the victim's property, reputation, body, or psyche. The mere fact that the wrongdoer has repented does not ease the victim's fear or resentment if only for the simple reason that the victim may not be sure of that repentance.

One might insist that those who are truly repentant will express their repentance in word and action and satisfy any claims for restitution that they have incurred, at least whenever such actions are possible. To be motivated to act in these ways is partly constitutive of what it is to repent. However, to claim that repentance will result in appropriate action is, at best, to give an incomplete account of our moral obligations. Consider, for instance, that we can express repentance in many ways and that people frequently disagree about which particular expressions are satisfactory. One might express one's repentance by offering the victim a monetary payment that goes beyond mere compensation, engaging in secret self-punishment, or writing a check to a charity. One might apologize directly to the victim, confess to a third party, or write a literary work that represents one's remorse and desire to change the past.[44] These different responses will be more or less appropriate depending on the details of the wrongs done and the circumstances of the involved parties. Still, it does not seem that we can make these distinctions simply by thinking about the wrongdoer's repentance and how it might be sincerely expressed. Instead, it seems that we should think about what the wrongdoers owe to their victims or communities *besides* their repentance.

3.6 *Repentance in Theology*

I have defended repentance as a valuable response to wrongdoing. Any response to wrongdoing that did not include genuine repentance would fail to be satisfactory. However, I have denied that repentance provides a sufficient account of atonement. The internal state of repentance, which is characterized by a remorseful acknowledgment of responsibility for wrongdoing and a recommitment to acting morally in the future, does not in itself guarantee that the victim's interests will be properly addressed. If we think of repentance as a state that requires both this internal change and its expression in external action, we are on the road to a better theory of atonement. However, the ideal of recommitting oneself to morality does not yet give us a sufficiently precise characterization of the external actions that are appropriate or required.

In drawing these conclusions, I appear to be placing myself in opposition to a widely held view (associated with some popular interpretations of Christian doctrine) that the internal state of repentance alone can suffice for moral and spiritual redemption. The Christian faithful are assured that if they sincerely repent, even if the moment of repentance comes on their deathbeds and allows no opportunity for further action, they will be redeemed. They are also directed to offer forgiveness to repentant abusers. Such heavy emphasis on repentance suggests that repentance must be a valuable thing indeed in order to deserve both God's and other people's forgiveness. A closer look at these views, however, reveals that desert has little or nothing to do with it. In Christian, as well as Judaic and Islamic, traditions the role of repentance in the redemption of the sinner says much more about God's merit than the sinner's.[45] Similarly, the requirement on human victims to forgive is frequently more directly rooted in the victims' needs and interests than in the merit of the penitents. In this section I argue that my critique of repentance does not stand in opposition to these religious views. Instead, I believe that the theologians and I are simply asking different questions.

In the Christian debates, theologians known as exemplar theorists argue that a theory of atonement centered on repentance is more consistent with the assumption of God's moral nature than is satisfaction theory.[46] Recall that, in satisfaction theory, the economic metaphor is thoroughgoing in the extreme. Every measure of sin must be repaid with the coin of suffering, either the sinners' own or that donated to them by others, especially by Jesus. The exemplar theorists object to the principle of vicarious punishment that is implicit in this framework, to the suggestion that God values human suffering as a good, and to the representation of God's forgiveness as an economic transaction.[47] Such views, say the exemplar theorists, fail to grasp the awesome nature of God's love and mercy. God does not require repayment through suffering. Instead, God forgives whenever sinners turn back toward him in repentance. The sacrifice of Jesus on behalf of humanity does not operate as some kind of cosmic restitution. Instead, Jesus's suffering and death serve the pedagogical purpose of inspiring human repentance, hence the label "exemplar theory."[48]

Despite the distaste that exemplar theorists express for satisfaction theory, the underlying metaphors of debt and repayment frequently continue to play a role. Rather than criticizing the satisfaction theorists for conceptualizing sin as the incursion of a debt, exemplar theorists often complain that the satisfaction theorists grossly misjudge the nature of the debt. Sin is so terrible and so pervasive that sinners cannot repay the debt, nor can others pay it for them. So, the only way to resolve the debt of sin is to forgive it. The creditor cancels the debt when the sinner repents. God's mercy takes precedence over his justice.[49]

Other defenders of exemplar theory attempt to resist the debt-and-repayment conception of atonement. It is not that our debt to God is greater than we can pay; rather, human beings have *nothing at all* that they could offer to God in repayment for sin.[50] In ancient religious practices, offerings of slaughtered animals or other goods were routinely made to the gods, who were imagined to take something from the offering that would somehow nourish, strengthen, or delight them. But in the great monotheistic traditions, these models of exchange lose their point. What could we offer to a being who is all-powerful and immaterial and who created everything in the universe in the first place? According to the satisfaction theorist, we could offer God our suffering. However, to imagine that God would intrinsically value our suffering is to conceive of God as less than perfectly benevolent. If there is anything at all that God wants from us, it is our free and reverent obedience to his laws. Nevertheless, this cannot be conceived of as repayment for sin since it is the substance of our moral duty at all times. Once again, repentance and reliance on God's mercy seem to be the only solution.

For our purposes, what is important here is how little these defenses of repentance actually say in favor of repentance itself. They do not present repentance as something so valuable that it earns God's forgiveness. Rather, forgiveness is not deserved at all but is mercifully granted to the undeserving.[51]

Similarly, when believers are instructed to forgive the repentant, they are not told to do so because of the intrinsic merit of repentance. Instead, the idea is that they must show mercy—they should give their abusers something better than they deserve—in the hope that God will respond mercifully to their own repentance in turn. In fact, Christians often take themselves to be bound to forgive even their unrepentant abusers in the same hope of mercy. The value of repentance itself plays no crucial role.

The defenders of repentance-centered theologies, then, do not generally claim that repentance deserves forgiveness. Perhaps this is why Anselm viewed repentance-alone theories of atonement as attributing moral laxity to God.[52] The exemplar theorists would say instead that their theory emphasizes God's loving nature. Either way, this debate does not support the conclusion that repentance is sufficient for atonement for those of us developing a moral theory of interpersonal atonement. While the human debt to God might be impossible to pay off, our debts to one another are frequently more manageable. While humans may have nothing to offer to God, there is much that we can offer to one another. Repentance is valuable, and wrongdoers must repent, yet repentance is not sufficient for atonement.

As presented here, repentance alone, especially a merely internal state of repentance such as could be had on one's deathbed, looks woefully inadequate as form of atonement. Why, then, have repentance accounts of atonement been so popular? Historically, theories that allowed for deathbed atonement, whether through repentance alone or vicarious satisfaction, became popular as a reaction to a medieval penitential system that was demanding, costly, and stigmatizing.[53] These days I suspect that defenses of repentance remain popular because they are usually addressed to questions that differ from the one asked here. Our question concerns how wrongdoers ought morally to respond to their wrongful actions. However, repentance is frequently the answer to questions about forgiveness.

If the question is "What does a wrongdoer need to do in order to gain God's forgiveness?" then "repent alone" is not an implausible answer. The great theological traditions hold that human sinfulness is extreme, what humans have to offer to God is negligible, and God's mercy and love are extraordinary. If God's forgiveness is to be attained, it may need to be through God's merit and not our own.

If the question asked is "When should one forgive one's fellow human beings?" once again it is not implausible to answer "When they repent." Yet, this does not entail that repentant wrongdoers have done all that is morally required of them. Victims might have good reason to forgive repentant wrongdoers other than that repentance has either earned or merited forgiveness. For example, although forgiving too quickly may be harmful to a victim's self-respect, setting the bar for forgiveness too high might also be to her disadvantage. Resentment is often a burden that prevents victims from living full lives. So victims might do best, from the point of view of their own self-interest, to forgive those wrongdoers who have met the rather minimal requirement of repenting. Additionally, one might argue that victims should forgive repentant wrongdoers in order to encourage those transgressors in their efforts to live better lives. However, neither of these arguments for the claim that repentance is sufficient for forgiveness shows that wrongdoers have fully satisfied their moral obligations when they have repented. Forgiveness and atonement are related concerns, as chapter 5 explains. At the same time, we must take care not to confuse an ethic of forgiveness with an ethic of atonement.

3.7 Conclusions

This chapter has explored the ideas that atonement consists in some kind of transformation and that repentance provides the key to this transformation. Our moral demands on the wrongdoer indeed include a number of demands for change. We want wrongdoers to change their course of behavior, their attitude toward their past actions, and their commitment to morality. We can even make sense of the ideas that we are asking them to change the contours of their very being or the meaning of the past. Wrongdoers are morally required to repent, but none of these claims captures all that we care about in the aftermath of wrongdoing.

Almost all of the ideals that we have examined in this chapter share a focus on a transformation of the wrongdoers.[54] It is *their* nature, *their* attitudes, *their* interpretation of the past, *their* future behavior, or *their* commitment to morality that must change. The interests or welfare of other people come into the picture only insofar as they are instrumental to achieving the desired improvement of the wrongdoer. This ignores the fact that wrongdoing is frequently committed against *another person*, who is equally real and valuable. The victim's interests in the resolution of wrongdoing ought to play a more central role. In chapter 4 I develop a theory of atonement that remedies this problem. It, too, can be described as aiming at a kind of transformation: the transformation of the relationships among wrongdoers, their victims, and their community.

| Reforming Relationships
The Reconciliation Theory of Atonement

4.1 Introduction

In the previous chapters we have examined several different conceptions of atonement: retributive self-punishment, the payment of restitution, personal reformation, and the transformation of the meaning of the past. While none of these conceptions of atonement can serve as a complete moral theory of atonement, each contains something important. At this point we have gathered pieces of the puzzle but have no coherent framework within which to organize them.

My conjecture is that the theories of atonement so far examined have all been of limited usefulness because they have all had too limited an understanding of the phenomenon of wrongdoing. Atonement cannot consist simply of "paying something back" because not all of what is wrong with wrongdoing can be conceived of in terms of debt. We should not focus solely on punitive suffering for the wrongdoer because in doing so we overlook the suffering of the victim. When we concentrate on compensating victims for the harms they have sustained, we lose track of the wrongfulness of the offense and the wrongdoer's particular role in that offense. Nor can atonement simply consist of the wrongdoer's moral transformation since there are usually more things in need of repair in the aftermath of wrongdoing than the offender's character.

In this chapter I develop a more comprehensive conception of wrongdoing and, to match, a more comprehensive conception of atonement. I believe that I can accomplish this by thinking in terms of the reconciliation of relationships among wrongdoers, victims, and communities and by keeping in mind how both harms and wrongs affect these relationships.

4.2   The Meaning and Consequences of Wrongdoing

We will have a better idea of what it means to right a wrong when we have a clearer and more comprehensive view of what wrongs *do* to their victims, to the wrongdoers themselves, and to the communities in which these people live and act. Jeffrie Murphy and Jean Hampton have argued that if one is properly to understand wrongdoing, one must recognize that wrongs have expressive power.[1] As Murphy puts it, "[moral] injuries are also *messages*—symbolic communications. They are ways a wrongdoer has of saying to us, 'I count but you do not,' 'I can use you for my purposes,' or 'I am up here on high and you are down there below.'"[2] When one person wrongs another, that person acts as if the victim's status does not preclude the action.[3] In wronging others, the offenders treat those whom they harm as having lower value than they, and the wrongful acts express this false and insulting view.

Wrongdoing typically causes its victims to feel resentment and other negative emotions such as anger or hatred. When the victims resent having been wronged, they protest the message that they are less valuable than the wrongdoers.[4] Through this resentment they reaffirm their own value. This is why many theorists worry that something is amiss when people forgive too easily or do not resent being wronged at all. Those who feel no resentment seem to fail to value themselves as people who are worthy of better treatment.[5]

Interpreting all wrongdoing as a form of insult may seem to treat it too lightly, however. The old adage "sticks and stones may break my bones, but words will never hurt me" surely underestimates the importance of insults. But, just as surely, one should recognize the different degrees of wrongfulness between a verbal insult and a bone-breaking attack with sticks and stones. All wrongs seem to be insults, but some forms of insult are much more harmful than others. As Daniel Farnham has emphasized, wrongful actions do not simply send messages about the victim's value; they also reshape the world so that the victim's value is not fully realized.[6] So we must attend to the ways in which particular wrongful acts harm victims and, furthermore, how the experience of being wrongfully harmed affects victims. Harm is present when some aspect of the victim's life, health, property, rights, reputation, or well-being has been damaged. The importance of these harms in and of themselves must be recognized. Moreover, harm is an additional cause for resentment and other negative emotions, which may be thought of as a second level of harm. The victims have not simply been damaged, as they may have been through a natural disaster or their own carelessness. They have also been damaged in a manner for which the wrongdoer is responsible and blameworthy. The harm they have suffered endures as evidence of the wrongdoers' insulting disregard for them.

Just as some forms of insult are more harmful than others, some insults are also more dangerous than others. The wrongful act functions as a kind of testimony that this sort of treatment of the victim is acceptable. If the victims believe that testimony, if any observers of the wrong believe it, or if the wrongdoers themselves are encouraged by the apparent acceptance of their claim to superiority, then further wrongs and further harms become more likely.[7] The severity of the wrong committed (e.g., a verbal insult versus an attack with sticks and stones) generally correlates with the severity of the future harms that the victim may reasonably fear. Any material or bodily damage caused by the original wrong will also continue to point to the possibility of future harms.

Perhaps for this reason, Pamela Hieronymi interprets wrongful actions not merely as insults but also as threats.[8] Trudy Govier and Wilhelm Verwoerd, taking up an image from Michael Ignatieff, talk about a "kind of 'nightmare time' [that] can result from reliving over and over again a wrong and the trauma that accompanied it."[9] In this way, "a past wrong may not *feel* past and may not be experienced by victims as past."[10] While Govier, Verwoerd, and Ignatieff address cases of gross human rights violations, a weaker version of this "nightmare time" accompanies less severe cases of wrongdoing as well. The general point is that past wrongs do not stay in the past. They continue to cause harm into the future. Hieronymi's explanation for this is that uncorrected wrongdoing is "a past action that persists as a present threat."[11] To forego resentment simply on the grounds that "what is past is past" would be to fail to recognize the potential influence of the wrongdoer's message that the victim is inferior.

One advantage of this account of wrongdoing is that it makes sense of the intuition that failing to atone for a wrong compounds the original wrong. To wrong another person is to insult and threaten that person. To do nothing (or to fail to do enough) to correct that action is to allow the insult and the threat to stand. It is to condone their continued influence. When one fails to atone, one suggests that one still views the victim as inferior and that one remains a threat to the victim. The obligation to atone, then, amounts to an obligation to cease wronging the victim.

Respect and esteem, both for oneself and for others, are shaped by social forces. They are influenced by how a person is treated, what is said about the person, and how that person sees others being treated. Being victimized can make one doubt one's own worth.[12] Victims of wrongdoing frequently wonder whether they somehow share the blame for the wrongful act. They criticize themselves for being bad judges of character or for failing to protect themselves properly. They wonder whether they asked for such abuse by being unlikable or bad people or by being perhaps too arrogant or too passive. Even people who do not normally suffer from self-doubt usually feel the need to defend themselves against wrongdoers' attempts to diminish them. Their resentment is evidence of this effort.[13] Thus, wrongdoing, in addition to damaging the relationship between victim and wrongdoer, also damages the victim's relationship to himself.

Because wrongs occur in a social world, they also have the potential to damage relationships among wrongdoers, victims, and third parties. Victims, thrown into doubt about whom they can trust, are sometimes alienated from their friends and neighbors in the wake of wrongdoing. When we view the wrong as an expressive act, we must also worry about how the community will receive that message. Any witnesses to the act or other people who come to hear of it may begin to view the victims (and perhaps people who are similar to them) as of lower value. Or they may instead sympathize with the victims and so be separated from the wrongdoers, feeling indignant toward and perceiving them (and perhaps people similar to them) as threatening.

Finally, wrongdoing may damage the wrongdoer's relationship to herself. When we violate norms that we ourselves accept as good and authoritative, we experience a kind of self-alienation. This feeling is expressed when people say, "I don't know how I will live with myself" or "I can't look at myself in the mirror." If our normative standards form part of our identity, then by breaking those standards we damage ourselves.[14] Wrongdoers, too, sometimes experience a kind of nightmare time after their misdeeds, in which they relive the past over and over again.[15]

In this section I have argued that we should conceive of wrongdoing not primarily as the incursion of a debt or as personal disorientation but as something that damages relationships. This is an account of wrongdoing in the sense that it is a description of what wrongdoing does. I do not mean to present it as a criterion of right and wrong, a theory that will tell us which actions are right and which are wrong. My suggestion is instead that thinking about the damage wrongdoing does to the relationships among victims, communities, and wrongdoers helps us better identify what a wrongdoer's atonement must accomplish.

Not everything that is wrong with wrongdoing can be reduced to the category of a relational harm. Certain harms caused by wrongdoing are indeed best understood in terms of debts. The destruction of property results in a debt, although wrongfully destroying property will harm a relationship as well. The advantage of thinking of wrongdoing as primarily damaging relationships is that it encourages us to attend to all of the parties who are negatively affected by wrongdoing and to identify the various kinds of harms that wrongs might cause. This was not true of the conceptions of wrongdoing that we examined earlier. Thinking of wrongdoing as the incursion of a debt, for instance, leads one to overlook harms to values that are not commensurable or fungible with other goods. On the other hand, when we think of wrongdoing as having harmed a relationship, we are thereby led to notice debts, as well as other kinds of harms. Debts intrinsically call for repayment, but they also need to be paid because unsettled debts linger as continuing reminders of the past wrong and as prima facie reasons to doubt the wrongdoer's recommitment to just action. These are relational harms. In fact, when unpaid debts do not cause relational harms (as when, for instance, debts are forgotten or involve minor sums), leaving them unpaid is a matter of negligible moral importance.

It is clear that some theorists find talk of damaged relationships unappealing. For example, when strangers wrong strangers, they argue that we cannot sensibly talk of a damaged relationship because there simply is no relationship. If there is no relationship, then we also cannot characterize the correction of the wrong as a case of reconciliation; yet, there are cases of satisfactory atonement in which no relationships are involved. Norvin Richards presents just such an objection:

> Consider the stranger whose car drenches you with mud. Having seen this in her mirror, she stops to apologize, insists on paying your cleaning bill, and so on. Surely it is possible to forgive this woman, just as it would be if she were an equally repentant friend. But to call this "reaccepting" her or "reestablishing our relationship" is rather strained: there was no relationship, and there is none after she drives away.[16]

However, I simply disagree with Richards's reading of the case. Wrongs done to us by strangers do involve relational harms, and the fact that the wrongdoer is a stranger makes those relational harms only more unwieldy.

Let us imagine alternative cases where a thoughtless driver covers us in mud and simply drives away, leaving us fuming on the street corner. In one case, the driver is a stranger, and in another we see that it is Bill, an acquaintance of ours. In the latter case, our relationship with Bill is damaged. We resent Bill and go over in our minds just what we will say to him when we see him again. The incident may put us in a bad mood that will affect our relations with others for the next hour, but our resentment is focused on Bill. When the driver is a stranger, we are also resentful. However, here our resentment, not having a clear object, spills over to others. Here our thought is not "Bill is careless and rude" but *Drivers today* are careless and rude." We continue our walk regarding all of the drivers along the way with suspicion, ready for similarly bad behavior from them and ready to unleash our pent-up resentment on the next driver we catch misbehaving. Similarly but much more severely, victims of unidentified criminals find the world at large a more dangerous place. They may regard every unknown person or everyone who somehow resembles the offender with suspicion and fear.[17] Being victimized by an unknown person does not prevent relational harms. In fact, it often increases them. When the stranger who has splashed us with mud stops to apologize and make amends, not only is our fleeting relationship with her improved, but our relationship to the community of drivers is improved as well. We continue our walk, if not quite "with our faith in humanity restored," at least with our relationship to other drivers normalized.

4.3   Atonement as Reconciliation

This interpretation of wrongdoing as damaging or threatening relationships suggests its own set of metaphors. A wrongful act distances people from one another. It tears apart social bonds. When past wrongs persist as present threats, people are separated from one another by fear and distrust. If this is the case, then to right the wrong is to repair this rupture. Successful atonement would be a matter of bringing people together again—or reconciliation. This brings us back to the idea of atonement as "at-one-ment" and recalls the *Oxford English Dictionary*'s definition of atonement as "the action of setting at one, or condition of being set at one, after discord or strife."[18] Besides images of reconciling and reuniting, the metaphors that are most appropriate to this theory of atonement include images of rebuilding, repairing, reforming, or healing. However, keep in mind that what is being repaired or reformed is not simply the victim's level of utility or the wrongdoer's character but primarily a set of relationships.[19]

The concept of reconciliation is associated with that of atonement in many theologies, including some of the theological systems mentioned earlier. For instance, retributive punishment and repentance are often represented as prerequisites to reconciliation with God. I have not highlighted the conciliatory dimensions of these theological traditions both in order to explore the independent value of concepts such as retribution and repentance and also because the value of reconciliation often does little independent work in these theologies.[20] It is often unclear whether retribution and repentance are justified simply because they are what God demands in return for reconciliation or whether retribution and repentance are also inherently just. Either way, we should not assume that what might secure reconciliation with a perfectly benevolent and invulnerable God would also achieve reconciliation with our resentful and insecure fellow humans.

In order to build a distinctively reconciliation-oriented theory of interpersonal atonement, we must ask the following questions: Who should be reconciled with whom? What sort of reconciliation is important in the aftermath of wrongdoing? Which values should reconciliation promote? What could merit this reconciliation?[21]

Presumably the relationships that must be repaired in the aftermath of wrongdoing are those that have been wrongfully damaged. As we have seen, that between the victim and the wrongdoer is merely the most obvious one involved. Wrongdoing can also damage or threaten the relationships between the wrongdoer and the community, the victim and the community, the victim and herself, and the wrongdoer and himself.

The goal of atonement should not be the restoration of whatever relationships existed before the wrong since those relationships might have been morally problematic or otherwise unhealthy. Both wrongdoers and victims may have legitimate grounds, independent of the fact of wrongdoing, for ending a personal or business relationship. Atoning friends and lovers will usually hope to be accepted back into their old roles by their victims, but love does not always survive wrongdoing, even when wrongdoers respond appropriately. The atoning wrongdoer hopes to regain his old feeling of self-worth, but he might well need to change his views about the proper basis for self-regard. In looking to account for a wrongdoer's *obligation* to atone, it is better to focus on the reconciliation of relationships that the wrongdoer is morally required to maintain. Furthermore, given that wrongs often take place among strangers—like the mud-splashing driver and her victim—we must identify a kind of relationship that actually exists (or should exist) in such cases.

The kind of reconciliation that is the goal of atonement, then, involves the restoration of a paradigmatically moral relationship. It is one wherein the parties regard one another and themselves as equally valuable moral persons. The term 'moral person' is ambiguous. I use it here in two of its possible senses. First is the Kantian idea of a moral agent as someone who is capable of judging right and wrong and making choices on this basis. According to Kantian theory, the capacity for moral autonomy is the source of human beings' moral status, a value all humans hold equally. Then there is the pedestrian notion of a 'moral person'—someone who is not only *capable of* judging but *likely to* judge right from wrong correctly and be properly motivated by these judgments.[22] Unlike moral status, moral standing—one's reputation as a morally good and trustworthy person—fluctuates over time.[23]

In order to bring these two ideas together, we can appeal to the idea of a moral community as one in which morality properly regulates the relations among the members. Given our status as agents, we are all members of the moral community. Nonetheless, not all of us are members in good standing because not all of us can be trusted to have committed ourselves to the values that are "constitutive of the bond between us."[24] Wrongdoing jeopardizes our deserved and our perceived place in the moral community, our *standing*, which is the degree of esteem and trust to conduct oneself appropriately that we merit within the moral community. In order to atone, the wrongdoer must regain the standing that he lost through his misdeeds and thereby reestablish a proper relationship to the moral community.

Reconciliation between wrongdoer and victim involves the restoration or establishment of a civil relationship between the victim and the wrongdoer.[25] When a wrongdoer atones, he gives his victim good reason to stop structuring their relationship to one another in terms of the roles of wrongdoer and victim[26] and "to eliminate the offence from the texture of their relationship and in that sense to 'annul' it."[27] The victim will have good reason to give up her resentment, fear, and distrust of the wrongdoer. Thus, this model of reconciliation fits well with the intuition that a wrongdoer who has fully atoned for wrongdoing has thereby provided the victim with good reason to forgive him.[28] The wrongdoer will have reestablished his reputation with the victim as a member in good standing in the moral community.

The wrongdoer's atonement should also aim to repair any damage done to the moral relationship between himself and the community and between the victim and the community. If the wrongful act gave the community any reason to doubt whether the victim or the wrongdoer is an equally valuable moral person or a reasonably trustworthy member of the moral community, then the wrongdoer should work to repair that impression.

The victim will be reconciled with herself when her sense of herself as an equally valuable moral person is restored. The wrongdoer can contribute to this end both by communicating his own renewed respect for the victim and by working to undo any damage he may have caused to the level of respect or esteem the victim is granted by the community.

In the aftermath of wrongdoing, the offender must also be reconciled with himself. He must once again be able to see himself as an equally valuable moral person. Reconciling himself to the idea that he is equally valuable means not just that he must not see himself as superior to the victim (as his wrongful action claimed that he was) but also that he must not see himself as inferior to the victim. The wrongdoer should avoid self-hatred. He must also make it the case that he can view himself as someone who can be trusted to perform morally acceptable actions in the future, which helps explain why personal reformation—"a change of heart"—is usually seen as so important to atonement. This need for reconciliation with oneself also explains why wrongdoers sometimes feel they must atone for wrongdoing even when their victims and communities have been quick to forgive them. Forgiveness may repair the wrongdoer's relationships with others, but it may not yet restore his view of himself as an equally valuable and trustworthy person.

The goal of atonement, then, is the reconciliation or reforming of the relationships among the wrongdoer, the victim, and the community. The ideal includes both the hope that the wrongdoer will come to merit restored standing in the moral community and that the other members of the community will have good reason to grant or recognize that standing. The wrongdoer's obligation to atone consists in an obligation to create the conditions in which such reconciliation can take place.

4.4   The Limits of Reconciliation

Before considering the ends and means of reconciliation in more depth, I consider some initial objections to the ideal of reconciliation as a model for atonement. In a variety of cases, reconciliation looks like an impossible goal or even an undesirable one. These objections will help us to explore the moral limits of reconciliation. However, in my opinion they will not undermine the connection between reconciliation and wrongdoers' obligations.

One might object to the reconciliation theory of atonement on the grounds that it is too ambitious. The form of reconciliation it identifies is complex and involves potentially many people and their most deeply held attitudes about themselves and others. It might seem that the duty to atone runs afoul of the principle that 'ought' implies 'can.' If this is what atonement consists in, then it lies outside the wrongdoer's grasp. It is true that many aspects of atonement are indeed out of the wrongdoer's control. She cannot ensure that the victim and the community will ever see her as a moral person again or guarantee that the victim's self-esteem will be restored. But, while these aspects of reconciliation are not in the wrongdoer's control, they are also not outside her influence. Except in cases of the most extreme harm or stubbornness, the attitudes and emotions of victims and community members will respond to new information about and new experiences with the wrongdoer. Although the wrongdoer cannot ensure that these other parties will lose their resentment or regain trust, she is obligated to provide victims and communities with good reason to do so.

The suggestion that wrongdoers should try to reconcile themselves with those they have harmed is often greeted with concern. For instance, the idea that someone who has sexually abused a child should approach that child in an effort to make amends is worrying indeed. Even if the wrongdoer has a sincere intention to atone, she risks doing greater harm than good by contacting the child. The reconciliation account of atonement can accommodate cases like these, however. Although wrongdoers have a duty to make amends, they are not morally permitted to atone in any fashion that would harm the people they have offended.[29] In the example of the sexual abuser, there may well be no way in which the offender could approach them in order to regain their trust. Yet, there is still important work for atonement to do. The wrongdoer can and should work to achieve reconciliation with the broader community and the ability honestly to regard herself as a morally trustworthy person.

It is surely true that some wrongs can never be righted. In some cases, the victim's death precludes a proper atonement. In other cases, the wrong is simply so horrific that nothing that the wrongdoer could do would provide the victim or the community with good reason to reconcile with her. However, the wrongdoer still has an obligation to atone. The wrongdoer's moral obligation to respond to her wrongdoing is a duty to repair the damage caused, to neutralize the threats her wrongful action created, to become a better person, and thereby to merit restored standing in the moral community. These are tasks that admit of degrees. Partial atonement is possible even when full atonement is not. This analysis allows one to acknowledge both that morality demands much from such wrongdoers and that, no matter what they do, their responses will never right the wrong.

The reconciliation theory of atonement offers an ideal. It conceives of the best case of atonement as one in which the wrongdoer has removed the reasons her misdeed gave the victim, the community, and herself to resent and be wary of her. It envisions the wrongdoer as reestablishing the circumstances wherein the parties involved can once again (or for the first time) relate to one another on terms of equal respect and even trust. To admit that this ideal is not always achievable but can only be approximated does not diminish its usefulness as a guide to action.

4.5   The Ends and Means of Reconciliation

Let us now consider the goal of reconciling relationships in more detail. We should keep in mind the conception of wrongdoing we have developed since wrongdoing is the problem that reconciliation is meant to solve. Wrongdoing sends an insulting and threatening message about the victim that has the potential to influence negatively the victim's view of herself, the community's view of both the victim and the wrongdoer, and the wrongdoer's view of himself in relation to others. To make amends one must reform these damaged relationships.

In order to achieve this sort of reconciliation, the wrongdoer's response will have to look both forward and backward. The response must look forward in the sense that it must provide good reason for the wrongdoer and others to accept that he can be trusted to act properly in the future. He will have to address the past in that he will have to acknowledge in a satisfactory way the facts about the wrongful act and his responsibility for it. He must also satisfy any moral claims against him—such as any debts he has incurred or legitimate calls for his punishment—if he is going to repair his relationships. No matter what other good he might do, any unsatisfied claims will linger as reminders of his past wrong and provide prima facie evidence that he has not truly accepted responsibility for his misdeed or committed himself to acting morally. In this way, unsatisfied claims remain threats to his standing in the moral community.

Reconciliation has three subgoals. These are objectives that must be met in order to merit the sort of reconciliation described here. First, the wrongdoer must morally improve herself. It is not enough to convince herself or others that she is trustworthy. She must actually become trustworthy. Second, the wrongdoer must communicate with the victim and in some cases the community in a way that withdraws the insult and the threat that the wrongful act expressed. Third, the wrongdoer must make reparation for the various sorts of harms she created. In standard cases of wrongs committed against others, all of these subgoals must be met if the wrongdoer is to count as meriting reconciliation.

The category of moral improvement itself has both backward- and forward-looking aspects. The backward-looking elements concern the agent's attitude toward the past. She must recognize that she was responsible for her past action, that it was morally wrong, and that the moral norm she violated was authoritative. She must recognize that she should not have performed this action, and she must care about this mistake. Besides this change of attitude toward the past, the wrongdoer must also resolve not to repeat such an action in the future and commit herself to reforming her character so as to be able to live up to this resolution.[30] She must actually behave better in the future with respect to this type of wrongdoing, or else her effort to atone will have failed and will have to begin anew. Moral improvement thus includes the sort of transformation frequently labeled 'repentance.'

The second subgoal of the reconciliation theory of atonement is the wrongdoer's communicative aim. As we will see, this end can be met by a number of different means. However, the main idea is that the offender must express—and express in a way that her audience will be likely to understand—a withdrawal of the insult and the threat that her wrongful act represented. She must send the message that she now recognizes that the victim is a person of equal moral worth to herself, that she should not have wronged him in this way, and that she intends not to repeat this sort of offense in the future. The communicative part of atonement is required by a duty to respect the victim and the need to halt any continuing harm linked to the expressive content of the wrongful act.

The third subgoal of reconciliation is the wrongdoer's obligation to make reparation for the other kinds of harms created, which may encompass material, physical, psychological, and relational damage. These various sorts of injuries often come in clusters. For example, physical harming can also create psychological, relational, and material harms (e.g., in the form of medical bills or lost earnings). Almost all cases of wrongdoing committed against another person involve some form of damage, even if only relational. As chapter 2 points out, not all of these admit of reparation in material terms. For instance, relational harms can often be repaired only by subtle, symbolically rich interactions between the wrongdoer and the victim such as an apology. In cases such as these, the reparative and the communicative tasks of atonement become one.

Most cases of atonement must include all three sorts of responses—moral improvement, communication, and reparation—because almost all wrongs committed against another person involve the problems that these responses answer. The three subgoals tend to support one another as well. Verbal communications of remorse, for instance, are often made more credible when reparations are offered. However, it is possible for an atonement to be satisfactory without serving all three subgoals. For an example we may recall the case discussed earlier, where I attempt but fail to break your favorite vase, and neither you nor anyone else ever comes to learn about this. Though I have wronged you, I have not harmed you. Here, in order to atone, it seems that all that is required of me is moral improvement. There is no harm to be repaired except the injury I have done to my own self-regard. Though I expressed an insult and a threat to you, neither you nor anyone else received the message. So the communicative requirement, which is usually part of atonement, seems to drop out in this case as well. The only way I could communicate remorse to you would be by telling you that I insulted you in the first place. To tell you this, it seems, would create harm unnecessarily.

Moral improvement, communication, and reparation are ends that offenders may achieve by various means. Particular means of atonement, such as an apology, may also serve more than one of those ends. The choice of means to meet the goals of atonement allows room for considerable cultural variation and personal creativity, which is an advantage of the account.[31] In the rest of this section I discuss some of the different types of means of making amends: emotions and attitudes, apologies, explanations, material transfers, care work, self-punishment, rituals, and future good behavior. I examine how each of the kinds of responses to wrongdoing contributes to the reconciliation of relationships and consider some objections to various acts of atonement.

4.5.1 EMOTIONS OF SELF-ASSESSMENT

The first atoning response that a wrongdoer must make to his misdeed is usually an emotional one. He must feel guilt and remorse. In this section I note briefly how the reconciliation theory of atonement supports this conclusion. I also evaluate the appropriateness of other emotions of moral self-assessment: shame, self-directed contempt, self-hatred, and humility.

In chapter 2 I argue that guilt is a natural consequence for an agent who believes that he has done something wrong, acknowledges the legitimate authority of that norm, commits himself personally to that norm such that he cares whether it is respected or violated, and acknowledges that he has violated the norm under conditions that neither justify nor fully excuse his actions. Remorse adds a wish to change the past. The emotion of repentance is remorse held specifically with respect to either moral wrongdoing or sin and joined with a commitment to change.

The reconciliation theory of atonement indirectly requires the emotions of guilt, remorse, and repentance by compelling the moral judgments and attitudes that cause these emotions. A commitment to morality includes both an intellectual and an emotional disposition. Thus, a failure to feel guilt and remorse in the aftermath of wrongdoing is grounds for denying that a wrongdoer has fully acknowledged his misdeed to himself or fully embraced the proper norms. Repentance, which not only looks back remorsefully to the past act but also rests on a resolution to pursue a better future, is the most appropriate emotional response to the past because of the more comprehensive judgments and the intentions it embodies.

Guilt, remorse, and repentance are also valuable as motivations to moral reform and deterrents against the recommission of wrongdoing. The experience of these emotions can aid the pursuit of the communicative goal of reconciliation as well. In order to atone, the wrongdoer must communicate respectfully with the victim (and perhaps the community) in a way that withdraws the insult and the threat contained in the wrongful act. A credible expression of guilt, remorse, or repentance to the victim is usually required if he is to accomplish this communicative task.

Victims and communities might be interested in guilt, remorse, and repentance for reasons that one could classify as reparative. They might wish for the wrongdoer's suffering simply as a form of compensation or retribution. As I have already argued, such desires are morally suspect. These painful emotions are valuable, but not because the wrongdoer's suffering is a good in itself. We can find a sufficient justification for the painful aspects of these emotions in the contribution they make to moral reformation and respectful communication.

Another emotion of self-assessment that a wrongdoer might feel is shame, which is an emotion that "requires an audience," as Gabriele Taylor puts it.[32] "The agent is seen as deviating from some norm, and in feeling shame he will identify with the audience's view and the consequent verdict that he has lost status."[33] This feature of shame makes it a controversial moral emotion. Some claim that shame privileges the appearance of virtue over its reality. Others fault it as being a heteronomous moral emotion and argue that only those feelings of shame that proceed from autonomously chosen standards and one's own evaluation of oneself should be counted as justified. In response, the defenders of shame have argued that we have good epistemic and practical reasons to be sensitive to other people's moral evaluations of us even when we disagree with those assessments.[34] In the cases that interest us, however, the agent is aware that he has done something wrong (as he understands wrong), and the question is how he should respond to that fact. His own evaluation of his action matches up with that of the audience (to at least a significant degree). The question, then, is whether it is appropriate for him to feel the shaming power of their gaze. I believe the answer is clearly yes. To reject the legitimacy of shame in such circumstances is to reject the legitimacy of the community's evaluative point of view. It would be to reject the legitimacy of the community's taking an evaluative stance toward the wrongdoer at all.[35] Such a thoroughgoing rejection of the emotion of shame would defend not moral autonomy but moral solipsism.

As in the case of guilt, this defense of shame does not rest on the idea that the wrongdoer deserves to suffer. Shame is painful, but its justification is not dependent on its painful nature. Instead, shame is an appropriate emotion because it acknowledges one's own fault, the authority of the norm that was violated, and the respect due to the community that shares a commitment to that norm.

Other critics of shame resist its characteristic focus on the actor rather than the act. In feeling shame, one more typically judges who one is rather than what one has done. One feels oneself to be seen as ranking low against some ideal of a good or virtuous person. Those who are committed always to "separate the sin from the sinner" will be made uncomfortable by the way shame seems to condemn the wrongdoer and not just the wrong. Bernard Williams accuses such critics of having a "characterless" view of the self, a view that not only is psychologically implausible but also leaves one unable to explain how the wrongdoer has come to commit the wrong and unable to recommend improvements that will encourage better future action.[36] Perhaps the critic of shame worries that the sort of self-condemnation that shame embodies does not properly value one's status as an inherently valuable moral agent, but this does not follow.[37] One might be making a judgment about one's moral standing rather than one's moral status.[38] I can judge myself to be a selfish person or a coward without denying that I have intrinsic moral value as an agent. In fact, it is only because I am a moral agent that I may be expected to live up to standards of benevolence and courage.[39] There might, of course, be people who judge themselves to be of low status and feel shame on this score. These feelings imply an unacceptable moral view and should not be encouraged. Nevertheless, not all cases of shame are like this, and thus we should not altogether reject shame as an emotion that can make a contribution to atonement.

Shame can be a means to atonement in the same way that guilt and remorse can. In feeling shame over a moral misdeed, one acknowledges that one's character or self (and not just one's action) has fallen short of an authoritative standard. Such acknowledgment is often crucial to one's moral improvement. The expression of shame to one's victim and community can enable reconciliation with them. Shame can also deter future wrongdoing, just as guilt and remorse do. Critics of shame may point out that shame typically inclines people to hide themselves and that this is incompatible with the work of atonement. However, when wrongdoers believe that they can do something to restore their moral standing and rid themselves of shame, this inclination to hide can be overcome.

Self-directed contempt and self-hatred for wrongdoing are more extreme cousins of shame. Self-contempt resembles shame in "presenting its object as low in the sense of ranking low in worth as a person in virtue of falling short of some legitimate...ideal of the person."[40] Self-contempt could involve a rejection of one's basic status as a moral agent. In this case, it would be a morally unjustifiable emotion. However, there are also reasons to worry about self-contempt when it embodies merely a judgment of low standing. Self-contempt, unlike shame, is also a totalizing attitude that colors one's perception of every aspect of the self.[41] A person who feels self-contempt is hampered from seeing himself as capable of improvement. He instead regards his alienation from other people and himself as the proper order of things rather than as a problem that he can and must fix. Hatred suggests an inclination to destroy its object.[42] A self-hating person will similarly lack the motivation and the optimism required to undertake the project of reconciliation and is likely to continue harming himself and others. While self-contempt and self-hatred may be excusable in certain cases and even be grounds for pity, they must be overcome if one is to achieve atonement.

Because the work of atonement must be protected from a potentially crippling spiral of negative feelings and attitudes, our list of the emotional responses that can aid atonement should include humility and the accompanying virtue of being a humble person. The wrongdoer must accept the fact that he is a fallible human being and have some compassion for himself as such.[43] The properly humble person will not let himself off the hook for wrongdoing. However, he will accept that his wrongful action or his vice does not account for the entirety of his value. A humble person will be better able to engage in the project of atonement than an unduly proud one who cannot live with the fact that he is flawed.

4.5.2   EMPATHY

A properly atoning wrongdoer must be moved emotionally by her violation of moral norms. However, this allows the wrongdoer's understanding of her action to remain too abstract. The problem with a wrong committed against another person is not merely that a *norm* or *rule* has been violated but that a valuable *being* who deserves respect has been harmed and demeaned. Just this distinction is missed by Jim in Joseph Conrad's novel *Lord Jim*. Jim is a junior officer on a ship in the South Pacific filled to capacity with Muslim pilgrims. When it appears the ship is about to sink, Jim and the other white crewmembers quietly escape in a lifeboat, leaving two native sailors and hundreds of sleeping pilgrims on board. As it turns out, the ship's bulwark miraculously holds, and the passengers on the ship are rescued many hours later. While it is true that Jim suffers greatly from guilt, remorse, and repentance, the focus of the caring that this embodies remains either too abstract or too self-centered. He had betrayed the trust of the pilgrims and the remaining crewmembers and exposed them to greater risk through his abandonment, but these aspects of the case seem to escape his notice. When Jim is in the lifeboat in the dark of night, he is tormented by imagined sounds of the pilgrims' terrible deaths. Yet, once he learns that they have survived, he seems to lose all interest in their part in the affair. It is not even clear whether Jim sees himself as having wronged the community of sailors as a whole, though Conrad portrays other members of the sailing profession as feeling that Jim has wronged them both personally and collectively. Instead, Jim sees himself as having violated a code of honor, a standard of manhood. The interpersonal dimension of his act is lost on him. As he sees his abandonment, it was an act of cowardice and a horrible personal failure, not a case of wronging other people. Thus, although Jim feels guilt and repentance, these emotions are improperly focused.

In order genuinely to acknowledge responsibility for the wrongful action, the wrongdoer should have a good understanding of what she has done to her victim. In order to gain such an understanding, another response from the wrongdoer seems to be required. The wrongdoer should empathize with her victim.[44] Of course, to empathize with the point of view of someone who has been wronged is to empathize with suffering.[45] It is to suffer oneself. So, once again, we have reason to believe that one cannot fully recognize that one is responsible for wronging another person without feeling pain.

Empathy has its critics, however. At least in some cases, the assumption that the wrongdoer can imaginatively enter the victim's point of view may be presumptuous to the point of offensiveness.[46] How could the prosperous, white, American farmer, paying exploitative wages to a desperately poor, undocumented worker from Mexico genuinely empathize with the worker's point of view? The farmer's epistemic access to the worker's situation is limited not only by a lack of interest but also by the great differences in their life experiences and worldviews.

While I think that this criticism is a valuable corrective, it does not convince me that empathy is unimportant to atonement. What it suggests is that empathy must be tempered by humility. To properly respond to what we have done, we need to consider the wrong from the victim's point of view. However, we, as wrongdoers, cannot simply assume that we are able to do this. Thus, we have here another argument for including communication with the victim as a part of atonement. We need to listen to what his experience of the wrong has been. This will help us to empathize, but we should still recognize that it may not be sufficient. The barriers to empathy may be insuperable. As I have already argued, however, we have reasons in addition to this for believing that atonement is not always possible. In many cases, it will be partial at best. Cases where empathy is impossible or inadequate are further examples of the limits of reconciliation as moral ideal. Still, partial atonement is valuable, and full atonement seems to require empathy.

4.5.3 APOLOGIES

Apologies are pointedly communicative acts such as utterances, writing, or even facial or bodily gestures that acknowledge some form of responsibility for a wrong and express a self-critical moral emotion.[47] This sketchy characterization of apology contains a number of elements that require further comment and explication.

First, apologies are communications and not just expressions. In order to apologize, one needs both an audience and an intention to make oneself understood. The communication need not be verbal. I might apologize to you through a regretful facial expression. Nonetheless, if you simply catch a look of regret pass over my face, one I had no desire to show to you, I have not apologized. Louis F. Kort argues further that the communication of one's regret must constitute a "gesture of respect."[48] A wrongdoer who simply reports his regret in an offhand manner in response to an interview question has not apologized, even if the interviewer happens to be the one wronged.[49]

Second, an apology must acknowledge the commission of a wrongful act or the holding of a wrongful trait.[50] This wrongful action or trait may belong to oneself, one's group, or someone for whom one is responsible. People understand themselves as capable of offering apologies for the actions of their compatriots, employees, and children, and these apologies are indeed accepted as such by their audiences. The possibility of apologizing for the actions or character of another person raises some puzzles. However, I delay further discussion of these until we turn to issues of shared responsibility in chapter 7.

The acknowledgment of wrongdoing that is required for an apology may be implicit, but it must genuinely be communicated to the audience. Phrases such as "I'm sorry" play a number of different roles. Sometimes they communicate sympathy alone. We say "I am so sorry" to someone who has lost a loved one. Following Aaron Lazare, we can call this the "compassionate" use of the word *sorry*.[51] At other times we say "I'm sorry" in order to provide what Erving Goffman calls an "account," a message that something that might have seemed to be a wrongful act really was not, either because it did not really happen or was unintentional, justified, or excused.[52] A person who accidentally and nonnegligently treads on another person's toe in a crowded room will sometimes say "I'm sorry" merely in order to express that no offense was meant. But in order for "I'm sorry" to count as an apology, the acceptance of responsibility for a wrong must be part of what is communicated.

It is sometimes difficult to tell whether the statement "I'm sorry" or even "I apologize" are being used as expressions of compassion, as exculpating accounts, or as genuine apologies. Politicians and other public figures frequently play on the ambiguity for their own advantage, hoping to be credited as having made amends while at the same time refusing to acknowledge (and sometimes explicitly denying) wrongdoing. A classic way in which to make such a nonapology is to say one is sorry that other people have become upset by an event, which one then goes on to suggest was misinterpreted, was none of one's responsibility anyway, or reveals the alleged victim's hypersensitivity rather than one's own shortcomings. Faux apologizing of this sort has now become a common practice, especially in the public sphere.[53] The most sympathetic reading I can put on this phenomenon is that it functions as a ritual of self-punishment or cleansing that is meant to have value in its own right. However, unless there is an acknowledgment of wrong, no genuine apology has been offered.

Even when "sorry" is used in its apologetic sense, debates may still arise about the adequacy of an apology. A proper apology must offer a satisfactory acknowledgment of the wrongful action or trait. However, the offender, victim, and community may not agree upon the representation of that action or trait. Which act is identified as wrongful? Was the offense intentional, reckless, or negligent? Which vice of character did it express, if any? Is the wrongdoer owning responsibility for all of the harms created or only some? Lazare claims that the process of apology is often one of negotiation.[54] Offenders sometimes make several attempts at characterizing that for which they are sorry in response to criticisms, demands, or cues they receive from their victims and communities. Extended negotiations over the content of an apology, as well as repeated, failed attempts at apologizing properly, are likely to undermine any confidence that the wrongdoer has a proper understanding of morality or is apologizing voluntarily. However, the presence of some degree of negotiation need not undermine the legitimacy of an apology. After all, a wrongdoer may not be able to understand fully what he did and the impact he had on his victim until his victim tells him, or he may believe with justification that the victim's perspective on the wrong is flawed to some degree.

Third, we should attend to the emotion or emotions expressed in apology. It is commonly said that remorse is the emotion proper to an apology. However, I am inclined to broaden the categories of emotion that one might express and still count as having offered an apology. This expansion is required when we grant that it is possible to apologize for one's group, proxies, and charges. In these cases, remorse does not seem to describe what the one offering the apology feels. Remorse is a form of regret (a pain with respect to the past) plus a wish to undo the past, but in these cases of apology, one never "did" the past in the first place. While the parent, boss, or compatriot of the wrongdoer may acknowledge accountability for the wrongful action, he need not be claiming direct, causal responsibility. For this reason, the more appropriate emotion for the apologizer to express seems to be regret, shame, or possibly grief rather than remorse. I might feel remorse for not being a better parent (a failure of my own), but I feel shame and regret that my child hurt another.

Regret and shame, then, in addition to repentance (which is more forward looking than mere remorse) and guilt, are emotions that may find expression in apology. In attempting to apologize, wrongdoers also sometimes express self-hatred or self-contempt, which I have characterized as problematic moral emotions. Such apologies are genuine but inappropriate. To apologize properly and in a way that contributes to one's meriting reconciliation, one should express the proper emotions—those that accurately represent the nature of one's connection to the wrong, condemns that wrong, and expresses respect for others without denying basic respect for oneself.

Apologies are associated with suffering, as frequently comes through in the words with which we apologize. The English word *sorry* is etymologically connected to *sorrow*. *Es tut mir Leid*, "it gives me sorrow," is a standard apology in German. In Spanish one says *lo siento*, "I feel it." The pain associated with apology is not limited to the pain of remorse or shame. To admit to wrongdoing and face the justified anger and resentment of one's victim can itself be a frightening or uncomfortably humbling experience. To apologize is to risk the possibility that one's victim will refuse to accept that apology.[55] Why should the wrongdoer submit himself to such unpleasantness?

As I have argued, the making of amends requires a communicative remedy because of the character and consequences of wrongdoing itself. To wrong someone is to express the view that the value of the injured party is not sufficiently high to preclude such treatment. The expression of this evaluation is both insulting in itself and threatening to the victim. To apologize is to correct the false claim about the victim's value and to withdraw the insult and the threat. When the offender properly apologizes for wrongdoing, he acknowledges that the victim deserves to have been treated better. He offers the injured party a gesture of respect. In showing his remorse, he lets the victim know that he does not take his mistake lightly but is instead emotionally moved by it.

The fact that apologies are ideally made directly to victims is telling. Communicating one's guilt and remorse through a third party is less worthy.

This is because the wrongdoer must do more than correct the false claim that resulted from his wrongful action. He must also redress the damage caused by the insult to the victim's self-respect or self-esteem. In apologizing directly to the victim in a fashion that gives her the opportunity to express what she will to him, the offender acknowledges that the victim's resentment of him is reasonable. He sends the message that her reaction matters to him, which is another way of acknowledging her status as a valuable person. For these reasons, apology can be empowering for the victim and aid the restoration of her relationship with herself.

In this way, apology helps to redress some of the harms that wrongdoing may cause, and so we can classify it as doing reparative work as well. Both Kathleen Gill and Erving Goffman resist talking about apology as a form of compensation for loss. "An apology is not a mechanism for offsetting losses," writes Gill. "It is instead a way to acknowledge the value of what was lost."[56] Goffman insists that an apology "is a matter of indicating a relationship, not compensating a loss," and adds that "a caution is implied for students who would apply an exchange perspective to all areas of social life."[57] Nonetheless, we can talk about apology as a form of reparation without buying into a model of compensation wherein one thing of value that was lost (e.g., the victim's peace of mind) is replaced with another thing of comparable value (e.g., a gesture of respect from the wrongdoer). Apologies repair harms not by compensating losses but by disarming threats to relationships. I believe it is helpful to talk about apologies as repairing harms because it is helpful to recognize that certain kinds of harms can be repaired best (and sometimes *only*) by things like apologies, which do not fit an exchange perspective. Harms to one's self-esteem, ability to trust oneself, and ability to trust others fall in this category.

In repairing such harms, apology removes some of the barriers to the reconciliation of the victim and the wrongdoer. Public apologies similarly aid the reconciliation of both the victim and the wrongdoer to the community. They serve this end, first of all, by setting the record straight about who was in the wrong. They also allow the community to hear the wrongdoer's message of respect for the victim and provide it with evidence of the wrongdoer's moral reformation. They play an especially important role in cases where a wrong done to one person sends an additional message of disrespect to people who are like the victim in some relevant respect. So, for instance, in making a public apology, an employer who has sexually discriminated against one female employee withdraws the insult and threat that his action implied for all of the women in that workplace. Public apology can play an important role even in cases where the victim has died. Though reconciliation with the victim is now impossible, apology aids the offender's reconciliation with the community and helps ensure that the victim is accorded respect in the memory of the living.

Apology can also contribute to the wrongdoer's moral improvement by reinforcing his own recognition that he has in fact done something wrong. It is one thing to make this judgment in private. It is quite another to say it aloud. The confession of wrongdoing to another person can make it seem more real and more important to the wrongdoer. Going back on such a judgment is also harder once it has been shared since withdrawing that judgment places a conversational pressure on the wrongdoer to justify his change in view.

In characterizing apology, some commentators describe it as a request for forgiveness.[58] This claim has intuitive appeal. It is further supported when we note that utterances like "please, forgive me" and "pardon me" are standard formulations of apologies. When a victim says, "I accept your apology," she implies that she thereby forgives the offender. However, the claim that an apology is always a request for forgiveness causes problems because it seems to render apologizing morally problematic in some cases. An apology, however meaningful it might be, will be grossly disproportional to some wrongs. To request forgiveness for such a wrong on the basis of an inadequate offer of amends would be presumptuous at best and possibly insulting or even harmful to the victim. In apologizing, one would be asking for a reconciliation one has not merited. One would be asking the victim to renew her trust even though one has not yet given adequate evidence of trustworthiness. The wrongdoer might wish for merciful reconciliation in such a case, but to request it strikes me as rude. If we are then to preserve the intuition that it is nonetheless appropriate and possibly even uniquely required for the wrongdoer to offer an apology in cases of grave wrongdoing, then we should not characterize an apology as a request for forgiveness. Such a request may be a common implication of an apology, but one can truly apologize and at the same time disown such an implication. Thus, the following would count as a genuine apology: "I don't expect you to forgive me. I'm not asking you to. But I want you to know how truly sorry I am for what I have done."[59]

Apology, then, can address all three of the goals of reconciliation as a communicative act, an aid to moral improvement, and a means of repairing certain forms of harm. However, the chief role of apology is usually the communicative one. While other forms of amends (e.g., material payments) also play a communicative role in certain contexts, apology remains special for many victims. In fact, some writers count apology as morally required for atonement.[60] In my view, what is required is a communication that sends the right messages. Such communication can take a number of different forms depending on the circumstances of the case and the culture. Still, in our culture it is rare for any other sort of response to wrongdoing to express the necessary messages and to express them in a form that victims and communities will understand as clearly as an apology. This is what gives apology its special power for us. A heartfelt apology will sometimes lead a victim to foreswear any interest in material restitution or punishment, while restitution and punishment are seldom described as obviating a victim's desire for an apology.[61]

4.5.4   TRUTH TELLING AND EXPLANATION

Apologies are sometimes simple acknowledgments of wrongdoing and expressions of remorse. At other times they include detailed confessions and explanations about what happened and why. Truth telling and explanation can perform reparative work even in the absence of an apology, so I list them here as a separate form of amends.

The "nightmare time" that follows victimization can be prolonged when victims are left unsure about what happened and why. Even if the explanation of the wrong is insulting or painful to hear, it is often more manageable for victims than uncertainty. Victims, especially of violent crimes or intimate forms of betrayal, are often left in doubt about their own behavior and their ability to judge others' characters.[62] "Did I ask for it somehow? Should I have known better?" Receiving explanations of the transgression from the wrongdoers can help them answer those questions and thereby help restore their ability to trust themselves and others.

The importance of truth telling is a frequent theme in the literature on political reconciliation and transitional justice.[63] Families of the murdered and the "disappeared" frequently express a need to know what transpired and where the remains of their loved ones lie. Such knowledge helps them find closure. It helps them to narrate the past to themselves as past.

4.5.5   MATERIAL REDRESS

The transfer of material goods from the wrongdoer to victims or communities can serve the ends of atonement in many different ways. These transfers may take the form of the return of wrongfully taken property or compensation for material kinds of harm, including things such as medical bills or lost earnings. Such responses to wrongdoing, which fit comfortably under the principle of restitution, can also be justified in line with the ideal of reconciliation. To respect others as valuable persons is in part to respect their property rights. Where the case of wrongdoing in question has violated those rights, the restitution of rightful holdings is called for.

However, material transfers can repair harms and wrongs in a broader sense of the term 'reparation.' Whereas restitution returns or compensates for losses that are commensurable and fungible, material reparations are sometimes meant to respond to nonmaterial sorts of harms or losses. An example of this broader sort of reparation would be monetary payments for pain and suffering, such as are routinely ordered in civil courts. Such payments are objectionable when they are represented as a form of restitution, which suggests that the value damaged and the value offered in response are fungible and that the latter could be exchanged for the former without loss. To suggest that money is a suitable restitution for pain and suffering is an insult to the victim. It treats the victim as an object rather than a subject.

However, we can understand reparation payments as attempting something other than restitution and thus as having a different significance. Reparation payments can be offered as a symbolic acknowledgment of responsibility and a sign of remorse and respect. While the direct harms of the wrongful act may not be reparable by material means, reparations can improve other aspects of the victim's life. So, although a reckless driver may not be able to give her victim back the use of his legs, she might help him pay for college. Her willingness to do this will demonstrate her caring for his well-being. In these ways, reparations show respect for victims. They serve as evidence to the victim and others that the wrongdoer recognizes and is moved by the recognition that she did something she should not have done. This provides some reason for believing that the wrongdoer may be more morally trustworthy in the future.[64]

In order to communicate these messages rather than the insulting suggestions of fungibility or the purchase of reconciliation, reparation payments must either be accompanied by other, perhaps verbal, forms of communication or else take place within a social institution or tradition of reparation payments that constructs such an acceptable meaning. There is always a risk of misinterpretation here. Victims and wrongdoers may not be sure that they have the same understanding of the symbolic value of the payment. They might also worry that third parties will place a shameful interpretation on the transfer, such as labeling it a payoff or hush money. However, other forms of atonement, such as apology and truth telling, can reduce these risks.

Within such a system of reparations, the size of the payment, though never strictly commensurable with the nonmaterial harms that were created, can symbolize the depth of the remorse the wrongdoer feels. Given this function of reparations, the amount of the transfer should often vary with not only the severity of the wrong or the harm but also the wrongdoer's means. A one-thousand-dollar reparation payment means something different when it comes from a wrongdoer who is a struggling graduate student as opposed to a wealthy movie star. The greater the sacrifice that is required to make the reparation payment, the more evidence we have that the wrongdoer is remorseful for her past action. In sum, what is repaired through reparation payments is the *relationship* between the wrongdoer and the victim, and this is accomplished through the communicative function of reparations.

Gift giving is another form of material transfer that may be a powerful means of atonement. Once again it is the communicative function of gift giving that connects it to the task of reforming relationships inasmuch as gifts can symbolize remorse, respect, and caring. Gifts and reparation payments have much in common, and in certain cases it can be hard to distinguish between them. Reparations are usually conceived of as a form of response that is owed or specifically required in some sense, whereas gifts are usually (but not always[65]) considered an optional form of response. Also, reparation payments usually take some standard form of wealth such as money. However, gifts may be more varied in form. The value that will be attributed to a gift is usually not just (and sometimes not at all) a function of its market value. Gifts often get much of their value by being beautiful or creative or by speaking to some particular aspect of the giver's or receiver's personality or circumstances. A handmade doorstop given by a movie star to her victim may communicate more of the right messages than a hefty reparation check ever could.

Both reparations and gift giving can also contribute to the wrongdoer's moral improvement, which is another aspect of reconciliation. The effort or sacrifice involved in paying reparations or giving a gift may help the wrongdoer induce repentance in herself, better remember her wrongful action, or deter herself from repeating such an action in the future.

While reparations and gifts are usually given to victims, they may also be offered to communities. Sometimes victims are resistant to receiving anything from their offenders. In such cases, giving to other people instead can send many of the same messages and serve many of the same reformative functions for the wrongdoer. When a symbolic connection exists between the victim or the wrong and the recipient of such transfers (e.g., the victim's favorite charity or a center for victims of similar crimes), communication of respect for the victim will be clearer.

4.5.6 CARE WORK AND SERVICE

The performance of service work for victims or communities is another way in which offenders can repair harms and send messages of respect and remorse. For many people, contributing their time and labor is much harder than simply contributing money. Care work especially—that is, work that involves responding directly to other people's physical, mental, or emotional needs and well-being (e.g., caring for sick or injured people, tending to children, or even preparing food for another)—requires us to deal with one another as embodied subjects of experience. Given that wrongdoing usually involves some degree of disregard for the experience of others, care work can be powerfully symbolic of a change of heart and a recommitment to a respectful relationship. This is especially true when the care work is somehow related to the wrongful act itself, as when a former criminal who used to prey on elderly people volunteers at a retirement home.

This last example might raise worries because it threatens to leave other people problematically vulnerable to the atoning wrongdoer, who may not actually have become sufficiently trustworthy. It reminds me of another example, one that has been recommended to me repeatedly when I have asked my friends and colleagues for stories of satisfying examples of amends. In the film *Gandhi*, a Hindu man who is guilty of having participated in a murderous riot against Muslims approaches Mahatma Gandhi in an attitude of repentance and asks what he can do to right the wrong.[66] Gandhi advises him to find a Muslim child who has been orphaned as a result of the ethnic violence and to raise him as his own son but also as a good Muslim. If the man has sincerely and stably repented, if he can overcome his ethnic biases, and if he is perceptive enough to understand how to serve the emotional and other needs of an orphaned, Muslim child, then this would be a powerful form of amends indeed. However, the risk is great.[67] Wrongdoers have a duty to make amends, but they are not permitted to atone in any fashion that would wrongfully harm or recklessly endanger others. The permissibility and advisability of care work as a form of atonement must be limited by this general principle.

A further aspect of care work that qualifies it as a form of atonement is the significant educational effect it can provide for the wrongdoer. In caring for others, he will learn about their needs, experiences, and points of view and thereby become better able to empathize with them. When the victim is resistant to the wrongdoer's attempts to make amends, service work for parties other than the victim is a means by which a wrongdoer can contribute to his own atonement while respecting the victim's wishes. In some cases, such service work may even convince the victim to allow the wrongdoer to make amends more directly. In sum, service and care work send conciliatory messages, repair harms, and both bring about and provide evidence of the wrongdoer's moral improvement.

4.5.7 SELF-PUNISHMENT

What role, if any, may punishment play in atonement? We have seen that some of the means of atonement I have already defended contain elements of suffering. Guilt and repentance hurt. Apology may be painfully humbling. Reparations and care work require loss and sacrifice. The specific question of this section, however, is whether the intentional self-infliction of a penance is defensible as such. I have in mind actions such as fasting for the purpose of producing suffering.[68] Can such actions be defended in terms of the reconciliation theory of atonement?

In chapter 2 I rejected the idea that the wrongdoer's suffering could in itself be defended as the main or final goal of atonement. The wrongdoer's suffering should not be seen as an intrinsic good. However, punishment can in certain circumstances be an instrumental good. Intentional self-punishment may be a means by which the wrongdoer can educate herself, strengthen her self-discipline, and deter herself from repeating her wrongful actions.

Self-punishment, when made known to others, may also communicate remorse and moral improvement to victims and communities. Morris has defended self-punishment along these lines in a way that closely parallels my earlier discussions of repentance and empathy. He cites an intimate tie between caring and pain: "Care for another, commitment to another, imply being prepared to sacrifice one's interests in avoiding pain, at least to some extent, to another."[69] Moreover,

> The satisfaction that one obtains in the self-inflicted or accepted pain here comes from the very character of the conduct as painful, for it is this that evidences how much what has been done counts for one and how much it means for one to restore. When doubt has been raised about care and commitment, assumption of pain is a preeminent mark of their presence.[70]

Self-punishment is capable of sending many different messages, the one Morris highlights among them. Given certain circumstances, self-imposed suffering is a sign that one cares about the victim's pain and thus is evidence that one is no longer discounting the victim's point of view as less important than one's own. These are precisely the messages that reconciliation requires. Thus, self-punishment might be justified as a means to communication.

Retributivists object to instrumental justifications of punishment. The usual objection provided in the literature on state punishment is that instrumental defenses treat the criminal as a mere means to some other good, which is in violation of the Kantian moral ideas to which I have already allied the reconciliation theory of atonement. Punishing a criminal simply to deter crime, says the retributivist, forces the criminal to suffer for the well-being of the rest of society, thereby treating the criminal as a mere tool for the benefit of others. This violates the idea that all people are of equal and incommensurable moral value. The same objection can be leveled at a communicative defense of self-punishment, such as the one Morris offers in the earlier quotes, in that it seems to place the end of communication with the victim and community above the dignity of the wrongdoer.

I believe that one can use the reconciliation theory of atonement to defend instrumental uses of self-punishment while avoiding this objection. The Kantian moral law, of course, is not that one cannot use oneself or other people as *a* means to some other good. The idea is instead that one cannot use oneself or other people as *mere* means. One must treat humanity, both in oneself and in other people, always at the same time as an end.[71] The relevant restriction here is that the self-punishing wrongdoer must treat herself as an equally morally valuable person. When self-punishment is used as a means to the wrongdoer's own moral improvement, this requirement is satisfied.[72] She would be using her suffering in order to nurture herself as a moral agent.

But what if the only end of self-punishment in a particular case were the communicative one? Would the wrongdoer be treating herself as a mere means if she punished herself *solely* in order to communicate remorse and respect to others? There is certainly something "in it" for the wrongdoer to engage in such communication. She has the potential thereby to regain her standing in the moral community, an interest that is fitting for a moral agent. One might also argue that the wrongdoer, in communicating her repentance through self-punishment, is expressing something that is distinctive to her nature as a moral person. Only moral agents can repent, after all.

While it is possible to defend self-punishment in a way that is consistent with the Kantian theory of human value, this does not entail that every case of self-punishment is permissible according to that standard. For example, although it seems possible that self-punishment could send messages about remorse and equal respect, punishment might also send quite different messages. It might express self-hatred. It might, as Hampton's defense of retributive punishment unintentionally did, suggest that the infliction of suffering is a way of actually lowering a person's moral status.[73] These messages are inconsistent with the Kantian theory of human value, upon which the reconciliation theory of atonement is based. What message self-punishment expresses in any particular case is a difficult interpretative issue that calls on the skills of psychologists and cultural critics, as well as philosophers. For this reason my position on intentional self-punishment must remain tentative. It may be an acceptable means to atonement in some cases, but it is one that we should treat with caution.

As I have suggested in the discussion of the moral emotions of guilt and remorse, suffering may be an ineliminable feature of atonement. Suffering, whether the relatively reflexlike suffering of the moral emotions or deliberate penances, can serve the goals of moral reformation and communication. However, this position is still importantly different from the retributive idea that suffering is the proper, overarching goal of atonement or the idea found in satisfaction theory that suffering is the coin that repays moral debts. Furthermore, too much emphasis on the wrongdoer's suffering might well undermine the project of atonement. Self-punishment can induce self-hatred. It can communicate a narcissistic or even sadomasochistic tendency in the wrongdoer as opposed to a sincere interest in repairing relationships with the victim and the community. I think this is at least part of what is going on when victims tell wrongdoers, with a note of exasperation, "Well, don't beat yourself up about it."

4.5.8 SUBMISSION TO PUNISHMENT

When the morally wrongful act falls under the jurisdiction of an authority who has a right to punish or penalize the wrongdoer—be it a state, an employer, or a parent—the wrongdoer's voluntary submission to that authority might also count toward the making of amends. This is true so long as the authority is legitimate, one's obligations to it are genuine, and the practices of punishment are justified. In order to reestablish oneself as a trustworthy member of the local community and as having recommitted oneself to the norms that one has wrongfully violated, one must accept the legitimate penalties that the community associates with those norms. It is a form of reparation that the local community specifies. Submission to punishment can potentially play a communicative role as well, although it is frequently unclear whether submission is motivated by remorse or a fear of greater penalties should one try to escape punishment. Submission to punishment at the hands of others might also have deterrent and educative effects similar to those of self-punishment.

4.5.9 RITUALS

Most cultures have some sort of ritual of atonement. In Western cultures, certain formulas of apology have a ritualistic kind of power in that a simple recitation of traditional expressions can improve relationships even when none of the participants in the ritual pretend that any deep emotion of remorse is behind them. Charitable offerings, confessions, prayers, and fasts often form parts of such ceremonies in Western religious contexts. Participation in these religious rituals, when made known to victims and communities, can contribute to interpersonal reconciliation. Rituals of atonement often contain the sorts of means (apology, repentance, self-punishment) that play the same sorts of roles (communicative, educative, reparative) that I have already discussed. By listing rituals as a separate category of means of atonement, I draw attention to the enormous range of actions that might count as atonement.

For example, a few years ago the *New York Times* described a ritual of atonement and forgiveness used by the Acholi people in northern Uganda:

> One after the other, [the wrongdoers] stuck their bare right feet in a freshly cracked egg.... The egg symbolizes innocent life, according to local custom, and by dabbing themselves in it the killers are restoring themselves to the way they used to be. Next, [they] brushed against the branch of a pobo tree, which symbolically cleansed them. By stepping over a pole, they were welcomed back into the community.[74]

Other parts of the atonement process in the Acholi community involve confession, apology, and material payments. The particular occasion of the use of the egg and stick ritual described in the article was the return to the community of former rebel fighters who were guilty of killing, maiming, and raping and also of abducting children to act as soldiers during the long-term civil conflict along the border with Sudan. While the Acholi community itself debates the sufficiency of these responses to wrongdoing and while we may well share their worries, my point is that even an act as seemingly simple as stepping in a raw egg can be *a* means of atonement.

The egg and stick ritual takes place within a context of socially constructed meanings—as, indeed, do all acts of atonement. The ceremony thereby acquires the power to communicate a number of relevant messages to the audience, including an acknowledgment of wrongdoing, respect, remorse, and a desire for moral improvement. Exactly what is communicated will depend on the details of the case, including the symbolic heritage of the ritual and the perceived sincerity of the participants. When a ritual is accepted as a meaningful and somber event, partaking in it can also help wrongdoers strengthen their resolve to change their ways. The reconciliation theory of atonement can recognize the power of such a ritual.

Of course, we need not accept all of the claims that are connected to particular rituals. We need not accept that ritual contact with water, oil, or raw egg, for instance, washes away guilt or that the mere utterance of a formulaic "I'm sorry" is a real apology. Nor should we endorse every ritual that is accepted as meaningful in a particular community as a legitimate means of atonement.

After all, some ceremonies may send messages or create harms that must be deemed wrongful in themselves by our moral theory. However, when there are customary rituals for sending the moral messages that need to be sent (acknowledgment of wrongdoing, renewed respect, a recommitment to morality), to fail to participate is to risk undermining one's other efforts at atonement.

4.5.10   FUTURE BEHAVIOR

Among means to atonement, we should not overlook the importance of better future behavior itself. The wrongdoer's forbearance from repeating her mistake when faced with the same opportunity or temptation is sometimes described as the most powerful sort of proof of the genuineness of atonement. Not only is such better behavior a requirement of moral improvement, but it may also play communicative roles in atonement. When victims or communities see that the wrongdoer refrains from repeating her wrongful action or generally improves her behavior, they receive the message that she is remorseful and that her attitudes have changed. This gives the victims and communities reason to trust the wrongdoer again.

In view of this long list of types of atoning responses, it is clear that the options are numerous and varied. In most cases, any particular form of response to wrongdoing can play multiple roles at the same time. However, the main roles of atoning acts are to promote the wrongdoer's moral improvement, to communicate respect and acknowledgment of wrongdoing to the victims and/or the community, and to repair the myriad forms of harm that wrongdoing creates. When these tasks are accomplished, the wrongdoer will merit redemption in the form of a moral reconciliation. She will have provided others and also herself with good reason to believe that she now accepts that her victim is a person equally valuable to herself and that she is now morally trustworthy (at least with respect to the sort of wrongdoing in question).

4.6   The Context Sensitivity of Atonement

Our experiences of doing wrong and forgiving others teach us that successful atonement is highly context dependent. The nature of the wrong and the extent of the harm it causes clearly affect what is required to make amends, but so do many other factors. I make a careless comment at a party that insults you. What must I do now? It depends. Are you my friend or my partner, or have we only just met? How many people overheard the insult, and how likely is it that the insult will lead them to have a lower opinion of you or of me? Have I done something like this to you or to other people in the past, or is this aberrant behavior on my part? Are there established norms or strong community preferences for some sorts of atonement over others, and are these consistent with the goals of reconciliation? Depending on how these various factors play out, it may be the case that a simple apology and short-lived experience of repentance will atone for the wrong. Or it may be that I must experience more severe remorse and also approach each of the witnesses personally to correct the impression that I gave of you. I may need to present you with a gift as a token of my remorse. The look on my face may count as an apology in certain circumstances, but in others I might need to apologize in formal language or even apologize to you in public.

The context sensitivity of the process of atonement is entirely predictable from what we have said about the goal of atonement. In atoning, we aim at restoring our moral relationships with other people and with ourselves. However, which relationships we must work to restore depend on which ones were actually damaged or threatened by the wrongful act. What we must do to restore our moral relationships with other people or ourselves will depend on the previous nature of those relationships, on the amount of strain that was placed on the relationships by the wrong, and on the legitimate expectations of the victims and the community.

The role of empathy in atonement deserves special emphasis because it is crucial to the process of making amends as a whole. Since proper and successful atonement is highly sensitive to context, in order to achieve reconciliation the wrongdoer must know whom he has wronged and in what ways. (What other relationships besides that between the wrongdoer and the victim have been damaged? How severe is the damage?) He must imagine what sorts of responses are most likely to heal these relationships, and in order to do that he must imagine what it is like to be this victim, what it is like to be wronged in this way, how this third-party spectator is likely to be affected by the wrong, and how these parties would likely be affected by various offers of amends. Performing such tasks well requires empathy.

We can all think of examples of failed attempts at amends, such as apologies that are ill timed, misdirected, or delivered in the wrong tone of voice. Reconciliation is not achieved when the act of atonement itself shows that the wrongdoer is reluctant, concerned only with his own suffering, or oblivious to the ramifications of his action. Sometimes acts of atonement fail not because they are not grand enough but because they are too grand. A husband complains to his wife that she always interrupts him when they are at parties. The wife reacts as if she must save their marriage from the brink of divorce—making heart-wrenching speeches about the importance of their relationship, investigating marriage counseling, or planning costly vacations during which they can work on their relationship. Perhaps her husband will be moved by her response, but he may be even more annoyed with her. The inappropriateness of her attempts to make amends may betray the fact that his wife simply does not "get it." She does not see that a good relationship means caring about the little things, as well as the big ones. Or he might wonder whether there are other wrongs of which he is unaware and for which she is expressing guilt. Her inappropriate attempt to make amends may leave her husband feeling more alienated from her than ever.

Empathy is important to the moral improvement of the wrongdoer as well. An ability to empathize with the parties affected by his misdeed will enable him to better understand the nature and significance of his transgression. In Conrad's novel, Jim's lack of empathy leads him to misdiagnose the wrongness of his action. An ability to perceive and empathize with other's experiences will aid the wrongdoer's efforts to behave better in the future.

Even the payment of reparations cannot be properly performed without empathy. In the aftermath of wrongdoing, *how* reparations are paid often makes a tremendous difference to the possibility of reconciliation. Reparations must be offered respectfully and in a way that communicates appropriate repentance. The timing and presentation of the offer must be sensitive to the needs of the victim. The form of reparations is sometimes a matter that requires great sensitivity to the victim's point of view. What can be offered as proportional reparation for a treasured possession, wasted time, or bodily injury? What form of reparation will send the message that the wrongdoer recognizes the extent of the harm caused without also suggesting that he hopes simply to buy reconciliation? To make reparations properly and to do so in the way that is most likely to serve the goal of reconciliation, the wrongdoer must understand the harm he has caused from the victim's own perspective. As these examples suggest, atonement is an art. It requires subtle, caring attention to other people's points of view and the ways in which people relate to one another. Successful atonement requires empathy.

4.7 *Conclusion: Reconciliation Theory and the Magdalen Penitents*

In the opening chapter I presented an extended case study of the Magdalen asylums in order to bring our attention to the obstacles and risks that face us in formulating an ethic of atonement. I conclude this chapter by applying reconciliation theory to that case. If it is to be a useful theory of atonement, it should be able to identify what was morally unacceptable about the Magdalen system and avoid the same mistakes.

As our earlier discussion shows, a long list of moral problems was associated with the Magdalen asylums. Yet many of the particular abuses can be traced to two main flaws: The penitents were robbed of their autonomy, and atonement was equated with degradation. Rather than emphasizing the importance of the inmates' taking responsibility for their own moral improvement and future behavior, the asylum system removed their powers of choice and limited their opportunity for free reflection.[75] The women and girls were either instructed or forced to imprison themselves in an institution where they would have no opportunity to make decisions about their sexual behavior, and they were often encouraged or coerced to stay there forever. They were prevented from discussing their previous behavior. Instead, they were continually presented with one moral view that they were supposed to accept uncritically. They were addressed as "children" and treated as such. Instead of being allowed the opportunity to repair their relationships with their families and their neighbors or even to accept responsibility for the children they bore, they were cut off from them and isolated as if their "sin" were contagious.

Such norms of atonement are inconsistent with the Kantian conception of human value and moral agency, which is at the heart of the reconciliation theory of atonement. Reconciliation theory requires wrongdoers to treat both other people and *themselves* as equally valuable moral persons. It demands moral improvement in line with a conception of morality that emphasizes autonomy rather than simple conformance to a set of externally legislated behaviors. In requiring wrongdoers to repair their relationships with other people, it recognizes the wrongdoers' moral potential rather than casting them aside as permanently untrustworthy. The Magdalen system violated these values of autonomy and dignity.

Furthermore, the punitive measures in the Magdalen system exemplify the misuse of suffering in atonement. While the suffering endured by the penitents was presumably meant to be either self-imposed or voluntarily accepted, that was not the case for many of the women and girls. Because of the lack of voluntariness, the punitive measures were incapable of performing the communicative work appropriate to atoning acts. The ones inflicting the punishment exceeded their legitimate authority by holding penitents against their will in violation of the laws of Ireland. The penitents were not morally educated by their suffering but terrorized by it. They were encouraged to deplore their bodies and their sexuality rather than to develop a self-respecting and responsible understanding of themselves as embodied, sexual beings whose choices would affect themselves and others in important ways. The fact that their communities did not see their suffering as either reformative or reparative is betrayed by the continuing stigmatization of those women who were released by the asylums. From the perspective of the reconciliation theory, it is no wonder that these women were not perceived as having restored their standing in their communities. The forms of atonement they underwent provided the community with no evidence that they had become trustworthy in the moral matters in question. Being terrorized into a fear of sex is not the same thing as developing a morally responsible character.

This chapter has argued that the wrongdoers' proper goal in atoning is a reconciliation of their moral relationships with themselves, their victims, and their communities. However, significant questions remain regarding the criteria of success for their atonement. From whose perspective do we judge whether the attempt at atonement is satisfactory—the wrongdoers', the victims', the communities', or perhaps some objective point of view? When is it appropriate to count the wrongdoer as redeemed? Chapter 5 addresses these issues, as well as the question of whether a wrongdoer can not merely merit but also *deserve* reconciliation.

| Forgiveness, Self-Forgiveness, and Redemption

5.1   Introduction

Up to this point we have been exploring what morality requires of wrongdoers. We have been asking how they must respond to their wrongful actions in hopes of redeeming themselves. In the last chapter I argued that the wrongdoers' proper aim is a kind of moral reconciliation with themselves, their victims, and their communities, wherein they both satisfy the claims against them and restore their standing as trustworthy agents. But if a reestablishment of trust is really the proper aim of atonement, then this suggests that wrongdoers cannot redeem *themselves* at all. If they are going to achieve redemption, they will need the cooperation of others.

The details of the reconciliation theory of atonement that I advocate suggest quite a significant role for victims indeed. The final correction of wrongdoing seems to depend on the victim's (and sometimes the community's) willingness to forgive or morally reconcile with an offender who has made a sincere and proportional atonement. However, in many cases the victim needs to cooperate with the wrongdoer in order for atonement to be made in the first place. Proper atonement requires respectful communication with the victim and other affected parties, and, to be respectful, that communication cannot be one way. The vital moral emotion of repentance is dependant upon an empathetic approximation of the victim's point of view, and this may be achievable only when the victim is willing to share her point of view. Many forms of reparation can be given to a victim only when the victim agrees to accept them. So, according to the reconciliation theory, atonement is frequently not just an action of the wrongdoer but also an interaction with a victim and perhaps a community as well.

However, if the wrongdoer needs the cooperation of the victim in order to atone, then it is in the victim's power to prevent the wrongdoer from making amends. She can inhibit the wrongdoer's ability to correct his wrongful actions. If the wrongdoer needs the victim's forgiveness or trust in order to count as redeemed, then his moral standing lies at her mercy. Given the fact that not all victims are wise or just, these apparent corollaries of the reconciliation theory of atonement should give us pause. Yet there are also good reasons, which I discuss later, for granting victims a substantial role in the resolution of the wrongs committed against them. The challenge for this chapter is to strike a balance between the legitimate interests of both victims and wrongdoers in laying out the terms of redemption. I am here concerned with what morality asks not just of wrongdoers but of victims and communities as well.

I begin the discussion by defining some terms, specifically the concept of forgiveness and its connections to moral reconciliation. In order to ask whether victims must extend either of these to atoning wrongdoers, we must clarify what we mean by these terms. First, however, we must say more about redemption. Whereas 'forgiveness' and 'reconciliation' have made their way into the secular philosophical literature, 'redemption' sounds a bit awkward even to my ears, and I use it with some trepidation. Still, we need some way of talking about the end state of cases of wrongdoing—some point at which we can describe the wrongful act as having been successfully resolved.

While wrongdoers should pursue forgiveness and reconciliation in atoning, these are no substitutes for atonement. As I argue in section 5.4, forgiveness and reconciliation offered preemptively do not achieve redemption for the wrongdoer. Yet, in section 5.5 I examine several arguments for the claim that wrongdoers also cannot achieve redemption by themselves. The victims must help them annul the wrongs. We may think of these as arguments for the victims' prerogative in the resolution of wrongdoing since they have options in their response to the wrongdoer. In section 5.6 I argue that such a prerogative is subject to significant moral pushes and pulls. The victim's role is not fully optional, that is, to be played however the victim wishes. Instead, there are right and wrong, better and worse, virtuous and vicious ways for victims to react to their offenders' attempts at making amends. These judgments rightfully affect our view of the wrongdoers' standing as redeemed.

Sections 5.7 through 5.9 of the chapter turn from victims to the other players in the story of reconciliation: communities and the wrongdoers themselves. I ask how communities should react to atoning wrongdoers.[1] Should their reactions be guided by those of the victims? How should they regard wrongdoers when victims are dead or otherwise absent or when victims react to atonement improperly? A resolution of the past also requires wrongdoers to achieve proper self-regarding attitudes. While it is appropriate to judge themselves negatively in response to their wrongful actions and to feel the corresponding painful emotions, atonement should change things. When do wrongdoers earn the right to forgive or reconcile with themselves, and of what does such self-forgiveness or self-reconciliation consist? Section 5.10 brings the chapter to a close by considering the issues raised by cases in which a full atonement and thus, apparently, a full redemption are not possible.

5.2 Redemption

Redemption is the term I have chosen to use for the proper end state of responses to wrongdoing. If 'to deem' something is to evaluate or place a value upon it, then when something is 'redeemed,' it has been reevaluated, and the connotation is that this reevaluation is a positive one. When one is redeemed, one has justifiably regained one's moral standing. In theological contexts, redemption is an end state in a much stronger sense than I mean here. To be redeemed there is to be finally and positively judged by God. Such redemption is totalizing and permanent. However, as I use the term, one can be redeemed for some failings but not others. For instance, one can regain one's standing as an ethical professional but still be suspect as a friend. One may also be redeemed after a particular instance of wrongdoing but later repeat the offense and lose one's standing once more.

In thinking of redemption as the proper end state of wrongdoing, it helps to return to our understanding of what wrongdoing does. We have described wrongdoing as an insult, a threat, and a cause of a variety of harms to victims and often communities. It also damages the wrongdoers themselves. Insofar as one's wrongdoing is detected, it tears at social bonds with others, and one's perceived standing in the moral community is lowered. As long as the past wrongful action continues to operate as a present threat and a plausible predictor of future behavior, the wrongdoer will not be granted the same level of esteem and trust as before but, quite sensibly, will be regarded with some level of resentment, indignation, and suspicion. This might have a number of further negative effects on others' willingness to interact and cooperate with the wrongdoer. If the offender is someone who cares about being moral or is at least sensitive to other people's opinions of her, she will also suffer a degree of self-alienation. Wrongdoing causes us to disapprove of ourselves and feel guilt, shame, or even self-hatred or contempt. These feelings are painful.

If these are the consequences of wrongdoing, its correction must involve repairing these consequences. Redemption consists in the satisfaction of moral claims stemming from the wrong, the normalization of one's standing in the moral community, and the establishment or reestablishment of good relationships with those affected by the wrong. This includes one's relationship with oneself. When one is redeemed, one is permitted to let go of the painful emotions of self-assessment that the misdeed caused. As I have said before, I do not think that we should describe the ideal end state as the full reestablishment of any previous relationship between wrongdoer and victim. There might be many reasons for either the victim or the wrongdoer to want to leave the friendship, marriage, or business partnership that they formerly had together, even if the wrong has been properly remedied. Some high levels of trust and intimacy may be emotionally impossible to reestablish once they have been upset. However, a wrongdoer can be redeemed in a moral sense as long as she can satisfy her obligations to others and reestablish her moral trustworthiness to the point that the victim and the community will no longer have any reason to continue to regard her with the suspicion and reserve that accompany the role of "wrongdoer." This type of reconciliation is what I term 'moral reconciliation.' In order to achieve this, the wrongdoer must regain her standing as a trustworthy member of the moral community, at least to a normal level in the moral matters in question.

This talk of trustworthiness needs to be made more precise. Karen Jones defines trust as "an attitude of optimism that the goodwill and competence of another will extend to cover the domain of our interaction with her, together with the expectation that the one trusted will be directly and favorably moved by the thought that we are counting on her."[2] To be trustworthy is to merit trust. But, of course, the scope of trust varies with the domain of interaction under consideration, and one can merit trust to different degrees. What level of trustworthiness is normal? Trustworthiness is surely role bound. The trust that is normal for a friend is different from that which is normal for a neighbor or a coworker. Take a case where a wife has cheated on her husband. In order to be redeemed with regard to this kind of wrongdoing, she must reestablish herself as trustworthy *as a marital or romantic partner*. She must atone in such a way that makes it reasonable to conclude that she could now be a faithful partner. Again, her relationship with the husband she betrayed may end. However, she can become trustworthy as a romantic partner to the point that even her ex-husband will recognize her as such. He might, for instance, have no particular worries about her faithfulness should she go on to marry someone he knows and likes.

When the wrongdoer is redeemed, the wrong has been dealt with, and all of the parties can now move on, leaving the roles of victim and wrongdoer behind. While the fact of guilt remains, it is now located safely in the past and need not negatively affect the possibility of good, normalized relationships in the future.[3] In their discussion of the aftermath of wrongdoing (which they frame in terms of the victim's forgiveness rather than the wrongdoer's redemption), Trudy Govier and Wilhelm Verwoerd highlight the importance of what they call "the releasing element."[4] This refers to the willingness of victims (and sometimes also communities) to grant that they no longer hold moral claims against the offender as a result of the misdeed.[5] In order to count as redeemed and retake her place in both the moral community and the particular community of friends or neighbors, the wrongdoer must be released in this sense. The victim, the community, and the wrongdoer herself should no longer see the wrongdoer as beholden to anyone in virtue of the past offense. Importantly, this requires not just a reestablishment of the wrongdoer's trustworthiness (a forward-looking good that is served primarily by personal improvement) but also a proper response to the harms that the past wrong created (a backward-looking good that is served directly by reparations and respectful communication). Of course, these values are tightly linked because the wrongdoer's responses to the harms, insults, and threats she created are prime evidence of her trustworthiness and may be crucial to restoring the victim's ability to trust her again. The victim might renew his trust in the wrongdoer before claims have been satisfied. However, if those claims remain inexcusably unsatisfied, this trust is neither merited nor likely to be stable. Govier and Verwoerd explicate the concept of release from moral claims in terms of counting a moral debt as paid. However, we can also associate this idea with the more relational metaphor of the parties' no longer occupying the roles of "the one wronged" and "the wrongdoer."

It is important to note that this model of redemption, with its associated metaphor of "putting the past behind one," is not possible in all cases of wrongdoing. After some wrongs, the only way to restore one's standing and reestablish oneself as trustworthy is continually to deal with the past. For example, part of what makes current-day Germany a trustworthy member of the community of nations is that the Nazi past is explicitly recognized to be relevant to current policy choices. A similar commitment to recognizing the continuing relevance of the past seems to influence the teaching of Alcoholics Anonymous that one remains an alcoholic for life. The point is not just one about the biology and psychology of addiction. It also suggests that, with regard to some flaws, one must be constantly vigilant in order to merit renewed trust. For instance, the adulterous ex-wife may be able to reestablish herself as trustworthy with regard to vows of sexual fidelity only by learning never to make such promises again. Being trustworthy requires knowing and acknowledging one's limits.

Full redemption is not possible in cases of wrongs that are so grievous and harmful that moral reconciliation and the restoration of trust and esteem for the wrongdoer will never be justifiable. However, even where redemption is not finally achievable, it can be approached or approximated. Thus, one's moral standing can be improved if not fully restored. I have more to say about such cases at the end of this chapter.

5.3   Forgiveness

I have strongly associated redemption with moral reconciliation, but most authors take the main issue in victims' responses to atoning wrongdoers to be forgiveness. Many are rather critical of an association between reconciliation and the resolution of wrongdoing.[6] Much of this skepticism stems from the fact that most writers think of reconciliation in terms of *personal* reconciliation (the resumption of a friendship, say) rather than the special notion of moral reconciliation that takes the central role here. Distinctively moral reconciliation and forgiveness are similar attitudes, and indeed many of the ways in which I have characterized moral reconciliation are drawn from other theorists' characterizations of forgiveness.[7] However, there are two attitudes here, and it is useful to distinguish between them. In this section I outline those differences and ask whether forgiveness, too, is tied to redemption and, if so, how.

Since the 1980s, the topic of forgiveness has attracted quite a lot of attention from philosophers, as well as psychotherapists and political theorists. The literature provides a number of compelling but incompatible characterizations of forgiveness. I suspect that this is due to the facts that philosophers attempt to stay true to ordinary conceptions and that the ordinary conception of forgiveness is multifaceted and disputed. A number of accounts of the term 'forgiveness' make equally good sense. In what follows I do not attempt to give *a uniquely correct* analysis of forgiveness. Instead, I discuss a particular moral attitude that victims hold toward wrongdoers and that is commonly named "forgiveness," compare it to the attitude I have already labeled "moral reconciliation," and then ask how each relates to the question of how to resolve wrongdoing.

The most obvious difference between moral reconciliation and forgiveness is that the former is normally thought of as a mutual relationship, whereas forgiveness is an attitude held only by victims toward wrongdoers. However, we can also talk about a unilateral variant of moral reconciliation: A victim may *reconcile herself to* the wrongdoer before the wrongdoer is ready to reestablish the relationship. We might think of this as a readiness to reconcile. Another difference is that most theorists agree that forgiveness is something that only a victim can extend.[8] However, there seems nothing awkward in saying that interested third parties can morally reconcile with a wrongdoer.

According to what one might call the standard account, to forgive is to overcome or foreswear resentment and other negative emotions (e.g., anger, hatred, contempt, disappointment), which are held toward the wrongdoer in virtue of the offense.[9] We define forgiveness as either the overcoming or the *foreswearing* of resentment and related emotions in order to recognize that a decision to forgive is not automatically followed by the dissolution of these emotions. Overcoming resentment frequently takes both effort and time and is not in the direct control of the victim. However, we can choose to forgive because we can choose to commit ourselves to ending our resentment, and we can lay down our claim to our continued right to those feelings.

Some writers add that these emotions must be foresworn or overcome for moral reasons.[10] A case where one ceases to resent simply because one has forgotten that one has been wronged is not a case of forgiveness.[11] However, precisely which sorts of reasons for abandoning resentment count as moral in the relevant sense and therefore as forgiveness is a controversial matter. If I abandon resentment of John because I learn that he was not the one who wronged me after all, then my reason is a moral one, but this is not a case of forgiveness. Some say that prudentially abandoning resentment in order to resume a full and happy life is genuine forgiveness, whereas others disagree. I am unable to go into these complexities here, so I opt for a generally inclusive notion of forgiveness, which allows that genuine forgiveness can be granted to wrongdoers for many reasons.[12]

Forgiveness and moral reconciliation often go together. I may forgive a person because I have come to see him as morally trustworthy again, or I may morally reconcile with a person because, once I have given up my resentment of him, there is no longer any obstacle to our normalizing relations. However, the concepts differ. One can forgive another person without morally reconciling with him. I might choose to forgive a person out of mercy, pity, or magnanimity or in hopes of inspiring his reformation, yet not consider him morally trustworthy. I might give up my resentment of him while fully expecting that he will wrong me again in similar circumstances and working to protect myself against that eventuality.

It also seems possible to morally reconcile with someone without forgiving that person. In morally reconciling, one trusts another person to act properly in the future in some respect. In forgiving, one gives up or foreswears one's resentment for something that lies in the past. The differing directionality of these attitudes can allow them to coexist in surprising ways. For example, I can resent you for risking my life by talking me on a dangerous expedition while at the same time trusting you and no one but you to protect my life now that we are in the midst of the adventure.[13] While such mixes of resentment and trust are possible, they are rare. Our reasons for resenting a person are almost always also those for distrusting that person with respect to future choices in that domain of action. Past actions are generally good evidence of both character and future action.

I can also imagine cases in which a victim will refuse, with justification, to abandon her resentment of the atoning wrongdoer even though she accepts that the wrongdoer has become a morally trustworthy person and has satisfied all of the moral claims against him. Even when wrongs have been repaired, the victim must maintain her sense that the wrong was a wrong and that she did not deserve such treatment. It could be that a particular victim needs to preserve her feelings of resentment in order to maintain this grasp on her self-respect and sense of justice. At the same time, the victim can recognize that the wrongdoer is now a person who owes her nothing, poses no threat, and is worthy of trust. This example and the previous one illustrate how trust and an endorsement of resentment can coexist. They suggest that one could morally reconcile with a wrongdoer while refusing to forgive him. Thus, moral reconciliation does not guarantee forgiveness.

Is forgiveness related to redemption? I have argued that in pursuing redemption the wrongdoer must seek moral reconciliation with the victim, the community, and himself. Must he also aim at achieving forgiveness? It seems that he should. After all, the victim's resentment is one of the generally harmful consequences brought about by the wrongful act. It is something from which both victims and wrongdoers might suffer. So, in order to right the wrong, the offender must try to eliminate that resentment. But sometimes victims remain resentful despite their agreement that the wrongdoer has adequately addressed the past. In some cases, this resentment might plague the victim but be due to the victim's own resentful nature rather than any failure on the wrongdoer's part. In other cases, like the one described earlier, the victim draws strength from her resentment and uses it either to help maintain her self-respect and her sense of right and wrong or to resolve not to reenter a personal relationship with the wrongdoer. It seems unfair to deny such a victim the right to resent the atoning wrongdoer so long as her resentment stays private and does not violate any legitimate claims of the wrongdoer, who *ex hypothesi* has made a proper atonement. Resentment is an internal state of the victim that does not necessarily manifest itself in action. On the other hand, because they are states of relationships, reconciliation and the granting of moral standing have both internal and external dimensions. In the end, I believe we should say that, in pursuing redemption, the wrongdoer must aim for both moral reconciliation and forgiveness, but he might achieve redemption when he secures the former but not the latter.

5.4   *Preemptive Forgiveness and Reconciliation*

In section 5.5 I ask whether actual moral reconciliation—as opposed to reconciliation that is merited or deserved but withheld—is necessary for redemption. (I have just claimed that actual forgiveness is not.) However, before considering those arguments, I explain that actual reconciliation and forgiveness are not *sufficient* for redemption. One can forgive and morally reconcile with a wrongdoer for purely prudential reasons or in hopes of inspiring repentance even when the wrongdoer has not improved herself one jot. Such wrongdoers should not count as redeemed even though they have been so lucky as to receive forgiveness and reconciliation. Sometimes people talk as though this is not the case. They describe wrongdoers as released from their obligations to their victims as soon as the victims forgive or reconcile. "You owe me nothing," the victim might say, "I forgive you." Such a view arises, I believe, from the debt model of wrongdoing. Just as financial debts may be forgiven rather than paid, so might moral debts. This is why forgiveness is so frequently associated with mercy and the avoidance of penalties.

Of course, these financial metaphors make a point. Some of the harms of wrongdoing actually take the form of debts to victims (such as the value of a ruined possession). The victim can forgive such debts, and that is the end of that issue. However, not all of what is wrong with wrongdoing can be properly conceptualized as a debt. We must also consider the insult to the victim and the implied threat of future wrongdoing. These and other forms of harm do not operate like debts. Your dear mother may well say to you, "Yes, you insulted and disappointed me, you broke my heart, but I love you, and I forgive you. Let's forget it." However, that does not mean you may forget it. Mother dear deserves your respect and repentance even if she is not willing to lay claim to it. You morally ought to become a better person than the one who wronged her even if she does not demand that you do.

A victim's willingness to reconcile with the wrongdoer may yet turn out to be a requirement of redemption, but it is not sufficient for it. Any forgiveness or reconciliation provided by victims simply out of magnanimity, hopes of inspiring reform, or even convenience or a lack of concern about the wrongful act do not reflect on the wrongdoer's moral desert in a relevant way. My position here contrasts with the sometimes magical way in which forgiveness is discussed—as if forgiveness by itself could eliminate guilt and put the past to rest, like the hand of God, which grants absolution and leaves the soul sparkling clean. Here in the natural realm, forgiveness is not so powerful, and wrongs are not righted so easily. It might seem as though they can be when they are very minor. Trivial wrongs may pose no plausible or significant threat for the future, and the only harm done is the resentment the victim feels and then relinquishes in forgiving. However, even in cases of minor wrongdoing, if the wrong suggests something negative about the wrongdoer's character, then there is more work to be done.

5.5   *The Victim's Prerogative*

A victim's forgiveness or willingness to reconcile is not a magic elixir that makes wrongdoing disappear into the past. However, victims and their responses to atonement are highly important to the resolution of wrongdoing because the wrongs we are interested in here are social in nature. They are problems in relationships. Govier and Verwoerd (as well as others) have discussed the "victim's prerogative" in the aftermath of wrongdoing.[14] The implicit idea, I believe, is that the resolution of wrongdoing and the possibility of the wrongdoer's redemption are dependent on the victim to some degree. While these writers talk about victim's prerogative *to forgive* rather than a prerogative to grant redemption, issues of redemption lie just below the surface. For example, Govier and Verwoerd examine victims' criticisms of the South African Truth and Reconciliation Commission (TRC) for claiming the right to forgive and reconcile with human rights abusers without the victims' having done so first. It is unclear what would be so important about the TRC's forgiving first—why it would seem like the usurping of the victim's right rather than a simple reconciling between the wrongdoer and the state—unless forgiveness or reconciliation changed something significant about the wrongdoer's general moral standing. Jean Harvey describes the victim's forgiveness as granting the wrongdoer "permission for a fresh start" and permission "not to continue calculating this act of wrongdoing into an account of her present moral status."[15] In this section I examine a variety of arguments that explain why a victim's acceptance of a wrongdoer's atonement is so important to the correction of wrongdoing. I concentrate first on a strong version of this idea: that the wrongdoer cannot by herself annul wrongdoing and that the victim's actual reconciliation with the wrongdoer is necessary for redemption.

First, let me make a stylistic note. In section 5.3 I argued that forgiveness, though valuable and a proper aim of the wrongdoer, is not necessary for redemption. If any victim reaction is to be necessary for redemption, it is moral reconciliation. However, the authors I discuss in this section do not draw the distinctions between forgiveness and moral reconciliation in the same way, and most of their arguments are stated in terms of forgiveness. I offer my apologies in advance for any confusion or awkwardness this may occasion.

Let us return once again to our understanding of what wrongdoing is and what it does. Notice that if the debt model of wrongdoing were right— if wrongdoing amounted to the incursion of a debt to the victim—then redemption would lie within in the wrongdoer's hands, at least in principle. The wrongdoer could earn redemption by paying back the debt. Were the victim to refuse the payment, then, following the logic of the metaphor, the debt would count as paid anyway. In such a system the victim's meaningful participation is not needed. Debts are described as "forgiven" when paid, but this type of forgiveness is so automatic that some would be inclined to call the use of the word "forgiven" here merely metaphorical and no longer deeply connected to the conception we have of the virtue of forgiveness.[16]

When we replace the debt model of wrongdoing with a relational one, things change. If what is wrong with wrongdoing is primarily the harm it does to the relationships among wrongdoers, victims, and communities, then to correct wrongdoing is to repair these relationships. However, the wrongdoer cannot correct her relationship with her victim unless the victim is willing to reciprocate, that is, unless the victim is willing to establish or reestablish a moral relationship with the wrongdoer. Redemption, then, requires the victim's participation. But need we go this far? Could it not be enough that the wrongdoer, through her own efforts, shows that she *merits* or *deserves* reconciliation? May we not count her as redeemed so long as she plays her role, whether or not the victim chooses to play his? The following arguments maintain that actual victim participation is required for full-fledged redemption.

The first set of arguments focuses on the idea that the victim has a special authority to either grant or ratify the wrongdoer's redemption. What we might call "arguments from authority" can be formulated in a few different ways. One might think that there is no fact about what merits reconciliation independent of the victim's own actual willingness to reciprocate. To say that a certain response objectively merits or deserves reconciliation is to risk falling back into the debt model of wrongdoing. In order to avoid such a view, perhaps we should simply recognize victims as having the special authority to say when the wrongs that have been committed against them are resolved.

However, this sort of defense of victim authority presents two problems. First, as we have already noted, some victims will count wrongs as annulled even when the wrongdoer has shown no moral merit whatsoever. Such unrepentant wrongdoers should not be counted as redeemed. Second and at the other end of the scale, other victims may insist on extreme or degrading forms of atonement in exchange for reconciliation. Victims do not have such unlimited forms of authority when it comes to reconciliation. Instead, they are subject to some form of justice—they are not morally permitted to set certain conditions for reconciliation. For instance, they cannot demand anything that is inherently wrongful, and they cannot justly demand an atonement that is disproportional to the harm, threat, or insult that constitutes the wrongful act.

The idea that the victim has a kind or degree of authority is compelling, though. Within the sorts of limits just noted, victims seem to have the right to dictate the terms of reconciliation to their abusers. Suppose Lisa cruelly ridicules Jennifer and Joe during a meeting at work, repents of her action, and goes to each of them the next day with a sincere apology and a lovely gift. Jennifer accepts, extends her forgiveness, and reconciles with Lisa. However, Joe refuses the gift and demands a public apology instead. It seems to me that he is justified in doing so.[17] Lisa's original offer of amends was sincere and meaningful, and both Jennifer and Joe may recognize that. Nonetheless, whereas Jennifer cares about being respected and esteemed by Lisa and takes the gift and the private apology as sufficient proof that Lisa does value her as a person and a colleague, Joe cares more about the harm Lisa did to his standing with the other colleagues in the office. Joe and Jennifer, as the victims, get to judge which aspects of the wrong are significant to them. Because they are different people, it is reasonable that they will disagree about what these are. In this way, victims have a limited authority to define what counts as meriting reconciliation.[18]

This example leads us to what we might call the "argument from epistemic authority," which suggests that victims have a say in what counts as meriting reconciliation because they have a privileged form of epistemic access to the damage that needs to be repaired.[19] They know best how they have been harmed and what will alleviate that harm. This is usually true, but it does not fully account for the victim's authority in such cases. Suppose that Lisa can foresee that it is not a good idea, for Joe's own sake, for her to make a public apology. Perhaps she knows that the other colleagues (competitive people who are proud of their thick skins) will see Joe as a weakling who cannot take professional criticism. Lisa should warn Joe that his choice of remedy will not have the effect he desires. However, should he insist on it anyway, it seems that Lisa must acquiesce. This case suggests that the victim's authority is not purely epistemic.

A further justification for the victim's authority is more directly tied to his status as victim. A large part of what is wrong with wrongdoing is that it is disrespectful to victims. In treating a victim as one would not want to be treated oneself, one acts on the assumption (or perhaps the wish) that the victim has a lower status than oneself. An important way for the atoning wrongdoer to reestablish respect for the victim—and, just as importantly, to *demonstrate* to the victim that respect has been reestablished—is to give the victim a say in what comes next. The wrongdoer must regard the victim as having limited authority in setting the terms for reconciliation and must regard the victim's forgiveness and reconciliation as relevant to the success of her own atonement.[20]

Our theory of wrongdoing also provides grounds for the victim's prerogative. Were wrongdoing equivalent to a debt of objective size, the victim's opinion as to the adequacy of the repayment would be irrelevant. However, if what is wrong with wrongdoing is primarily the damage done to relationships, repairing wrongdoing requires re-earning the victim's trust. To do so, we must be responsive to the standards of trustworthiness the victim embraces.

A final set of arguments for the claim that wrongdoing cannot be annulled without the victim's participation starts from the now-familiar claim that both wrongdoing and atonement are expressive acts. Atonement somehow corrects or changes the meaning of the past wrong. Pamela Hieronymi, reacting to Aurel Kolnai's work on forgiveness, argues that wrongdoers cannot change the meaning of the past all by themselves because that meaning is essentially social.[21] A wrongful action sends insulting and threatening messages whether or not the wrongdoer intends it to do so. The act has the meaning it does because of social conventions that attach to such events. For example, romantic infidelity signifies disregard even if the one cheating hopes that it does not. If the meaning of the wrongful action has its source in social conventions rather than the wrongdoer's intentions or attitudes, then the wrongdoer cannot change the meaning of that action merely by changing her intentions or attitudes.

Similarly, the offender's repentance cannot make her a "new" person, one who is importantly different from the one who committed the wrong, because our identities are socially constructed as well. Hieronymi writes, "if we understand the [wrongful] event as carrying broader, social meaning, and if we understand one's identity as at least partially constituted by how one is perceived by others, then we can…start to see why one's repentance and change in heart requires ratification by others."[22] This ratification, according to Hieronymi, is what the victim provides through his forgiveness. The victim, and presumably the community as well, thereby help the wrongdoer change the meaning of the past.

In support of this social theory of the meaning of the past, Hieronymi offers a further argument. She claims that "If the meaning of the event and his own moral standing were the sole property of the offender, we would be left without a way to understand either the pain of remorse or the desire to seek forgiveness."[23] If I could change the meaning of the past simply by now disapproving of my past action and if I could nullify the claim I previously made by now declaring that I take it back, why would I also suffer over it? The work would be done. What more would there be to bother about? Remorse includes a wish to change something that one does not have the power to change. Similarly, if I could change the significance of the past myself, whether through repentance or a richer form of atonement, why would I also reach out for forgiveness and reconciliation? Why would that be necessary? The fact that I do feel both remorse and the need for forgiveness, argues Hieronymi, is evidence that I cannot change the significance of the past by myself.

Hieronymi provides us with another intriguing, if not fully convincing, reason for thinking that the project of redemption requires the victims' participation. She suggests that attached to every wrongful action is a kind of harm the offender cannot repair.[24] The wrongdoer can redress many forms of harm—she can pay for destroyed valuables or medical bills, and she can bolster the victim's self-esteem and reestablish his reputation in the neighborhood—but one sort of harm will always be left with the victim. He has to live with the fact that he was wronged and that this particular person wronged him. He must "incorporate the scars that bear [her] fingerprints into the permanent fabric of [his] life."[25] This is something that must be done if the wrong is to be resolved, but only the victim can do it. "Forgiveness is not simply a revision in judgment or a change in view or a wiping clean or a washing away or a making new….The wrong is less 'let go of' or washed away than it is digested or absorbed."[26] If some of the damage that wrongdoing creates can never be removed by the wrongdoer but instead must be accepted by the victim, then the wrongdoer can never correct, annul, or resolve her wrongful act all by herself. In order for the roles of "wrongdoer" and "victim" to be abandoned, the wrongdoer requires the victim's merciful cooperation.

This strikes me as a powerful interpretation of what forgiveness amounts to in certain cases, such as those involving traumatic and permanent physical injury. Here, significant harms touch on the victim's psyche in such intimate ways that the wrongdoer's ability to make reparation is seriously limited. Here, indeed, are permanent scars that bear the wrongdoer's fingerprints in a very painful way. However, this is precisely the sort of case where the wrongdoer is *unable* to offer proportional amends. The stronger claim (which Hieronymi may not mean to make)—that *all* cases of wrongdoing involve such permanent scars or that wrongdoers could never give their victims good reason to incorporate the fact of the wrong into the narratives of their lives—is mistaken.

There are many wrongs that, once addressed by the wrongdoer, would only fail to be forgiven by a victim who is laboring under some vice, misinformation, or mental incapacity. To insist that all wrongdoing involves a kind of harm that is irremediable by wrongdoers encourages an improper view of human life. We live in necessary proximity to and cooperation with other flawed people. To continue to insist on a reason for resentment even when the wrongdoer has performed the thoroughgoing sort of atonement under consideration here would display either a desire for complete control over the events in one's life that seems unhealthy or else a deluded sense of one's own virtue in comparison to others. This is the kernel of truth, I believe, in the idea that we should all be forgiving people since none of us is perfect. The virtuous person has a modest understanding of his own and other people's moral fallibility.[27] This does not mean that the victim should always forgive or forgive in advance of atonement. However, it does mean that the victim should be willing to accept the general, though defeasible, principle that wrongs can be remedied. Were he in the role of wrongdoer, he would hope that others would accept this principle. I agree with Hieronymi's basic point that, in order for a wrong to be resolved, the victim must add her own efforts to the process. However, it seems that we can also say that sometimes it is proper that the victim add those efforts—that not to do so would be criticizable.

In this section we have seen arguments that suggest that wrongdoers cannot correct their wrongful actions all by themselves. They need the participation of victims and perhaps even communities. Taken in the strong form—as the claim that wrongdoers are redeemed only when they achieve actual reconciliation with their victims—the moral fate of wrongdoers is unacceptably vulnerable to their victims. Redemption is important for wrongdoers after all, and victims are sometimes hard hearted, inappropriately self-righteous, or even malicious. So, while I think that these arguments give us good reason for assigning an important, even authoritative, role to victims in our theory of redemption, their prerogative comes along with responsibilities. We must have some standards for the behavior of victims.

5.6   The Victim's Duties

In thinking about the ethics of victims, a few things are fairly straightforward. First, neither victims nor their proxies can demand that wrongdoers make amends by performing actions that are inherently wrongful. Reports that victims' families and tribal authorities in parts of Pakistan and Afghanistan sometimes demand the rape of a female relative of a rapist as a form of redress provide particularly horrifying examples.[28] Second, a victim cannot justly demand a form of atonement that is disproportional to the wrong committed. I may not demand a public apology when someone negligently treads on my toe, or ten million dollars for a cup of coffee spilled in my lap. As the example of the insulted coworkers, Jennifer and Joe, suggests, people sometimes have differing points of view regarding the nature and importance of the harms, insults, and threats connected to wrongdoing. I have argued that victims' points of view on such questions deserve special status. Thus, our notion of what counts as a proportional atonement must necessarily remain somewhat loose. But, as a start, we can say that an atonement is proportional to a wrong if the victim judges it to be proportional, as long as the victim is well informed, rational, and not influenced by any salient vice (such as greed or arrogance).[29]

The main question that interests me in the ethics of victims, however, is whether a victim can rightfully refuse moral reconciliation with a wrongdoer who has made sincere and proportional amends. Part of our notion of atonement includes the idea that the wrongdoer satisfies the moral claims against him that stemmed from the wrongful act. A victim would surely be wrong to accept proportional monetary reparations for harm caused and yet refuse to relinquish at least that part of her moral claim against the wrongdoer. The wrongdoer clearly deserves to have that particular debt erased. However, moral reconciliation also involves the idea of renewed trust and normalized relations with the wrongdoer. I have suggested that victims sometimes display a vice in refusing such reacceptance. However, could a wrongdoer ever *deserve* these things? Could the wrongdoer ever deserve to be released from the victim's claim to a right to treat him as a wrongdoer?

Could he ever earn the right to protest his victim's continued suspicion, displays of resentment, criticism, refusals of cooperation, or reminders of the past?

One might think that the answer to these questions has simply been built into the theory of atonement already presented. In chapter 4, the argument for the reconciliation theory of atonement proceeds by identifying a victim's moral claims and legitimate reasons for resentment and then prescribing whatever would properly respond to those reasons. Atonement withdraws the insult and the threat that wrongdoing contained, communicates respect, redresses the harms caused, and reforms the wrongdoer. Insofar as a wrongdoer's atoning efforts fail to do these things, the atonement is not appropriate and proportional. Atonement, it seems, is simply defined as just that which will give the victim sufficient reason to forgive and morally reconcile. If a wrongdoer has really atoned, then the victim must forgive and reconcile.

However, matters are not as straightforward as this line of argument makes them appear. Many theorists argue that forgiveness is, by its very nature, a kind of gift that victims extend to wrongdoers and not the sort of thing that can be earned. We might say the same thing about moral reconciliation, which involves a renewal of trust, and trust too is frequently considered to be a kind of gift. Forgiveness and trust may be merited. Some people are clearly better candidates for receiving such treatment than others. However, according to this view, forgiveness and trust cannot be deserved. The crucial difference between merit and desert is that, if the victim refuses to forgive or reconcile with a wrongdoer who deserves such treatment, the victim thereby wrongs the wrongdoer.

First, let us consider the claim that forgiveness is by its nature a gift and so not the sort of thing that can be deserved or regulated by duty. I do not consider the intriguing objection that this view rests on an inaccurate understanding of how gifts operate in our moral world and that gifts are indeed heavily tied up in the logic of obligation.[30] The idea that forgiveness is a gift, freely given and never deserved, is frequently cited as simply part of our cultural understanding of forgiveness. Insofar as an argument is offered, it is usually that we need to see forgiveness as a gift in order to explain why a forgiving nature seems to be a virtue distinct from justice. In speaking of the just person and the forgiving person, different figures come to mind.

This argument is flawed, however. Forgiveness is an attitude that victims hold toward wrongdoers and consists in the overcoming or foreswearing of resentment and other negative attitudes caused by the wrongful act. This attitude can be held virtuously but also viciously, as when forgiveness condones wrongdoing or displays a want of self-respect.[31] *Forgivingness* is a virtue that characterizes a person who is particularly ready to forgive and frequently forgives before forgiveness is fully merited. The forgiving person hits the golden mean between the vices of moral laxity and lack of self-respect on the one hand and hard-heartedness on the other. In this way, one can recognize that there is a distinctive virtue related to forgiveness, yet make room for the idea that forgiveness is sometimes deserved. The forgiving person forgives whenever justice requires forgiveness but also when it does not.[32]

Another argument that one might offer for the idea that forgiveness is a gift rests on the observation that it always seems inappropriate for wrongdoers to *claim* a right to be forgiven. The wrongdoer who criticizes the victim for failing to forgive comes off as objectionable. However, as Norvin Richards has argued, the explanation of this phenomenon may depend on something other than the claim that forgiveness cannot be deserved:

> First, demands are by nature rather unendearing. Since the object is to return to someone's good graces, demanding to do so is often simply bad strategy. Second, there are obviously special difficulties for the other party in abandoning hard feelings "on demand."... Third... what you really want is for the forgiveness to flow effortlessly from a reserve of affection for you, once the other person understands your version of events, how devastated you are by what you have done, and so on. That is not what you would get by demanding to be forgiven.[33]

Furthermore, some cases of a wrongdoer's demanding forgiveness or at least complaining about not being forgiven do not rankle. When one family member continues to vent her resentment at another although the wrong was minor, lies far in the past, and has been addressed by the wrongdoer, our sympathies usually lie with the wrongdoer. We not only believe that the victim displays a vice but also see the wrongdoer as unjustly burdened by this vicious behavior.

However, we need not even press this issue of whether forgiveness can be deserved, I believe. If we stick by the definition of forgiveness as overcoming or foreswearing resentment and other negative attitudes and if we continue to see forgiveness as an internal state of the victim, then we might say that the victim can viciously refuse to forgive without actually wronging the wrongdoer. The wrongdoer is not wronged until the victim's lack of forgiveness is manifested in action, and this sort of wrong seems to me to be more productively described as a failure of moral reconciliation rather than a failure of forgiveness. Were the victim to fail to forgive and yet reconcile, the wrongdoer would not be negatively affected. The victim's criticizable failure to forgive would be her own private vice and not a wrong committed against the wrongdoer. So let us move on to the question of whether *moral reconcilia-tion* can be deserved by wrongdoers or whether it is a gift.

The argument for thinking that moral reconciliation must always be a gift freely given rather than something regulated by desert and duty centers on the connection between moral reconciliation and renewed trust. When the victim morally reconciles with the wrongdoer, she accepts that he is once again trustworthy, at least to a normal level in the moral matters in question. However, to judge someone to be trustworthy is to make a pre-diction about his future behavior. It is, in part, to judge how he will act in the future when faced with various options, temptations, and pressures. Such judgments about the future are almost always underdetermined by present evidence. The wrongdoer cannot normally prove definitively to a victim that he will never commit such a wrong again. Sometimes he can, of course—as when a wrongdoer has become so physically infirm that he is incapable of committing just that type of wrong again. However, evidence of inability to reoffend is not evidence of trustworthiness in the moral sense relevant here. It is not evidence that the wrongdoer has become the sort of person who sees moral matters in the right light and who now respects the victim properly and sees the error of his past ways and so is worthy of the restoration of standing and civil contact that comes with moral reconcili-ation. To judge someone as trustworthy is to make a judgment about his character and not just a predication about his behavior. However, the state of one's character, too, is the sort of thing that resists definitive proof. If wrongdoers can never give victims conclusive evidence of their moral trust-worthiness, then trust and reconciliation will always require a generous leap of faith from victims. Wrongdoers will never be able to *earn* renewed trust and moral reconciliation.

Plausible though this line of thought is, however, I argue that it is mis-taken. My argument, in its briefest form, is that if we consider moral trust to be the sort of thing that cannot be deserved and cannot be re-earned after wrongdoing, we will all be the worse off for it. A preferable moral system is one in which a certain level of moral trust is legitimately presumed and in which a withdrawal of trust is justified only if there is a credible reason to withhold it.

In defense of moral trust, we may cite Hobbesian sorts of arguments about the value of cooperation that is possible only when suspicion is kept at bay. We might also add Annette Baier's pointedly anti-Hobbesian argument regarding trust, which she characterizes as "accepted vulnerability to anoth-er's possible but not expected ill will (or lack of good will) toward one."[34] She contends the following:

Trust is much easier to maintain than it is to get started.... Unless some form of it were innate, and unless that form could pave the way for new forms, it would appear a miracle that trust ever occurs. The postponement of the onset of distrust is a lot more explicable than hypothetical Hobbesian conversions from total distrust to limited trust.[35]

In Baier's view, the benefits that are characteristic of communities and relationships that involve trust are available to us only because trust is prima facie justified. It is a status we grant to one another in the absence of a good reason to withhold it.

Among the communities that are characterized by this kind of trust is the moral community as a whole, the community in which agents regard their relations with one another as regulated by morality. Christopher Bennett writes, "the agent we recognise as a fellow member [of the moral community] is an agent we trust (at least in the absence of evidence that we ought not to trust) in various forms of social cooperation. We trust such agents, for example, in the sense that we leave our interests vulnerable to them."[36] In order to reap the benefits of life in a moral community, then, we must trust one another; and that trust cannot await positive proof of trustworthiness. It must be considered prima facie justified.

One must point out, however, that wrongdoers are precisely those people who have given us good reason to withhold trust. The question then becomes, how can trust be restored? Does it now require a positive proof of trustworthiness? Or does it require merely that the particular evidence of untrustworthiness be countered? I suggest that the idea that trust is originally prima facie justified points to the latter response. If positive proof of trustworthiness is so hard to attain and if the benefits of trust are as valuable as we have claimed, these are reasons for allowing trust to be regained in line with a less demanding standard.[37] As Baier points out, "One thing that can destroy a trust relationship fairly quickly is...a rigoristic unforgiving attitude on the part of the truster.... If a trust relationship is to continue, some tact and willingness to forgive on the part of the truster and some willingness on the part of the trusted...to be forgiven...seem essential."[38]

Harvey worries about the conception of an "indestructible ledger" that records our moral failures and forever affects our moral standing.[39] "There is the danger of being morally immobilized: venturing nothing, staying out of close relationships, and avoiding positions of responsibility, so as to risk the least possible failure."[40] Were we to count the renewal of trust as requiring a guarantee of proper behavior in the future, the benefits of trust would be lost.

Wrongdoing is simply too common. So we have reason to make the renewal of trust a more achievable goal, at least for what we might call the normal range of moral wrongs that affect most of our lives. This brings us again to the old adage that we should be forgiving (or at least willing to reconcile), given that we will need to be forgiven ourselves someday. A moral system that provides a road back from wrongdoing to trustworthiness will be generally beneficial.

One might reasonably object that to deny that trust can be re-earned is not to close the door permanently on wrongdoers. Though trust once lost cannot be re-earned, it can be granted. Redemption is possible, according to such a theory, but only through victims' supererogatory mercy, generosity, or compassion. However, although I grant that victims deserve considerable leeway in the resolution of wrongdoing, I cannot agree that the granting of moral reconciliation is always a matter of supererogation. For a victim to fail to morally reconcile in response to a thoroughgoing atonement, I believe, would be to fail to show proper respect for the wrongdoer. It would be to deny his status as a moral agent.

Harvey presents an argument of this type for a moral obligation to reconcile with atoning wrongdoers.[41] She emphasizes the connection between the concepts of moral progress and free choice:

> I believe that the idea of such a cumulative moral status [i.e., the indestructible moral ledger] is at odds with the concept of a genuinely fresh choice and the related concept of an agent's moral progress. In the relevant sense, it is not true that once a thief, always a thief. Without the possibility of fresh choices and moral progress, the commitment to a life of moral endeavour makes little conceptual sense.[42]

If we are truly to regard people as moral agents, we must regard them as capable of making free choices, for which they may justly be held morally responsible. But to regard them as capable of making free choices, Harvey suggests, is to grant that they are capable of moral improvement. It is to grant that, although they may have made poor choices in the past, it is within their power to make better ones. According to Harvey, to deny that victims could ever be obliged to reconcile in light of a wrongdoer's atoning action would be to suggest that moral progress is not really possible. "Such a commitment to a life of moral endeavour in spite of moral failures," she concludes, "is not just something each of us should undertake, but something that we should support in others."[43] Not to recognize and nurture moral progress is to deny moral agency.

This line of reasoning makes sense of the emotional reactions a wrongdoer often experiences upon having her attempts to make amends rebuffed. Imagine someone who has wronged another person, sincerely felt sorry, but then had her apology rejected, her repentance greeted with skepticism, or her offer of reparations scorned. In such a case, most of us would feel slighted and even demeaned. Why? In trying to make amends, the wrongdoer acts as a moral agent should, but the victim does not recognize her as such. Treating someone as a responsible moral agent requires treating her as an agent with responsibilities. This requires allowing her to fulfill those responsibilities. By failing to recognize or actively opposing the wrongdoer's atoning actions, the victim seems to be treating her as if she were something less than a moral agent.

These arguments regarding the ethics of victims suggest that they have both negative and positive duties to those who wrong them. They must not victimize the wrongdoers in return by abusing the prerogative they have as victims to demand and set the terms of atonement. Any demands must be reasonable, proportional, and not inherently wrongful. Additionally, I have argued that victims would wrong their wrongdoers were they not to meet appropriate offers of amends with their moral reconciliation. A failure to forgive in the same circumstances would exhibit a vice on the victim's part; it would not, however, wrong the wrongdoer so long as moral reconciliation is achieved.

To this list of moral restrictions and requirements we must add another. This one is a corollary of the duty to morally reconcile with a wrongdoer who has atoned. If I have a moral duty to reconcile with those who make sincere and proportional amends, then it would surely be unfair of me to avoid incurring an obligation to reconcile with a particular wrongdoer by preventing her from making such amends. If I have a duty to reconcile with those who make proper amends, then I have a duty not to interfere with their attempts to make amends, other things being equal.[44]

What precisely does the victim's duty not to interfere include? Surely, permanently cutting off all communication would be a significant kind of interference. While amends may take many forms, the role of communication with the victim is central to the task of redressing the insults and threats contained in wrongdoing. So, communication should be permitted unless there is a stronger reason for prohibiting it. Interaction between victims and their wrongdoers is, of course, a very tense thing that frequently involves as much miscommunication as communication. We might be tempted to add as a moral rule for victims that they should not attempt to provoke wrongdoers who try to communicate with them in an atoning fashion. However, victims often provoke shame-faced wrongdoers in an attempt to test whether their remorse is genuine. I do not want to deny that this is sometimes a legitimate strategy.

Another question about the details of victim/wrongdoer communication is whether victims owe it to their abusers to share their side of the story. I have suggested that proper repentance requires wrongdoers to try to understand what it was like for the victim to be mistreated. Does that mean that the victim must be willing to express such things to the wrongdoer? Here, again, it is hard to say anything precise. For some victims and for some wrongs, to relive the event by talking about it with the person who caused that event is surely too much to ask. However, victims who do not find the harms too traumatic or too personal to discuss should do so when asked respectfully. In such cases, they would be helping the wrongdoer with something morally important at little cost to themselves.

Regarding the aspects of atonement other than communication—reparation and personal reformation—what is asked of victims is similarly limited. Some forms of reparation (e.g., "Let me make it up to you by taking you to lunch") might require a degree of intimacy with the wrongdoer that the victim must be free to decline. Victims are permitted to turn down sincere and proportional offers of reparation in that they are not obligated to accept the particular things offered. At this point, the victim might explain why that mode of reparation is unwanted and suggest something more agreeable. However, if an adequate and respectful offer of restitution or reparation has been made and simply declined, the victim is obligated to acknowledge that the harms caused have been redressed. Personal reformation is an aspect of the wrongdoer's atonement that involves the victim less directly. The victim is not required to try to inspire the wrongdoer's moral improvement. The communicative and reparative tasks of atonement are tied to personal reformation, and so in allowing these first two tasks to be performed, the victim contributes in an appropriately modest way to the third as well.

In general, to say that victims should not interfere with wrongdoers' atonement is not to say that they must accept any form of amends that wrongdoers think to offer or let the wrongdoers choose the timing of these amends. Victims can legitimately demand a cooling off period before listening to their abusers' apologies and offers, given their own psychological needs. Furthermore, the victim's duty not to interfere with the wrongdoer's atonement is merely a prima facie duty that can be cancelled out by other considerations.

For instance, some wrongs are so traumatic that even the most minimal contact with the wrongdoer would involve additional harm to the victim. Some wrongdoers are so dangerous that the reestablishment of civility should not be risked. A grown child whose parents have continually and significantly undermined his self-respect throughout his life may justifiably cut off all relations with them, thus denying them the chance of making proper amends. However, we can accommodate this judgment without denying a general duty of victims to allow amends to be made. Wrongdoers are not morally permitted to make amends in any way that would cause additional, significant suffering or risk to the people they have harmed. Repeated patterns of wrongdoing and repentance can also annul the victim's duty to allow amends to be made insofar as victims can justifiably take these patterns to be evidence of insincerity. The mistreated lover who knows from experience that her lover can talk her into a forgiveness that he does not deserve may refuse to listen anymore. The neighbor whose behavior is explosive and unpredictable may be avoided without injustice. In general, the victim's right to self-protection trumps his duty to allow amends to be made when the two come into conflict.

Still, one might object that even the relatively modest, prima facie duty I have ascribed to victims to allow their wrongdoers to make amends to them, in addition to a duty to morally reconcile with those wrongdoers who have made amends, unfairly burdens victims. I hope to have forestalled this objection in cases involving particularly severe wrongs, threatening wrongdoers, or vulnerable victims. However, this objection can also be pressed in cases of minor wrongdoing. Consider, for instance, the following reflection from Jeffrie Murphy on the burdens of receiving amends:

> I must confess . . . that I have grown a bit tired of receiving unwelcome and time-consuming apologies from people (often former students) in various twelve-step programs—people, often totally unremembered by me, who seem to believe that they have done me some injury in the past for which they must atone. I generally let them go on with it because they are so very earnest and it seems so very important to them, but I also generally feel trapped and start to develop some resentful feelings of my own about being dragged into somebody else's agenda.[45]

As Murphy describes these cases of minor, half-forgotten, or completely forgotten wrongs, such interactions provide nothing of value for the victim. The reception of amends is presented as a tiresome act of charity that is wheedled out of the victim.

Murphy makes two different points in the preceding passage that are well worth acknowledging. First, he is right that a wrongdoer's atonement can be burdensome and annoying to the victims and that this should be avoided. We might also argue that, if a person truly does not feel insulted or threatened by a past action, then (at least as long as his lack of resentment is not itself a product of his victimization by this offender or others or of a lack of self-respect) one did not really insult or threaten him. One only risked doing so. Such risks are morally problematic, but the atonement they call for is limited to personal reformation—a change in the wrongdoer's character—rather than an atoning interaction with the intended victim. If the wrongdoer's moral improvement would be aided by performing some outward act of atonement, she can find a recipient other than the reluctant intended victim—such as a charitable organization or the sympathetic audiences that one finds in the sort of twelve-step programs to which Murphy refers. However, and here is the second point, Murphy is also right when he politely listens to these tiring apologies. After all, these people *are* so very earnest, and it *is* so very important to them.

Lots of humorists these days take aim at twelve-step programs, and the jokes are often funny. Representing self-improvement and atonement as a recipe to be followed is absurd, and the very notion of a twelve-step program invites such a charge. Some also suspect that twelve-step programs simply replace one addiction with another, a self-involved obsession with atonement. Another explanation is just the point that Murphy makes—that an atoning wrongdoer's earnestness will seem a bit silly to a victim who has truly forgotten or forgiven because it will be a disproportional response to the significance of the wrong as the victim perceives it. However, I think another, more troubling source of the humor is skepticism that atonement and redemption are possible. As I have argued here, the ideas that wrongs are always irreparable and that moral trust can never be re-earned should not be endorsed. A moral community guided by such ideas leaves everyone worse off and manifests disrespect for moral agents, their capacities, and their well-being.

5.7   The Community's Place

The moral reconciliation that constitutes the resolution of wrongdoing sometimes involves not just victims and wrongdoers but communities as well. This is because the damage that wrongdoing creates sometimes involves the relationships between both victims and wrongdoers and their communities, such as circles of friends, neighbors, and coworkers. According to standard accounts, third parties cannot forgive. However, members of communities do form negative emotions as a result of wrongdoing (notably, indignation, anger, disappointment, hatred, and contempt). Such negative emotions are regularly overcome or foresworn even though philosophers do not normally label this phenomenon "forgiveness." Moral reconciliation, specifically the reacceptance of the wrongdoer as a person in good moral standing, is surely something that communities do. So, in this section, I consider whether the community's moral reconciliation is necessary for the wrongdoer's redemption and how the community's reaction should relate to the victim's reaction.

These issues are made more complicated by the fact that there are many types of communities and their relationships to wrongs, wrongdoers, and victims are quite varied. It is often unclear whether community members have any rightful stake in disputes between wrongdoers and victims. To illustrate this complexity, I recount an episode from my own experience that I have always found a bit perplexing. I once had a friendship with a woman I will call Ann. Ann had recently experienced a traumatic breakup with a long-term partner who had been unfaithful to her. Her self-esteem was low, and in an attempt to raise it and perhaps revenge herself on her former partner, she immediately started a relationship with a new man for whom she felt no real affection. She treated this man poorly. As Ann's friend, I pointed out to her that the new boyfriend was being hurt and deserved respect and consideration. She responded in ways that I took to communicate cold-heartedness to his suffering and even glee at now playing the role of wrongdoer rather than victim in a romantic relationship. From that point on, I withdrew (gracefully, I had hoped but apparently not) from the friendship. I felt that this episode revealed that Ann was uncaring and untrustworthy, and I did not wish to continue a close relationship with her.

A mutual friend who had been privy to these events, Teresa, questioned me about my new distance from Ann. When I explained, I was surprised that Teresa replied with anger. She believed that I was mistreating Ann in two ways. First, she thought it was wrong for me to sanction Ann for wrongs she had done not to me but to someone completely unconnected to me. It simply was not my place to do so. Second, she argued that it is a friend's proper role to remain loyal even when one's friend does something morally wrong. Ann had trusted Teresa and me with the story of these events because she needed to talk about them. To penalize her for it was not worthy behavior from a friend.

On the second issue, I believe Teresa was right. Friends do commit themselves to being especially tolerant of one another's failings. One can communicate moral disapproval to a friend while remaining a friend. There are limits, of course. Some acts of wrongdoing justify breaking the bonds of friendship, but Ann's misdeed did not reach those limits. However, was Teresa's first charge also justified? Was it simply not my place as an uninvolved third party rather than a victim to sanction Ann by allowing her misdeed to affect our relationship? When, if ever, may third parties legitimately respond to wrongdoers with indignation, alienation, criticism, or sanctions?

Sometimes third parties are indirectly harmed by the wrongful acts. A racist insult aimed at one employee also harms those coworkers who share his ethnicity. The mother of an abused child, who suffers from her child's suffering, is indirectly harmed by the abuser. We can think of the coworkers and the mother as secondary victims.[46] This status gives them reason of their own to resent, to claim a right to apology and reparation, and perhaps to impose sanctions when those claims are not met. It also gives them the status to forgive in their own right.

However, other third parties are simply bystanders, as I was in the case of Ann's mistreatment of her new boyfriend. Teresa's argument seems to be that mere bystanders—parties who are neither victims, secondary victims, nor recognized authorities—have no right to sanction moral wrongdoers with their anger and indignation (what Mackie called the "retributive emotions"),[47] withdrawal of regard, or social distancing. One might try to resist Teresa's view by defending the idea that informal communities, such as neighborhoods or circles of friends, have a right to punish wrongdoers by noncoercive means such as anger and social withdrawal. One could point to good consequences that may be achieved through these forms of social punishment. Being under the moral gaze of our fellows, who will react with disapproval, indignation, and distrust when we act inappropriately, provides a powerful motivation to maintain our commitment to morality.[48] Although Ann was not sufficiently moved by her victim's expressions of hurt, she might have been moved by my disapproval. Sometimes victims need bystanders to come to their aid in their disputes with wrongdoers. There is much to be said for this line of thought.

However, we need not approach these issues with a model of punishment. While Ann may well have felt sanctioned by my withdrawal of friendship, I did not conceive of my actions in those terms. For me, the issue was one of relationship and trust. I had a relationship with Ann that left my interests vulnerable to her goodwill and moral competence. In learning about her mistreatment of another person, I had reason to doubt her character and so to be concerned about my own relationship with her. While Teresa is right that friendship should have inclined me either to weigh the entirety of evidence about Ann's character in her favor or to take a greater leap of faith for Ann, neither friendship nor the fact that I was not the victim of the wrong negates the evidential import of Ann's misdeed. Our actions affect other people's estimations of our characters and our trustworthiness. This is neither surprising nor regrettable. Third parties do not need a right to punish in order to be justified in changing their view of a wrongdoer and her moral standing.

On the other hand, there is a virtue in minding one's own business. The difficult task is to find the boundaries of this virtue. When should we keep our noses and our judgments out of other people's affairs, and when would doing so amount to abandoning our commitment to the moral community? I have no satisfactory answer to this question. However, as a starting point, we can suppose that it is usually illegitimate for us to search for moral wrongdoing on the part of others unless we stand in particular roles that require us to do so (such as a parent or an auditor) or we have some evidence that wrongdoing is going on and that the victim might need our help (such as when we suspect the neighbors are abusing their children). However, when we are faced with compelling evidence that a wrong has taken place, it is both predictable and good that we are affected by that fact.

A bit more manageable are questions concerning what might be done about community members' indignation and estrangement when we assume these are indeed legitimate, as well as what might be done about the resentment and moral claims of secondary victims. Atonement, which requires wrongdoers to repair the myriad sorts of harms they caused and reestablish their moral trustworthiness and which I have claimed can earn the moral reconciliation of the primary victims, also addresses the moral concerns of these parties. As in the case of unvirtuous victims, if community members wrongfully refuse to reconcile with properly atoning wrongdoers, then those wrongdoers should be counted as deserving moral redemption.

If a wrongdoer achieves moral reconciliation with the victim but does not, for some reason, sufficiently communicate or address the concerns of her atonement to third parties who have a legitimate interest in the case, then the wrongdoer has not fully corrected her wrongful act. She has not fully reached redemption. In this way, third parties have a kind of prerogative in the resolution of wrongdoing, similar to that of victims. They may decide what (within reasonable limits) counts as a sufficient assurance of renewed trustworthiness and refuse to extend their reconciliation until that assurance is provided.[49]

According to Govier and Verwoerd, however, we should say that the moral prerogative held by the primary victims is stronger than that granted to secondary victims or legitimately concerned bystanders.[50] Victims can make demands as to what forms of amends should be made, and those of primary victims should come before those of secondary victims in most cases.[51] Furthermore, it is generally inappropriate for those third parties who are legitimately affected by the wrongdoing fully to reconcile with offenders before the victims do because, in doing so, the third parties would show a disrespectful attitude toward the victims, their suffering, and the claims they retain against the wrongdoer. However, if victims are unreasonably reluctant to morally reconcile, third parties can legitimately proceed to do so. In cases where the victims are dead or otherwise unavailable but meaningful forms of atonement have been performed, communities can restore their trust in and esteem for the wrongdoer while at the same time recognizing that some legitimate claims against the wrongdoer have gone tragically unresolved.

5.8 Self-Forgiveness and Reconciliation with Oneself

In order for wrongdoing to be resolved, wrongdoers must repair their relationships with themselves, as well as others. They may experience a number of negative moral emotions in the aftermath of wrongdoing: guilt, shame, self-directed hatred or contempt, self-alienation. Wrongdoers sometimes feel they "won't be able to live with themselves" or "look themselves in the mirror again." The resolution of these negative emotions is sensibly labeled "self-forgiveness." Like the forgiveness of others, self-forgiveness involves either overcoming or foreswearing certain negative emotions about the wrongdoer that are occasioned by the wrongful action. Self-forgiveness resembles the forgiveness of others in additional ways as well. Quelling these negative emotions about oneself may require significant effort and time even when one has committed oneself to self-forgiveness. Also, self-forgiveness is sometimes appropriate and sometimes not, sometimes virtuous and sometimes vicious.

In addition to self-forgiveness, we should consider a self-regarding form of moral reconciliation. When a wrongdoer becomes morally reconciled to himself, he comes to see himself as a moral person in both of the relevant senses of that term. First, he accepts that he is an agent with intrinsic moral value and equal to all other persons. This means both that he abandons the claim to superior status that was implicit in his wrongful action and that he does not let his moral failings convince him that he is an inferior being. Second, he comes to see himself as a moral person in the sense that he regains confidence in his own goodwill and his ability to follow the norms of morality; once again he grants himself a normal level of esteem with regard to his moral character. He arrives at the point where he can honestly believe that he has satisfactorily answered the moral claims against him and that he will act properly when faced with similar choices or temptations for wrongful action in the future.

I have claimed that victims can morally reconcile with yet refuse to forgive their wrongdoers. A similar split is possible in one's self-regarding attitudes. A wrongdoer might continue to resent himself—to feel guilty—and to own rather than to foreswear that feeling while at the same time accepting that he has redressed the past and become a trustworthy person. A lack of self-forgiveness can be a terrible force in one's life, destroying one's relationships and possibility for happiness.[52] However, when a lack of full self-forgiveness is combined with moral reconciliation with oneself, these harms are unlikely. In fact, there are advantages to not forgiving oneself fully for serious wrongs but instead maintaining some feelings of guilt in virtue of one's past actions. The ability to tap into a reservoir of guilt and shame might well be part of what helps one to maintain one's moral character. Jeffrie Murphy quotes J. L. Austin as having once asked, "How many of you keep a list of the kinds of fool you make of yourself?"[53] I imagine most of us do carry around such lists, and we do not wish to forget at least some of the items on those lists too quickly or to cease feeling the pangs they occasion. Complete self-forgiveness is not always desirable.

The person who deserves to be described as redeemed may not fully forgive himself for a wrong. He might retain some painful feelings. Moral reconciliation with oneself, however, as long as it is deserved, seems like an indisputable good that must be achieved if we are to say that the wrongdoer has corrected the past. Thus, moral reconciliation with oneself seems to be a requirement of redemption, while self-forgiveness may be desirable to different degrees in various cases, depending on the consequences of continued guilt.

The question then is, When are a wrongdoer's moral reconciliation with himself and self-forgiveness morally appropriate? Predictably, my view is that these attitudes should be dependent on atonement. A wrongdoer who has neither faced up to his responsibilities to his victim and his community nor improved himself is not warranted in regarding himself as morally trustworthy. A wrongdoer who has not adequately addressed his wrongful action does not deserve release from his guilty feelings because the factors that justify those feelings remain in place. The insult and threat that he issued by his wrongful action are still in effect. The harms have not been repaired. His wrong continues, and so his awareness of that responsibility and the pain this awareness causes should continue as well. In section 5.5 of this chapter I argue for a moral prerogative for victims in the resolution of wrongdoing. This implies that a wrongdoer's self-regarding attitudes should generally be guided by a victim's willingness to reconcile. Before wrongdoers fully reconcile with or forgive themselves, they should generally secure the moral reconciliation of their victims (and at times their communities).[54] Exceptions are valid, however, in cases where victims are unreasonably or viciously resistant to moral reconciliation. Cases in which the victim is dead or otherwise unreachable are complicated, and the final section of the chapter addresses these. However, in some cases, atonement is impossible, and so self-forgiveness and self-reconciliation are not justified. In such cases, one ought to feel remorseful, to hold oneself in low esteem, and to doubt one's moral competence for the rest of one's life.

These ideas stand in contrast to the view popularly held in contemporary culture, as well as in psychology and philosophy, that self-forgiveness is always appropriate and desirable. For some, self-forgiveness and self-acceptance are elements of mental health.[55] Others defend these attitudes in more explicitly moral terms. Margaret Holmgren gives a particularly powerful defense of a right to self-forgiveness, while starting from a Kantian moral background and an understanding of wrongdoers' moral obligations that are very similar to my own. She concludes that self-forgiveness "is appropriate and desirable from a moral point of view whether or not the offender can fully atone for the wrong and whether or not the victim is willing or able to forgive her."[56] Given our similar background views and our starkly contrasting conclusions about self-forgiveness, I examine Holmgren's arguments in depth.

According to Holmgren, self-forgiveness is appropriate and morally desirable as long as the wrongdoer goes through a process in which she deals with the wrongful act.[57] This process, which is very similar to the atonement process I have endorsed, involves acknowledging and taking responsibility for the wrongful action, recognizing that the victim is an equally morally valuable person who should not have been treated in this way, allowing one-self to feel the negative emotions like guilt that are caused by the wrong-ful action, reforming one's character and behavior, and offering apologies, restitution, and other remedies.[58] The first of Holmgren's list of steps in the process of self-forgiveness, however, is for the wrongdoer to "recover enough self-respect to recognize that she is a valuable human being in spite of what she has done."[59] This element—this recognition of one's intrinsic moral worth, which follows from one's status as a moral agent—is to Holmgren the most important. Self-improvement may falter. Restitution and apolo-gies may be impossible. However, as long as the wrongdoer comes honestly to the recognition that she is a morally worthy being despite her wrongful action, it is both permissible and desirable that her negative emotions of guilt, self-hatred, and self-contempt subside.[60] In coming to realize that she has intrinsic moral worth, she will come to see that she deserves her own love, compassion, and acceptance, no matter what her past actions have been. Since all human beings are, in fact, intrinsically morally worthy, self-forgiveness based on such recognition is always desirable.

For Holmgren, self-forgiveness is justified by taking the right moral view of things. It requires the realization that both you (the wrongdoer) and your victim have equal and intrinsic moral worth. These values made the past action wrong, but they also make the elimination of guilt and self-hatred appropriate. Continued guilt and self-hatred, in Holmgren's view, are incompatible with the recognition of one's true value. The wrongdoer need not continue to feel guilt because "she need not renounce herself as a person."[61]

Herein lies the problem. If coming to the proper moral view of things always renders the negative emotions of self-assessment inappropriate, then how can Holmgren avoid saying that these emotions were inappropriate all along? If I commit a wrong and feel guilty about it, am I not, in her view, regarding myself as morally inferior? If so, then in feeling guilty, I am not simply holding a mistaken view of myself; I am *wronging* myself. I am treating myself as something less than a moral agent. Thus, it is morally wrong to feel guilt. Similarly, if my victim resents me, he is wronging me as well because he is failing to recognize the fact of my intrinsic worth.[62] But surely these are unacceptable claims, and if Holmgren's position on self-forgiveness implies them, we have reason to reject her position.

In Holmgren's defense, we should note that she does not herself label the feeling of guilt as wrongful. In fact, she actually includes emotions like guilt as a step in the self-forgiveness process: "A wrongdoer must allow herself to experience the feelings that arise for her in connection with an offence."[63] As examples of such emotions she lists grief, guilt, remorse, and revulsion. Experiencing such emotions is important because "[the wrongdoer's] feelings serve to connect her with the reality of what she has done, the value of the victim, and the importance of her moral obligations."[64] Holmgren also grants that such negative emotions can motivate a wrongdoer to perform the other tasks that are called for in the aftermath of wrongdoing, such as apology and restitution. However, as I read Holmgren, these passages are not so much endorsements of the emotions of guilt and self-hatred as they are decisions to tolerate them as natural and somewhat useful mistakes that wrongdoers make. She neither demands that wrongdoers feel guilt nor criticizes those who feel none. Instead, she merely says that "a wrongdoer must allow herself to experience the feelings that arise for her." Holmgren seems to believe that these emotions will occur and that it is better to let oneself experience them than to deny or repress them. Yet, guilt and self-hatred are still a kind of mistake, which is evident in the claim that they will permissibly subside once one takes the proper Kantian view of one's unalterable moral status. I suspect that Holmgren does not label the feeling of guilt as wrongful because she sees it as falling under the category of excuse.

I believe that this view of the negative emotions of self-assessment as excusable moral mistakes is itself a mistake. The problem stems from two related sources. First, Holmgren does not distinguish between moral status and moral standing.[65] Second, Holmgren fails to recognize some relevant distinctions among the various self-directed emotions. I address these points in turn.

I have been using the terms 'moral status' and 'moral standing' to match up with the two meanings of 'being a moral person.' One has moral status as long as one is a moral agent, a being who can have a sense of right and wrong and can guide one's actions in accordance with such judgments. To have moral status is to deserve what Stephen Darwall calls "recognition respect."[66] One must treat oneself and others as having intrinsic moral worth, which means, among other things, that one cannot be treated as a mere means to others' ends. Moral status is not altered by wrongful actions because the wrongdoer retains the capacities that are definitive of moral agency. However, moral standing is a different matter. It relates to whether a moral agent does *in fact* live up to her moral capacities. Wrongful action appropriately affects the agent's reputation in a moral community. She does not merit the same level of trust and esteem as someone who has acted well. Darwall uses the term 'appraisal respect' to refer to the reaction we have to this variable kind of standing.[67]

Holmgren is right that wrongdoers retain their moral status. She is also right to say that all wrongdoers should recognize and respect that they have such moral status no matter what they have done. However, she does not sufficiently address their moral standing, which *is* affected by the misdeed. When someone commits a wrongful act, we have reason to see her (and she has reason to see herself) as less trustworthy in moral matters. Wrongdoing is evidence of a failure of either goodwill or competence (which we might think of as a developed capacity) in the moral matter at hand. Our level of appraisal respect for the wrongdoer is appropriately lowered. Insofar as the wrongdoer is sensitive to her failings, she will make a similar judgment of her own standing. This judgment of compromised standing should underlie the wrongdoer's emotions of guilt and shame and should be addressed if the wrongdoer is justly to overcome or foreswear these emotions and forgive herself.

Let me emphasize that to judge that a wrongdoer's deserved moral standing has been lowered by a wrongful action is not to deny that she has moral status. In fact, if the actor does not have moral status—if she does not have the capacity for moral sense and responsible action—it would be inappropriate and probably impossible for her to feel guilt over the action. Thus, the feeling of guilt does not deny one's moral status; it presupposes it.[68]

After having done something morally wrong, one may feel not just guilt but also shame, self-hatred, or self-contempt. Holmgren is right to worry that some of these self-directed emotions include negative judgments about one's moral status and that these are incompatible with a proper view of human value. However, Holmgren's mistake is to assume that all of the emotions of negative self-assessment are of this type. Some of these emotions—and I put moral guilt and at least some forms of shame in this category—include or imply judgments that one's moral *standing* is relatively low. Such judgments and emotions are justified in cases of wrongdoing. On the other hand, self-hatred and self-contempt deserve Holmgren's criticism. They seem to mark out the self as either a legitimate target for destruction (in the case of self-hatred) or a withdrawal of recognition respect (in the case of contempt). They represent the self not just as having made bad choices or developed a bad character but as falling into a moral class altogether different from that of other people. Such emotions are impermissible (if frequently excusable or even pitiable).

Certainly, theorists disagree over these interpretations of the emotions of self-hatred and self-contempt. Some are inclined to put shame in the category of moral emotions that inappropriately judge moral status and not just standing. I am not interested in pursuing those debates further here in large part because I believe they quickly turn semantic. Human beings are capable of a huge variety of emotions based on judgments of complex and often vague or confused content. We should not expect this range of phenomena to divide neatly into the linguistic categories at hand. However, I suggest that when one looks at the literature in which philosophers try to defend hatred, self-hatred, contempt, and self-contempt as permissible attitudes, one finds that the debate usually turns on the distinction between status and standing (recognition respect and appraisal respect).[69]

If I am right about these issues, then guilt and shame are frequently perfectly appropriate reactions to wrongdoing. They are not simply natural but also misguided reactions to our misdeeds and character flaws. They incorporate negative judgments of our moral standing that are called for by an honest acknowledgment of the fact that we have done wrong, that we are responsible for our misdeed, and that we have not yet righted that wrong. The painful nature of such emotions shows that we do not simply judge ourselves negatively but also care about those negative judgments. We care about the fact that we have wronged another person, fallen short of our principles, or adopted the wrong principles and so earned our fellows' mistrust. In order legitimately to let go of our negative self-regarding attitudes, we need to earn a positive reevaluation of our moral standing. We need to fulfill our obligations to those we have harmed, reform our behaviors and characters, and communicate our respect and renewed commitment to morality to our fellows. In order to merit self-forgiveness and our own reconciliation, we must properly atone.

5.9   The Victim's Prerogative to Guide Self-Forgiveness

I have suggested that the wrongdoer's self-forgiveness and moral reconciliation with herself should be guided, all things considered, by the reactions of victims and sometimes communities as well. As I have argued in this chapter, these parties play a role in determining when atonement is adequate and credible and thereby help determine when wrongdoers may revise their self-regarding attitudes. Holmgren, on the other hand, rejects any such victim prerogative to set the terms of self-forgiveness. According to Holmgren, although it is right to respect a victim's decision to forgive or refuse forgiveness: "The responsible offender will not wait to forgive herself until her victim forgives her, nor will she refuse to forgive herself on the ground that it is her victim's exclusive right to do the forgiving. Instead, she will respectfully separate herself from her victim's attitudes and work on her own."[70] Holmgren makes three arguments in support of this rejection of a victim's right to guide self-forgiveness.

First, recall that, on Holmgren's account, forgiveness is always a matter of coming to the proper moral view of things. More specifically, it is a matter of recognizing that the wrongdoer (whether oneself or another) retains her moral status despite the wrongful act. The wrongdoer can and should reach this judgment independently of whether the victim or the community draws the same conclusion. The victim has no prerogative here because the moral facts are independent of his opinions of them. I reject this argument because I reject the theories of forgiveness and self-forgiveness that underlie it, and I do so for the reasons already given. Forgiveness and self-forgiveness are not properly secured simply by accepting the wrongdoer's *status* as a moral agent. Instead, forgiveness, self-forgiveness, and reconciliation should correspond to the wrongdoer's restored moral *standing*—to her efforts to atone and the evidence this provides of her renewed trustworthiness. As I have also argued, the victim deserves a limited authority in deciding when the wrongdoer has shown herself to be trustworthy. To leave such judgments solely to the wrongdoer would fail to respect the fact that the wrong was a wrong against a particular victim, who deserves to be treated with respect. It would also risk self-deception since wrongdoers are predictably flawed judges of their own characters, merits, and trustworthiness in the moral issues at hand. Limited and reasonable input from victims and communities is desirable. Thus, whereas Holmgren is right that wrongdoers need not appeal to others to validate their moral status, when the question is one of moral standing, it makes sense to include victims' and communities' points of view.[71] Moral standing is relational in ways moral status is not.

Holmgren's second argument against a victim's prerogative to guide self-forgiveness charges that such a prerogative would leave victims vulnerable to new abuses. If wrongdoers need victims' forgiveness in order to forgive themselves, then this makes it likely that wrongdoers will approach victims not out of proper respect and an honest attempt to right the wrong but out of need and even desperation:

> If [the wrongdoer] performs acts of penance and expresses her regret strictly for the victim's sake, to promote his welfare or to help him know that he is valuable, she behaves in a respectful manner. But if she presses her apology and performs acts of penance to get her victim to forgive her, her behavior is self-centered, manipulative, and inherently disrespectful of her victim.[72]

In order to illustrate her point, Holmgren takes up the case presented in Simon Wiesenthal's *The Sunflower*.

In *The Sunflower*, Wiesenthal reports an encounter he had with a repentant and mortally wounded member of the SS while Wiesenthal was assigned to a work detail in a hospital. Wiesenthal was at that time an inmate of a concentration camp. The dying soldier had asked a nurse to bring him a Jew, any Jew. He proceeded to confess to Wiesenthal his participation in a horrifying massacre of a group of Jewish villagers, explain his background and motivations, express great remorse, and ask Wiesenthal for his forgiveness. Wiesenthal listened to the entire confession in silence while performing a few small acts of kindness toward the soldier such as giving him water. However, when asked for his forgiveness, Wiesenthal left without a word.

The main question of Wiesenthal's memoir and the responses that follow from a variety of philosophers, theologians, and other thinkers is whether Wiesenthal's reaction to the soldier was correct. Holmgren, however, approaches the text by asking whether the repentant Nazi acted correctly. She concludes that he did not and traces a large part of his fault to his assumption that he needed a victim's forgiveness in order to forgive himself. That assumption leads him to mistreat Wiesenthal. First of all, the soldier

> presses Wiesenthal to forgive him for selfish reasons...he fails to respect Wiesenthal's need to come to grips with his own feelings in his own time. Second, the soldier imposes an unfair burden on Wiesenthal, who is already severely burdened at the time. It is not Wiesenthal's responsibility to assuage the soldier's guilt or to establish for him that he is worthy of love and acceptance.[73]

While I agree with Holmgren's assessment of the soldier's behavior, I cannot agree with the conclusion she draws from it. She argues that it would have been better if the soldier had forgiven himself first. "He could have told Wiesenthal, without need or desperation, that he hoped he would find it in his heart to forgive him someday, and then he could have died in peace."[74] In general, it is Holmgren's position that "it is...morally preferable for an offender to forgive herself before she seeks either her victim's forgiveness or full reconciliation with her victim."[75]

In the context of the *Sunflower* case, I find this a rather shocking suggestion. This wrongdoer is guilty of such a horrendous deed that full atonement is impossible. Furthermore, the soldier's absorption with his own bodily and moral suffering, the apparent abruptness of his change of heart, and the evidence that he continues to lack proper respect for both his direct victims and for Wiesenthal are reasons to doubt that he has morally improved himself in the necessary ways for self-forgiveness to be justifiable.[76] The soldier has not met—and could not meet—the criteria for the process of self-forgiveness that Holmgren herself lays out.[77] Holmgren has chosen an example that is not likely to bolster her argument.

However, beyond the particular details of this SS soldier's lack of desert of self-forgiveness, I find something troubling in the recommendation that wrongdoers should forgive themselves before approaching their victims with apologies and restitution. Holmgren is right that it is selfish, disrespectful, and manipulative for a wrongdoer to seek forgiveness simply in order to free herself from her own negative moral feelings. However, I find it arrogant, disrespectful, and manipulative in a different way for a wrongdoer to approach her victim and to say, "I have forgiven myself, I am at peace, and I hope you will forgive me someday, too." If we were to agree with Holmgren that self-forgiveness turns on a judgment of moral status, such a statement might be rather rude to say aloud but not mistaken in any deeper sense. However, I have argued that the issue is one of moral standing and trustworthiness. In this case, reporting to one's victim that one has already forgiven and reconciled with oneself is much worse than rude. It says to the victim, "I'm okay now, deserving of the trust and esteem of my fellows in the moral community. I ask your opinion on this matter as a courtesy and to evince my good moral character to you and others but not because anything you might have to say could legitimately influence my opinion on the matter. I hope someday you are as enlightened with respect to my moral standing as I am."

To commit a wrongful act against another person is not just to have an incorrect view about the moral status of human beings.[78] It is not simply a mistake in judgment that can be corrected by getting one's moral views in order. Nor is wrongdoing simply evidence of a bad character that can be repaired through personal reformation. To wrong another person is to insult, threaten, and harm *that particular person*. Such wrongs are events that take place in relationships among persons. This means, among other things, that what a wrong meant, what it did, what effect it will have on the future, and how it may be put to rest are all going to be influenced by the points of view of both the wrongdoer and the victim (and usually others as well). To claim a right to self-forgiveness in the absence of a serious moral interaction with one's victim is to ignore the significance of the fact that he was the victim. This wrongs the victim a second time.

Holmgren provides a third and final argument against a victim's prerogative to guide self-forgiveness. Having suggested that the need for a victim's forgiveness could place an unfair burden on the victim, she also acknowledges that some victims want wrongdoers to come begging for forgiveness. This sort of supplication helps the victims regain their sense of self-respect. But Holmgren suspects that a problematic moral view lies behind a victim's interest in gaining such attention and being granted such authority: "By catering to [the victim] in this way, [the wrongdoer] also enables [the victim] to remain stuck in a set of attitudes that are unproductive for him. He will be much happier and more empowered if he stops seeking external approval and recognizes for himself that he is a valuable human being who deserves to be treated well."[79] Again, I believe this reading of the victim's interest in a prerogative to forgive places undue emphasis on status rather than standing. The victim may be assured of his intrinsic moral worth yet still care that he is shown respect in his community. As we learn from Hegel, having intrinsic value is one thing, but having that value realized in the social world is something else. Holmgren's position undervalues the fact that both our self-evaluations and the respect we receive from others are influenced by how we are treated. Nor is this fact something to be lamented. As Hieronymi puts it:

> being threatened by another's disregard does not betray a failing or weakness. . . . contrary to the advice we give schoolchildren, we ought to care about what other people think. To not care about what you think is not to care about you. To disregard your evaluation is to disregard you. Respect for you as a fellow human being commits me to caring about your evaluation.[80]

Victims are right to resent being treated poorly, and they are right to value the respect and authority they are granted when wrongdoers work to gain their forgiveness and moral reconciliation.

Holmgren is surely correct that victims sometimes value having a prerogative to forgive for the wrong reasons and that wrongdoers sometimes pursue forgiveness in self-centered ways. However, we may criticize such persons without denying the special value of victims' forgiveness or the general idea that their forgiveness and readiness to reconcile should guide self-forgiveness and self-reconciliation.

Let me summarize my view of moral reconciliation with oneself. I believe that this reacceptance of oneself as a moral person in good standing is justified when the wrongdoer has made a full and proper atonement and when the victim and any other relevant parties have received that atonement with an attitude of moral reconciliation. The victim has the role of ratifying the wrongdoer's atonement and determining whether her standing as a trustworthy member of the moral community (with regard to the moral issues in question) is to be restored. The victim deserves this role because of his epistemic and other forms of authority. However, if he abuses his authority by reacting viciously or if he is improperly informed about the wrongdoer's atonement (through no fault of the wrongdoer), then the wrongdoer may proceed to reconcile with herself. The conciliatory or nonconciliatory reactions of community members should also guide the wrongdoer's self-regarding attitudes in some cases in virtue of the fact that they are either indirect victims or have epistemic authority in judging the wrongdoer's trustworthiness. However, if these community members react in ways that are vicious or improperly informed (through no fault of the wrongdoer), then the wrongdoer is justified in reaccepting herself as morally trustworthy. Important though the reactions of victims and communities are, however, they do not suffice to justify reconciliation with oneself. If victims and communities extend their moral reconciliation before the wrongdoer sincerely and reasonably judges herself to deserve it, then self-reconciliation must wait.

The conditions for appropriate self-forgiveness are similar to those for appropriate reconciliation with oneself. Self-forgiveness should respond to one's atonement and the reasonable reactions of one's victim and one's community. The only difference is that, in some cases, a continued refusal or inability fully to forgive oneself will serve the end of the agent's renewed commitment to morality without unduly burdening her own life. Where this is true, a degree of continuing guilt or shame is proper. However, these emotions should not attack one's moral status and should be tempered as a result of one's atonement.

Other writers argue that emotions such as self-love, self-directed compassion, and humility play a role in restoring one's regard for oneself in the aftermath of wrongdoing, and I agree.[81] While there is a danger of forgiving oneself too quickly from either self-love or moral laxity, proper self-forgiveness and self-reconciliation require humility and measured compassion. For instance, in her discussion of the vice of being unforgiving toward oneself, Robin Dillon links proper self-forgiveness to having an appropriate view of one's fallibility.[82] One must take responsibility for one's failings but not demand perfection from oneself or set the bar for renewed self-trust too high. To do so would fail "to respect our human reality."[83] In this way, too, self-forgiveness and moral reconciliation with oneself have much in common with their other-directed counterparts.

5.10   *Partial Redemption*

I have allowed wrongdoers to consider themselves redeemed—to consider their past failings as no longer affecting their deserved moral standing—in cases where victims and communities react improperly so long as other conditions are met.[84] However, in other cases we might be also tempted to let wrongdoers off the moral hook even though they have failed to achieve actual moral reconciliation with their victims or their communities. Where victims have either died or cannot be found by wrongdoers, amends cannot be made to them. Yet the wrongdoers in these cases may have engaged in significant self-reformation and other meaningful forms of atonement. In still other cases, wrongdoers owe a material restitution they can never pay due to poverty or other forms of blameless incapacity, although they complete the other tasks of atonement. Sometimes reformed and well-meaning wrongdoers are not morally permitted to approach their victims because the victims, due to a particularly sensitive constitution that involves no vice on their part, would be too traumatized by further contact. Or it could be that the wrong was so severe or so horrifying that the very idea of reparation makes no sense, and no fitting apology could be expressed, yet the wrongdoer has undergone such a dramatic internal transformation that we are tempted to say that she is a new person.

Holmgren appears to take the position that self-forgiveness (and presumably redemption) should be granted in all of these cases because "as Kant pointed out, 'ought' implies 'can.' An offender is not obligated to do what she cannot do. Once she has done her best to atone for the wrong, she has fulfilled her moral obligations to her victim."[85] If wrongdoers ought to atone, then whenever they have done their best they should count as having atoned and therefore as deserving redemption.

However, in the correction of wrongdoing, the principle that 'ought' implies 'can' does not seem to apply. Wrongdoing sometimes admits of only a disappointing and inadequate resolution. One's relationships can be damaged beyond repair. Not all instances of wrongful harming admit of correction. These are simply facts of our moral world with which we must live. Wrongdoers must do their best to correct wrongdoing, and, by definition, they cannot do more than this, but doing their best does not guarantee redemption. It is not always enough to restore their moral standing—to reestablish them as trustworthy and deserving of normal levels of esteem in the moral community.

I believe the only sensible way to respond to cases like these is to take them one by one in full detail. The theories of atonement and redemption defended here present ideals that frequently can be only approximated in real life. Luckily, redemption, the restoration of moral standing, moral reconciliation, forgiveness, and self-forgiveness come in degrees. Although some wrongs cannot be fully repaired, wrongdoers and their relationships can be made better. These improvements are morally, personally, and socially valuable. At the same time, a sense of partial redemption can coexist with a degree of lingering guilt and regret and a continuing sense of indebtedness. This view may be troubling to those who view self-forgiveness as a requirement of mental health. However, I am more inclined to agree with Murphy, who argues that most of us can and should retain some degree of guilt for our past actions. "These burdens may properly humble us without crippling us," he writes. "It is, after all, possible to have a somewhat tragic view of human life, including one's own, without being destroyed or defeated by that view."[86] In fact, I suspect that most of us are rather too adept at living with our guilt and self-recriminations, which is why so many wrongs go uncorrected.

CHAPTER SIX | # Making Amends for Crime
Restorative Justice and the Liberal State

6.1 Introduction

In this chapter our focus shifts formally from cases of private wrongdoing to cases of legal wrongdoing. The issues that dominate philosophical discussions of crime have already drawn our attention repeatedly. Debates regarding the state's response to crime form the main arena in which secular philosophers have addressed the more general question of how to correct wrongdoing. Some theorists insist that criminal wrongdoing deserves retributive punishment. Others believe that it calls for the deterrence, rehabilitation, or moral reformation of the offender and that the criminal justice system should organize itself to promote such outcomes. A few others argue that the state should focus its efforts on compensation for the victim. In the preceding examination of interpersonal atonement I have argued that each of these conceptions of the resolution of wrongdoing—retribution, personal reformation, and restitution—is inadequate inasmuch as wrongdoing requires a more thoroughgoing making of amends. It requires moral reconciliation, with the subgoals of moral improvement, respectful communication, and reparation. If reconciliation is the ideal resolution of a case of moral wrongdoing, it seems likely also to be the ideal outcome of a response to criminal wrongdoing. Should we then conclude that the criminal justice system ought to promote moral reconciliation?

A number of people in law, criminology, and social justice circles seem to be drawing this conclusion. Under the heading of "restorative justice," they advocate a radical reenvisioning of the purposes and practices of the criminal justice system so that it will come to promote the reconciliation of offenders, victims, and local communities. Reconciliation, when conceived merely as a normalization of relations among the parties to a conflict, could be achieved in a number of ways. The parties might genuinely forget about the crime. The victim may simply forgive her abuser without having received any form of corrective response from him. Reconciliation might even be brought about by the forceful imposition of a punishment on the wrongdoer. From this perspective, many different theories of criminal justice could claim to have an interest in reconciliation. However, the restorative justice movement is distinctive in that it considers the atoning efforts of criminal wrongdoers to be a crucial ingredient. Here we see a fundamental distinction between restorative justice and other approaches to crime.

Paradigmatic restorative justice practices allow criminal offenders a remarkably active role. In some cases, offenders actually help determine what their sentences will be. They suggest ways they might make reparation, react to the suggestions of others, and agree (or refuse to agree) to a particular resolution. They are allowed and encouraged to right their wrongs through direct communication with their victims, the payment of reparations, and efforts at personal improvement. The offender's capacity for positive, constructive action is recognized, and she is treated as an agent and not a thing, as a subject and not an object. In this way, restorative justice systems promote the moral ideal of atonement that I have advocated here.[1]

However, this very connection will suggest to some that restorative justice is misguided as a theory of criminal justice. How could the state possibly contribute to the distinctively moral project of atonement since atonement requires the wrongdoer's sincere repentance and voluntary efforts? By definition, sincere and voluntary responses cannot be compelled by the state. Attempts by the state to use the criminal justice system to persuade offenders to make amends threaten to undermine any credibility that a sincerely repentant offender might otherwise have. Thus, atonement appears to be a moral ideal that the state simply *cannot* pursue. Furthermore, one might argue that the state *should not* pursue this moral ideal. Is it proper for the state to concentrate its efforts on encouraging offenders to fulfill their moral obligations? Shouldn't the liberal state stay out of the business of morality and remain neutral among competing conceptions of the good? Doesn't the blurring of the line between legal and moral realms actually undermine respect for agency, the very value that I have invoked in defense of restorative justice?

In this chapter I explore the tense relations among the moral ideal of atonement, respect for the agency of the offender, and the role of the liberal state. First I introduce the central values and practices that tend to be presented under the banner of restorative justice. I highlight how they cohere with the moral theory of atonement that I have advocated in earlier chapters. Then I further develop the two lines of critique already mentioned: that the making of amends is neither a possible nor an appropriate goal for the liberal state. In the latter category I examine two main objections: first, that restorative justice violates the principle of liberal neutrality, and second, that restorative justice improperly limits the state's interest in crime. While many of the worries raised against restorative justice can be answered satisfactorily, in the end I am able to lend only tentative support to the restorative justice project.

6.2 Restorative Justice: Values and Practices

Restorative justice is sometimes characterized as a social movement rather than a theory.[2] Its advocates are united by what they oppose as much as by what they favor. The target of this opposition is the reigning criminal justice system, in which offenders are tried and convicted by juries or judges and sentenced to jail or prison (or more commonly, where similar sentences are determined through plea bargaining between the prosecution and the defense attorneys). This system, it is charged, rarely makes anyone better off. Victims frequently find the process alienating and sometimes even describe it as a further victimization, given practices such as the adversarial cross-examination of witnesses and the conceptualization of offenses as crimes against the state as opposed to individual human beings.[3] Offenders are usually not helped in any way by being sent to prison. Prisons have become such overcrowded and dangerous places that confinement arguably amounts to a cruel punishment. Offenders are further alienated from the community.[4] Contra the "moral education" defenses of punishment, what most criminals seem to learn in prison is that conflict is the norm and violence is its proper response.[5] Some argue that the humiliation of punishment typically turns into a rage that inspires further wrongdoing.[6] Prisons that release these people back onto the streets do not make communities safer.

While the critique made by restorative justice scholars is that standard, punitive sentencing practices help none of the parties who are affected by the original crime, the positive view is that a just response to crime will help *all* of these parties. The core idea of restorative justice is that our response to criminal wrongdoing should aim at the healing, reintegration, or reconciliation of the victim, the community, and the criminal himself.[7] "Among the losses victims, offenders or communities might want restored are property loss, injury, a sense of security, dignity, a sense of empowerment, voice, harmony based on a feeling that justice has been done, and social support."[8]

In addition to these results, restorative justice is committed to certain procedural norms. Tony Marshall characterizes restorative justice as "a process whereby all the parties with a stake in a particular offence come together to resolve collectively how to deal with the aftermath of the offence and its implications for the future."[9] Sentencing procedures ideally involve input from each of the relevant parties—victims, offenders, and local communities. Participation by these parties is key to the very idea of restoration. In order to explain this, let us consider a paradigm restorative sentencing practice known as a sentencing conference.[10]

During a sentencing conference, offenders are placed in direct contact with those they have harmed. They are asked to talk with their victims and community representatives. Both victims and offenders are encouraged to bring members of their support networks (e.g., family members, friends, pastors, teachers), and these people are allowed and encouraged to take part in the conversation. Offenders are expected to explain why they acted as they did and to listen to what the other parties have to say to them. Offenders are not required to apologize or express remorse, but they frequently do.[11] The discussions in sentencing conferences explore the various effects of crime—not just the cost of damaged property, say, but also the fear, anger, and sense of vulnerability that victims and community members experience. These conferences explore both the causes and the effects of crime (e.g., addiction, poverty, frustration, broken support networks). The task of the meeting is to come to a reparation agreement. The terms are set out in a contract that is signed by the parties and approved by a judge. If the offender fails to live up to the terms of the contract, she is sent to a more traditional court, where she will be sentenced by a judge.

Reparation agreements frequently require material restitution, community service, or service directly to victims. Drug rehabilitation and job training are also likely to appear in reparation agreements because the parties are encouraged to take a comprehensive view of crime. The wide-ranging conversation brings their attention not just to material and physical harms but also to psychological and relational damage. The discussion highlights the injuries that result from crime and those that lead to it. As a result, the interests in compensation for the victim and personal reformation for the offender become intertwined to such a degree that they are not always distinguished. In this way, sentencing conferences enable and encourage communication, reparation, and personal reformation, the three components of a proper offer of amends.

Advocates of practices such as the sentencing conference argue that they offer benefits to victims, offenders, and communities. The most obvious one that restorative justice practices offer to victims is restitution. However, advocates often put more stress on the immaterial benefits that may be gained. The syndrome of victimization involves a diminished sense of order and autonomy, feelings of alienation from other people, and uncertainty about whom one can trust.[12] Sentencing conferences aim to help with all of these problems. Victims generally feel empowered by playing a significant role in determining what the offender will do to repair the wrong. Having had an opportunity to confront the offender and express themselves in a context in which they are set up as figures of consequence and dignity, victims feel that they have regained some control over the situation. The presence of a supportive community, here in the persons of family, friends, and neighbors, helps rebuild one's ability to connect with and trust other people. John Braithwaite claims that victims who participate in conferences of this sort are easier on offenders, more likely to express forgiveness than victims whose cases are handled by the standard court system, and more inclined to be satisfied with restitution and offender rehabilitation as opposed to punitive measures.[13] "Victims are punitive interlocutors in traditional Western justice systems because they are denied a voice in the outcomes. When they are given a voice in a conference, they tend to go in angry and come out more forgiving," argues Braithwaite.[14]

Offenders are also more likely to benefit from participation in sentencing conferences as opposed to standard sentencing procedures. Most obviously, they are spared the pain of the punitive treatment that they would otherwise face. They are also more likely to be given an opportunity for rehabilitation. Their chances of actual rehabilitation are expected to be higher since offenders who have met with their victims are better able to understand the consequences of their actions. Rehabilitation (whether from criminality, substance abuse, or any other destructive pattern of behavior) is more likely to succeed if it is pursued voluntarily.[15] Furthermore, many supporters of restorative justice believe that alienation and feelings of worthlessness are important factors that contribute to crime.[16] By being given an opportunity help determine their own mode of reparation for their crime, offenders are treated as responsible and morally competent agents who are capable of making reasonable moral judgments and abiding by them in the future. The presence of family and friends—gathering around and focusing on helping the offenders—rebuilds the community ties they need to restore their self-esteem and avoid crime in the future.

A recurrent theme in the literature on restorative justice is that crime should be understood as a breakdown of community.[17] This involves the claim both that crime tears community ties and also that a failure of community is one cause of crime. Sentencing conferences aim to strengthen communities. As Braithwaite puts it,

> The genius of the conference is...that it is a meeting of two communities of care, rather than a meeting of two individuals, as in traditional Western mediation. While the criminal trial assembles in a room those who can do the maximum damage to the other side, the conference assembles those who can offer maximum support to their own side, be it the victim or offender side.[18]

The involvement of the family members, friends, and community representatives sends the message that both crime and healing are communal issues. The relevant communities not only voice their opinions about what the sentence should be but are often put to work to ensure that the sentence succeeds in its restorative goals as well. Families may be asked to commit to counseling, and teachers agree to keep in closer touch with the parents of troubled juveniles. In drunk-driving cases, friends may be asked to hold the offender's car keys on weekend nights or to serve as designated drivers. In cases of spouse abuse, members of the extended family sometimes volunteer to move into a troubled household to help disrupt the patterns of mistreatment.[19] It is believed that when such relationships are strengthened, communities receive both the direct and the indirect benefits connected to lower recidivism rates.

One question we must ask about sentencing conferences and similar programs is whether they work. Do they really reduce crime, increase the chance of successful rehabilitation, and serve the victims' psychological needs? Social scientists are busy studying these issues, and early reports look promising, though there are significant worries about sampling. As things stand, sentencing conferences are an optional sentencing procedure used in just those cases in which they are most likely to succeed. For example, such methods are primarily practiced in juvenile justice systems, where offenders may be more impressionable. Restorative practices are also found in tribal justice systems in New Zealand and North America,[20] but these may be among the few communities left in the contemporary world where communal ties are strong enough to do the work asked of them.[21] The crimes redressed in sentencing conferences are almost exclusively the less severe sorts (property crimes or assaults rather than rape or murder), which are more amenable to reparation. Restorative sentencing practices are also commonly used in plea bargains. District attorneys are most apt to offer this option when they believe offenders will participate successfully.[22] Victim participation is also voluntary, and the victims most likely to volunteer may be those who are most disposed to benefit from such an experience.[23] These worries about the empirical evidence are important and deserving of careful scrutiny, but our focus here is on the justice of such practices. Does restorative justice present a defensible and compelling conception of criminal justice?

The affinities between restorative sentencing practices and the moral ideal of making amends are clear. Restorative justice practices enable and encourage criminal wrongdoers to atone. Their atoning responses ideally take the form of respectful communication with victims and affected communities, the reparation of material and nonmaterial harms, and personal reformation. The atoning criminal aims to restore or develop morally appropriate relationships with her victim, her community, and herself. It is worth emphasizing how distinctive this interest in the wrongdoer's atonement is. Standard, punitive criminal justice systems not only fail to encourage the making of amends but also actively prevent it.[24] Communication between wrongdoers and victims is discouraged or prohibited. Incarceration severely inhibits most offenders' ability to pay restitution. Personal reformation is also hard to achieve in prison, where violent conflict is pervasive.[25] Elsewhere I have argued that, if treating someone as a moral agent requires treating that person as an agent who has moral obligations, then criminal justice systems that prevent offenders from making amends might be guilty of injustice.[26]

Restorative justice systems, in providing offenders an opportunity to make amends and especially in giving them an active role in helping to determine what form those amends should take, seem to show respect for offenders' moral agency. They are treated as people who are capable of both understanding and being motivated by their moral obligations to others. However, in the remainder of the chapter I consider the charge that restorative justice's seeming respect for offenders' moral agency is illusory and that the liberal state neither can nor should pursue the making of amends by offenders.[27]

6.3 Objections to the Possibility of State-Enforced Atonement

Let us begin with the objection that the ideal of atonement as reconciliation is an impossible or self-defeating goal for the state to pursue. As our moral theory has claimed, atonement can be made only through the voluntary efforts of the offender. An offer of amends must include sincere communication and an improvement in the offender's character and behavior.

Reparations must not only be offered but also be offered for the right reasons. Anything short of this simply does not count as a genuine offer of amends.[28] I have also argued that victims' input on the adequacy of atoning responses and their willingness to reconcile with wrongdoers are crucial to the success of atonement. Thus, their voluntary participation is also required. How could the state plausibly claim to be pursuing the goal of reconciliation if the making of amends is so clearly out of the state's sphere of control?

In response, the defender of restorative justice can point out that *pursuing* a goal is not the same thing as *guaranteeing* that it will be met. Even though the state cannot guarantee that offenders will be repentant and victims willing to reconcile, it can try to create conditions in which this is more likely to happen. Restorative justice practices are designed to do just that.

The objector might retort that the state's attempt to encourage the making of amends will backfire and inhibit reconciliation instead. In most actual systems of restorative justice, restorative sentencing practices are made available as alternatives to punitive sentencing practices. If offenders do not participate in these restorative programs or if they fail to negotiate a resolution with their victims, they risk serving jail time. Given this highly undesirable option, one might charge that offenders are coerced into offering restitution, which disqualifies any such offer as an act of atonement.[29] Even if an offender's experience in a sentencing conference inspires sincere remorse and a desire to right the wrong, one might argue that he is coerced nonetheless. Furthermore, the possibility of punishment if restorative justice procedures do not come to a resolution gives offenders good reason to fake a sincerity they do not feel and victims good reason to be suspicious of any expressions of remorse. In these ways, the use of the criminal justice system to pursue amends might be self-defeating.

In any criminal justice system backed by the punitive power of the state lies an element of coercion. However, voluntariness comes in degrees. If restorative justice programs allow the offender at least a significant degree of latitude in his response and if the victim and the community members are able to tell when the offender is being sincere, then the making of amends remains a possibility. While the offender's actions are easy to coerce, his attitudes remain more under his control. It is the offender's attitudes—his repudiation of the past, his respect for the victim, and his good intentions for the future—that transform mere restitution into atonement. Because sentencing conferences include intense and unscripted interactions between victims and offenders, we have grounds for believing that they provide reasonably good access to one another's frames of mind.

6.4 Objections from Liberal Neutrality

Let us now turn to the objection that the making of amends is a goal that the criminal justice system *should not* pursue. In both theory and practice, restorative justice is concerned with the reconciliation of the parties affected by crime. Yet, as Timothy Garton Ash has objected, "taken to the extreme, the reconciliation of all with all is a deeply illiberal idea. As Isaiah Berlin has taught us, liberalism means living with unresolvable conflicts of values and goals."[30] Amy Gutmann and Dennis Thompson concur: "Reconciliation of this comprehensive sort is...deeply undemocratic.... A substantial degree of disharmony is not only inevitable but desirable. It can be both a sign and a condition of a healthy democracy."[31] Meaningful liberty requires the freedom of individuals to develop and pursue their own conceptions of the good, at least within reasonable limits.[32] To the extent that a criminal justice system tries to enforce a particular, contestable conception of the good on citizens, it is illiberal. It violates the principle of liberal neutrality (i.e., the idea that the liberal state must be neutral among reasonable conceptions of the good).[33]

How, precisely, is restorative justice meant to violate liberal neutrality? The general objection, as I interpret it, can take three more specific forms, each of which requires a direct response. First, restorative justice seems to aim at the personal reformation of the criminal, which presupposes some conception of the good. The personal reformation that restorative justice has in mind is not merely outward improvement. The goal is not merely that the offender stops acting in ways that are deemed criminal by the state. Instead, the emphasis on face-to-face interactions and deep and wide-ranging communication about the causes and effects of crime suggests that the goal is the offender's internal improvement—a change in her point of view, values, or motivations, where those are be judged to be lacking according to some moral standard. The state uses its monopoly on force in order to pursue this objective.

A second way in which restorative justice seems to violate liberal neutrality is in the influence it apparently hopes to have not just over the offender's moral views but also over those of the victim and the community. Reconciliation—where this involves a renewal of civil relationships, release from continuing moral claims, and the normalization of levels of trust standardly leading to forgiveness—is held up to victims and communities as the ideal resolution of crime. Once more, this presupposes particular and controversial moral views: here, about the value and appropriateness of particular forms of relationship and of reconciliation and forgiveness as responses to offers of amends.

The third aspect of restorative justice that seems to put it in opposition to liberal neutrality concerns the particular nature of the sentencing agreements that may emerge from restorative justice processes. When individual victims confront individual offenders to discuss what was done, why it was wrong, and what should happen next, contestable moral values come to the fore. The participants in a sentencing conference give voice to their own conceptions of the good, their views of God, the value of community, and their valuations of class, race, family, and gender. Participants argue from their personal conceptions of the good to specific demands that will make up part of the negotiated sentencing agreement. The state then enforces this agreement. It might turn out, then, that state will require offenders to perform certain actions that could be defended only from a particular point of view. For instance, the state might find itself monitoring and enforcing an offender's regular attendance of a certain church service or religious education class, if such attendance was part of the sentencing agreement. More worrying still, the sentencing agreement might be the result of negotiation with one or more conceptions of the good that are not merely contestable but patently *unreasonable*. For example, a sexual offender may receive a lighter than usual sentencing agreement because he, his victim, or the community representatives proceed from the point of view that the victim was partly responsible for her victimization because she wore revealing clothing.[34] When the state is put in a position of enforcing such an agreement, is it not also put in the position of endorsing the illiberal moral views that lead to the agreement? Let us consider each of the three versions of the critique from liberal neutrality in turn.

6.4.1   ENFORCING PERSONAL REFORMATION

The objection to making personal improvement a goal of the criminal justice system has precedent in the literature on rehabilitation and moral education theories of punishment.[35] The suggestion that the state could have a legitimate interest in changing not simply the behavior of criminals but also their moral views or personalities has been seen as a gross overstepping of the legitimate bounds of the state into the realm of private conscience. Even if an offender's character or moral views are unreasonable—as when, for example, the offender views other people as mere means to his own pleasure and convenience—it is not clear that this is any of the state's business. The state has a legitimate interest in curbing the harmful and illegal behavior that would likely follow from such unreasonable states of mind. Nonetheless, were the state to try to change the offender's character or beliefs, it would violate the offender's freedom of conscience.

However, restorative justice theorists can defend their interest in the offender's moral improvement against this objection. While it is true that the liberal state is committed to freedom of conscience and the pluralism of reasonable conceptions of the good, there is no point or value in denying that liberalism is committed, at its core, to certain moral values—specifically the freedom and equality of persons.[36] These values undergird the liberal state's commitment to freedom of conscience, as well as the other defining aspects of the liberal state, such as democracy and the protection of other basic rights. While the liberal state values neutrality among reasonable conceptions of the good, the values of freedom and equality define the bounds of the reasonable. If this is the case, then the state can use the criminal justice system to educate the citizenry about the moral importance of following just laws without violating its commitment to neutrality about *reasonable* conceptions of the good.

Of course, restrictions on what the liberal state can do in attempting to educate its citizenry certainly exist. Brainwashing, for instance, is out of bounds since it would itself violate the principle of respecting freedom. Liberal moral education, then, must be education that approaches its subjects as free and equal persons, which suggests that such education may not be based on coercion. Yet, as we have already noticed, criminal justice systems, even those based on restorative justice models, are inherently coercive. How, then, could it be permissible for the liberal state to use the criminal justice system as a means of education?

Here, the restorative justice theorist might appeal to an argument that Hampton makes in her defense of the moral education theory of punishment.[37] She argues that, although the criminal justice system includes an element of coercion, the educative element itself is not coercive. According to Hampton, the educative work of punishment is performed through the expressive content of the punishing act. The idea is not to punish the offender until he has changed his moral views or character but to inflict a punishment on him in order to communicate to him that the community finds his behavior wrongful. The punishment is made proportional to the crime in order to convey the severity of the wrongdoer's guilt in the eyes of the community. The offender may listen to this moral message and reform himself, reject it, protest against it, or simply refuse to hear it.

Similarly, the restorative justice theorist hopes that the offender will learn a lesson through listening to his victim, having to explain and evaluate his own actions, and making reparations. However, whether this moral improvement actually comes about is up to the offender himself. He may well refuse to listen to the moral message he is being sent. Furthermore, restorative justice systems allow the offender ample opportunity to pointedly reject those messages. He can disagree with the alleged victim, voice his own interpretation and evaluation of his actions, refuse to agree to a particular restitution, and even opt out of the restorative process altogether. In this way, restorative justice better serves the offender's freedom of conscience than does a moral education theory of punishment.

Following Hampton's lead, then, the restorative justice theorists might argue that the use of a criminal justice system to pursue the personal improvement of criminal wrongdoers is compatible with the nature of a liberal state as long as its methods of moral education are compatible with the offender's right to form his own conception of the good. Restorative justice procedures, which make offender participation optional and allow the wrongdoer the opportunity to voice his own views, appear to be consistent with such agency. One could certainly say much more on this topic, but we have here at least the beginnings of a defense of restorative justice's interest in the personal reformation and moral education of criminal wrongdoers.

6.4.2   COERCING RECONCILIATION
AND FORGIVENESS

However, criminal offenders are not the only apparent targets for the moral lessons implicit in restorative justice procedures; so are victims and communities. These procedures are designed to encourage the restoration of the relationships among victims, communities, and offenders, which includes some ideal of reconciliation and arguably even forgiveness. However, people differ over the value and appropriateness of forgiveness and reconciliation. Even among those who might think that we have a moral obligation to reconcile with and forgive those who have harmed us (or perhaps only those wrongdoers who have also offered appropriate amends), few would agree to permit the state to enforce such a moral obligation.

This particular version of the objection from liberal neutrality was raised against the restorative efforts of the Truth and Reconciliation Commission (TRC) in South Africa.[38] In response, it was emphasized that, during the TRC hearings themselves, victims were allowed to express their refusal to forgive and the policy was neither to discourage nor criticize these victims.[39] Similarly, although restorative justice theorists and practitioners may value restorative justice for its ability to promote forgiveness, the state neither presses nor even asks victims to forgive their offenders. The general agenda for a sentencing conference includes discussion of the character, causes, and effects of the crime and the design of a restitution plan that the parties themselves judge to be appropriate and fair. The state asks but does not require that the participants come up with a plan that makes possible the settlement of their dispute. It need not ask them to reconcile as friends or family members but as fellow citizens.[40] For many participants, such a request raises issues of apology, repentance, forgiveness, and more personal forms of reconciliation. However, this is a consequence of their own moral understandings and expectations rather than any state requirements that are inherent to the restorative justice process.

Restorative justice, its advocates emphasize, is what the participants make of it.[41] Their own judgments of what restoration means or of what forms of restoration will satisfy them—whether mere restitution, genuine repentance, or forgiveness—are left to the people who are stakeholders in the conflict. When victims are empowered in determining what counts as an appropriate sentence and when they meet their offenders face-to-face, they come to see them as individuals rather than simply causes of harm.[42] Forgiveness under such circumstances should not be a surprising reaction. Nonetheless, to say that the system makes forgiveness a reasonable reaction for a wide range of victims is different from saying that it enforces forgiveness.

Thus, in opposition to the objection that the state is forcing a particular, contestable moral conception onto victims, one might rather argue that restorative justice systems better enable victims to live in accordance with their own conceptions of the good than do standard, punitive criminal justice systems. While the theory and rhetoric of restorative justice are clearly interested in reconciliation, victims may voice their own views of what, if anything, could earn reconciliation in the case at hand. They are free to demand that their own standards for the making of amends are met (within limits). If their demands are not met to their own satisfaction, they are free to object, withhold forgiveness, and even bring the restorative justice proceedings to a halt.

6.4.3   ENFORCING PRIVATE CONCEPTIONS
OF THE GOOD

Do restorative justice systems instead give *too much* latitude to differing conceptions of the good? In section 6.4.1 I suggested that we can defend subjecting criminal offenders to the moral lessons of the liberal state, but can we defend subjecting them to the moral lessons of their fellow private citizens? The moral education efforts of the liberal state are permissible insofar as they focus on the core values of liberalism—freedom, equality, human rights, and perhaps the obligation of citizens in a just state to obey the law. These values define the limits of reasonable disagreement in the liberal state. However, the values that fellow citizens are likely to try to impress upon one another in a sentencing conference are much more varied and contestable.

Recalling the earlier examples, we might find victims insisting that their offenders attend a specific form of religious instruction, or a sexual assault victim might be talked into agreeing to a light sentence for her abuser because he and the community representatives insist that she take partial responsibility for her attack. Given that the state would enforce negotiated sentencing agreements, it would enforce the particular values that shape these agreements. In the religious instruction case, it would be required to enforce a conception of the good that, while reasonable, is also outside the scope of the state's legitimate interest. In the sexual assault case, the state would lend credence to a moral view (that women have at best a limited right to bodily integrity) that stands in opposition to core liberal values.

Various responses to these objections are open to the restorative justice theorist. The most radical one insists that a just sentencing agreement is whatever the particular stakeholders agree upon. If the offender and the victim agree that religious education is desirable and appropriate in a particular case, then who is the state to disagree? The offender could, after all, opt out of the sentencing conference if he believed that the victim's insistence on religious instruction was an infringement of his freedom of conscience. Similarly, the sexual assault victim could opt out of the process if her offender tries to make her share the blame for the offense. In both examples, the cases would be turned over to a punitive sentencing procedure.

This response is inadequate, however. For one thing, given the strength of offenders' interests in avoiding imprisonment and victims' interests in receiving some degree of restitution, these parties might agree to the negotiation even if they believe that their rights are not being properly respected. Second, especially with regard to the sexual assault example, we see the danger of making the parties themselves responsible for defending their own rights. If a woman has been raised in a community that constantly sends her the message that to express sexuality is to ask for male aggression, we should not assume that she both recognizes and has the courage to insist upon her rights.

In response to such worries, restorative justice theorists sometimes emphasize the importance of procedural safeguards, which could take a number of conceivable forms.[43] For example, well-trained mediators should be both willing and able to intervene in a sentencing conference in order to help particular participants perceive and defend their own rights. Restorative systems can give either mediators or judges the power to invalidate sentencing agreements. This might be done by setting minimums or maximums on restitution agreements and placing limits on what sorts of things these agreements can include (e.g., disallowing required attendance of religious services). In these ways, the state could be given a kind of veto power over restorative justice procedures in order to ensure both that unreasonable conceptions of the good are not allowed to rule the day and that reasonable conceptions of the good are not applied in ways that interfere with the rights of others. The difficulty of designing and implementing such procedural safeguards (especially in a way that continues to permit the high degree of stakeholder autonomy that restorative justice values) should not be underestimated. However, this line of response to the objection seems promising.

Still, a fundamental issue remains to be addressed. Even when reasonable limits are observed and protections of rights are in place, restorative justice systems put offenders in the position of being morally educated *by other private citizens* under the auspices of the state. In order to come to a sentencing agreement, the offender needs to respond to and to some degree satisfy the victim's conception of justice. This feature of restorative justice procedures reflects the claim that crime must be "given back" to the stakeholders.[44] Instead of continuing to conceive of crime as a wrong committed against the state, restorative justice advocates claim, we should see it as a conflict among offenders, victims, and (more remotely) their local communities. We should allow these stakeholders the power to resolve their disputes as they deem appropriate. Thus, the state should be relegated to a supporting role. Fully to evaluate the third version of the objection from liberal neutrality—that the state should not place offenders at the mercy of their fellow citizens and their private conceptions of the good—we need to evaluate this reconception of the nature of criminal wrongdoing.

6.5 Objection to the Conception of Criminal Wrongdoing

Nils Christie's essay "Conflicts as Property" is a classic source for the restorative justice movement's claim that we should stop conceiving of crime as an offense against the state and instead enable victims and offenders to reclaim the controlling interest in the issue of crime.[45] Christie views the sorts of conflicts that lead to criminal and civil trials as valuable events in human lives. Conflicts and their resolution provide an opportunity for activity, meaningful participation with others, and the clarification of norms.[46] The modern state, in Christie's view, robs citizens of these opportunities by overrepresenting them, putting all of the meaningful interactions in the hands of professionals, and imposing strict and limited interpretations on what is relevant and valid in settling a conflict. Victims are the main losers in this scheme:

> Not only has [the victim] suffered, lost materially or become hurt, physically or otherwise. And not only does the state take the compensation. But above all he has lost participation in his own case. It is the Crown that comes into the spotlight, not the victim. It is the Crown that describes the losses, not the victim. It is the Crown that appears in the newspaper, very seldom the victim. It is the Crown that gets a chance to talk to the offender, and neither the Crown nor the offender are particularly interested in carrying on that conversation. The prosecutor is fed-up long since. The victim would not have been. He might have been scared to death, panic-stricken, or furious. But he would not have been uninvolved. It would have been one of the important days of his life.[47]

Offenders lose something valuable through the state's control of conflicts as well, argues Christie. "The offender has lost the opportunity to explain himself to a person whose evaluation of him might have mattered. He has thereby also lost one of the most important possibilities for being forgiven."[48] Rather than being "a participant in a discussion of how he could make it good again," the offender is left "a listener to a discussion—often a highly unintelligible one—of how much pain he ought to receive."[49] Through the state's regulation, "conflicts are taken away, given away, melt away, or are made invisible."[50]

Christie is surely right to emphasize that victims and offenders have a fundamental and meaningful stake in the resolution of crime. However, his analysis does not tell us why the state is justified in using its monopoly on the legitimate use of coercive force to bring these parties to the negotiating table. Furthermore, Christie's argument for the significance of victims' and offenders' interests does not entail that the state has no stake of its own in the resolution of crime. We must inquire further into the state's relationship to criminal justice. In the remainder of this section I consider a traditional, Lockean argument for conceiving of the state as a stakeholder in the resolution of crime. In critiquing this Lockean model, we will have the opportunity to reformulate and evaluate the restorative justice position on the role of the state.

According to one popular tradition, extending from Locke through the work of Robert Nozick, citizens have a slate of fundamental rights that are independent of any membership in a state.[51] This set of rights includes rights to life, bodily integrity, and property.[52] It also includes a natural right to retaliation and reparation, i.e., a right to use force in order to punish or secure compensation when one's rights have been violated or threatened. This right to retaliation and reparation is viewed as an obvious corollary of the others. A right to property is meaningless unless I also have a right to demand compensation when my property is damaged or taken. If I have a right not to be killed or injured, then I have a right not just to defend myself in midst of an attack but also to retaliate in way that will both deter future attacks and assert the claim that I have been treated in an unacceptable way. Similarly, the alleged wrongdoer has his own fundamental rights to life, bodily integrity, and property, so he has a right to resist unjustified or disproportional claims to retaliation or reparation from the alleged victim. This framework of fundamental rights supports the intuition that both victims and offenders are legitimate stakeholders in wrongdoing and that each has a right to make claims regarding retaliation and reparation.

According to this Lockean model, the state becomes a stakeholder only when citizens forfeit their rights to retaliation and reparation to the state in return for increased security. Such forfeiture is a rational move because individuals are likely to find that they are not particularly effective in securing satisfactory resolutions to their grievances. Furthermore, if citizens were to judge and pass sentence in their own cases, the argument goes, the result would be violent chaos. Each would judge her case to her own advantage, frequently unreasonably, and this would spur destructive cycles of vengeance. For these reasons, citizens transfer their rights to retaliation and reparation to the state, which is given the monopoly on the legitimate use of force. Violations of particular citizens' rights are redefined as violations of the state's rights. According to this model, the state's interest in crime is dependent on that of individual victims. The state comes to have a right to use force in response to crime in virtue of a social contract designed to protect and enforce individuals' rights. However, on this account, the state comes to be a stakeholder in the conflicts among its citizens only by supplanting the victim.

Christie's critique might lead us to conclude that the Lockean social contract goes too far. In order to bring security and end cycles of vengeance, the state must take control over the process by which guilt is determined and control offenders to ensure that justice is done and that offenders are not penalized in excess of their desert. But surely it can achieve these goals without demanding that citizens completely forfeit the rights associated with their status as victims. Citizens need not give away their right to articulate their own demands, formulate their own conceptions of appropriate redress, or receive reparations. Rather, they must forfeit only their right to use coercive force in securing that redress. Instead of redefining itself as the victim, the state can simply take on the role of regulating and aiding victims as they assert their own rights. The state is legitimized in using its coercive power as a limited agent of the victim rather than as the victim itself. Such a system, it seems, would still be able to provide security while maximizing the protection of individual rights. In this scenario, the state loses its status as a stakeholder in crime because the victim retains the right to retaliation and reparation. Surely not all advocates of restorative justice would be happy to adopt a revised Lockean argument of this sort, but it does provide a rationale for giving the state a role in resolving crime while at the same time denying that the state is an independent stakeholder in crime.

Notice, however, that this revised Lockean framework presupposes an extremely limited view of the role and purpose of the state and only thereby its limited view of the state's interest in crime. In contrast, we should note that crime violates not just the rights of particular victims but also the state's right to pass authoritative laws and its monopoly on the use of coercive force. The state must respond to crime in order to reassert its own rights and to preserve the normative force of the law.

Furthermore, many people believe the liberal state is charged with not just the protection of citizens' rights but also the promotion of their well-being. Crime threatens the well-being of more members of the state than those who have had their rights violated. It creates fear, increases the perceived need for greater security measures, and weakens trusting relationships among citizens. These considerations give the state as a whole an interest in crime that goes beyond its obligation to aid the primary victims in the defense of their rights.

Finally and as we have already noted, the liberal state is committed to the ideals of freedom and equality. This commitment requires the state to take a more substantive role in the response to crime than restorative justice processes allow. Other writers have framed this sort of objection by pointing out that, under restorative justice systems, it is possible for similar crimes to receive very different sentences.[53] For example, one criminal might be required to pay a hefty sum of money whereas another is sentenced to drug rehabilitation and community service. The very possibility of such inconsistency, it is argued, violates the liberal commitment to equality.

Restorative justice advocates may respond that sentences that appear unequal on the surface might reflect a sensitivity to context legitimated by a deeper, more informed interest in moral equality. Quite different restitution agreements could communicate similar degrees of condemnation of the criminal act, result in comparable improvements for the community, and be equally effective in reforming the criminal.

I agree that we cannot immediately conclude that moral inequality is the result of differential sentencing. However, we have other grounds for thinking that restorative justice processes might conceal moral inequality. As we have already noted with regard to the sexual assault example, particular restitution agreements among victims and offenders might embody the stakeholders' inegalitarian moral views. Furthermore, it seems highly likely that morally neutral differences in race, gender, class, education, physical strength, or linguistic abilities will give some parties greater bargaining power within a sentencing conference.[54] In order to prevent such outcomes, the state must restrict the range of agreements that can be made. Its duty to take such an action is not based simply on its obligation to help particular victims assert their rights to retaliation and reparation, as the Lockean model suggests. Were the state to allow such an inegalitarian outcome to stand, it would harm the interests of more people than just the victim. As Feinberg and Hampton have argued, the state's actions are expressive.[55] Were the state to allow and enable an inegalitarian resolution of the sexual assault case, it would send the message that male desire could diminish women's rights to bodily integrity. Were the state to consistently enforce less demanding restitution agreements for offenses against black victims, it would send the message that the rights of blacks are less significant than those of whites. Such a role would make the state complicit in an unjust system of norms that would wrong women and blacks generally. The expressive function of the state's actions and its duty to promote and defend freedom and equality within its borders suggest that the state has a stake in the resolution of crime that goes beyond its role in defending the rights of particular victims and offenders.

To repeat, I agree that the severity of a social condemnation of crime is not simply equivalent to the sum of restitution dollars demanded or the number of hours of community service required. Such differences could be consistent with equally earnest condemnations of crime and instead reflect culturally differentiated views of how crime should be resolved or the differences that exist in the resources offenders can muster in order to make amends. We need to consider more features of the context in order to interpret the moral messages a particular sentencing agreement sends about crime and human value. However, since we know that inegalitarian prejudices persist in our society, we need to take steps to prevent their influence in our criminal justice system.[56]

The operation of conscious or unconscious prejudices is not the only threat to the egalitarian operation of restorative justice processes. The phenomenon known as "adaptive preference formation" also causes problems.

Individuals' preferences are shaped by their understanding of what is possible and what is normal. Faced with difficult circumstances, people tend to lower their expectations and revise their preferences in order to avoid disappointment.[57] Imagine, then, two cases of property theft that are to be resolved through sentencing conferences. In the first case, the victim lives in a local community where property theft is rampant. The victim, though wronged and harmed by the action, views the event as a predictable, normal experience. Her friends and neighbors, who take part in the conference, share this view. In the second case, the victim lives in a community where property crimes are relatively rare. This second victim experiences the theft as an outrageous violation, and her friends and neighbors endorse her view. It seems reasonable to predict that the sentencing conference in the first case would result in a less severe evaluation of the wrongness of property theft than the second one. Because the parties in the first community expect less security of property, when property rights are violated they express less severe moral condemnation. In the second community, the theft is marked as more wrongful. The phenomenon of adaptive preference formation has the potential to result not just in differential sentencing but also in differential condemnations of crime. A state that allows the first community's meager expectations to influence the moral evaluation of crime may rightfully be charged with permitting moral inequality to flourish within its borders. It would be complicit in processes that reinforce the view that the rights and well-being of the people in the first community are less important than those of the people in the second community. When the state fails to condemn morally equivalent crimes with equivalent severity, it becomes complicit in a system of inequality.[58]

The liberal state is not and should not be morally neutral. It ought to promote certain values, including the welfare and moral equality of its citizens, both those who are immediately affected by a crime and those who are not. Because the state is so powerful, the messages it sends through its responses to crime are influential. The state expresses who is valuable and to what degree, and it reshapes the social world of its citizens in line with those views. For these reasons, the state has a stake in the resolution of crime that is broader than its duty simply to aid particular victims, offenders, and even local communities in coming to a negotiated resolution. It has both a right and a duty to express its own views about what counts as an acceptable and satisfactory resolution. The state should not replace the victim, but neither should it be a neutral bystander or a mere servant.

This line of argument should not lead us to reject the ideal of justice as restoration. In fact, we can restate the preceding critiques in restorative terms. While Christie and others aim to restore the relationships among offenders, victims, and local communities, they ignore the relationships among these parties and the state. Criminal wrongdoing damages the relationship between the offender and the state as a whole by both challenging its laws and threatening and insulting (at least many of) the citizens whom the state represents. Furthermore, the state's response to crime is one of the most important forums through which it maintains its relationship with the citizenry, a relationship that ought to be marked by equal respect and concern. Given restorative justice's emphasis on rebuilding damaged relationships, it ought not to ignore those that involve the state as a whole. Thus, my argument criticizes not the general principle of restoration but the particular formulations of restorative justice that fail to recognize the state as an independent stakeholder in crime.

Earlier we considered the suggestion that the state should participate in restorative justice procedures in a regulatory fashion by setting minimums or maximums on sentencing or exercising veto power over restitution agreements. However, this latest line of argument instead suggests that the state deserves its own place at the negotiating table. Perhaps the sentencing conference model of restorative justice could accommodate such a role for the state, but it is not immediately obvious how that might be done or whether such a change would be compatible with the commitment to empowering victims, offenders, and local communities.[59] Should the state be granted bargaining power equal to that of the victim in negotiating a settlement agreement? Should its influence be greater or smaller than this? Should legal professionals or a jurylike panel of citizens represent the state? Can the state participate as an equal party to the negotiation, or will the perceived authority of the state's representative have a silencing effect on the other parties, leaving them in a subordinated role? Simply bringing the state to the table in something like a sentencing conference might create as many problems as it solves.

We began this inquiry into the state's stake in crime in order to ask whether it is permissible for the state to use its power to put offenders in the position of being morally educated by other private citizens. Such a role for the state would be defensible if we concluded that the victims and offenders are the only real stakeholders in crime and the state is merely a servant to the interests of these parties. Instead, I have argued that the state has a broader constituency and a distinctive agenda that gives it an independent stake in the resolution of crime. While I approve of restorative justice's interest in empowering both victims and offenders in the criminal justice system, the liberal state should not simply endorse whatever outcome the other parties to the conflict decide upon.

6.6   Conclusion

As I have indicated throughout this chapter, I have significant questions and worries about restorative justice. However, the main focus here is the compatibility of restorative justice, with its interest in the moral project of making amends, and the liberal state. I have argued that restorative justice is more compatible with the principle of liberal neutrality than it may have appeared at first. However, the tensions between restorative justice and liberalism can be resolved only by granting a greater role to the state than many advocates of restorative justice would find acceptable.

The restorative justice movement is animated by values that I have defended in earlier chapters—atonement, moral reconciliation, and respect for the autonomy of both victims and offenders. Nonetheless, the task of putting these values into practice in a criminal justice system is daunting. Restorative justice is new and different, whereas the punitive criminal justice system is established and familiar. However, we know that criminal justice as it is currently practiced in the West is seriously flawed. In the United States especially, crime rates remain high, prisons are bursting at the seams, and offenders frequently emerge from prison more psychologically damaged, more likely to reoffend, and less able to reintegrate into communities than they were before incarceration. In most philosophical discussions of criminal justice, theorists simply try to give better reasons in defense of what we already do—put offenders in prison. But an honest look at the current state of criminal justice in the United States suggests that a much more radical change is needed. As disconcerting as restorative justice can sometimes be, it has at least this advantage: It is a theory that clearly has implications for practice.

CHAPTER SEVEN

Collective Atonement

Making Amends to the Magdalen Penitents

7.1 *Introduction*

What becomes of an ethic of atonement when wrongs are committed by groups? Can states and other institutions atone, or is atonement possible only for individuals? Is atonement required when the group's misdeeds lie so far in the past that current group members played no role in their commission? The very category of collective responsibility for wrongdoing raises hackles. For some, the worries are metaphysical. They ask whether we can meaningfully and accurately describe collectives as agents. In this chapter I assume that some sense can be made of collective agency. Groups such as states, churches, and corporations play too significant a role in our lives for any other answer to the metaphysical problems to be plausible. For other critics of collective responsibility, the concerns are moral. Is it fair, they ask, to hold all of the group members responsible for wrongs that only a subset of the group caused? Is it fair to hold current-day members accountable for the actions of their predecessors? Moral objections to collective responsibility are almost always objections to demands for correction. Critics reject the idea that corrective measures can be either forced upon or demanded of the group as a whole. They deny the appropriateness of collective punishment, collective compensation, or collective atonement.

Were we to endorse a retributive model of the correction of wrongdoing, attributions of collective responsibility would be objectionable indeed. To hold a group responsible for wrongdoing would be to legitimate either the infliction or the self-infliction of suffering proportional to the severity of the wrong. But to punish a group is to punish the individuals in it. In many cases of collective wrongdoing only a few of the members of the wrongdoing group can plausibly be counted as deserving punishment at all, and no particular member deserves a punishment proportional to the entirety of the wrong. So, to endorse collective responsibility, according to this model, would be to advocate treating individuals more harshly than they deserve. If, however, we can build a satisfactory model of the correction of wrongdoing without retribution, then we may be able to avoid this line of objection to collective responsibility.

By "collective compensation" I refer the practice of holding a group liable to pay restitution to either individual victims or a victimized group. The basic principle that victims deserve to be compensated for wrongful harm is quite straightforward and uncontroversial.[1] However, in cases of collective wrongdoing, it raises both moral and practical objections.[2] Some dispute the fairness of charging the entire group with debts incurred by merely a subset of its members, especially if the perpetrating members have all passed away and the current members played no role in causing the harms. Even when the principle of collective compensation is accepted, practical objections to its application arise. In debates about restitution for slavery in the United States, for instance, critics highlight the difficulties of choosing a sensible method of identifying both the wrongdoing group, which is liable to pay, and the victimized group, which has a right to receive restitution. Critics defend statutes of limitation or argue that there is no rational way to measure the amount of compensation owed.[3] Others object to the symbolic meanings that would accompany the payment of collective compensation. Members of the wrongdoing group often feel that the payment of compensation would be not simply a return of property to its rightful owner but also an admission of collective guilt that they feel justified in resisting.[4] Furthermore, members of the victimized group sometimes fear that acceptance of compensation for an evil such as slavery would suggest that the wrong was *compensable*.[5] Perhaps a dollar amount could be placed on the value of unpaid labor, but no amount of money could compensate for the wrongness of forcing others to labor against their will, the total restriction of personal freedom, continual humiliation, the destruction of families, rape, torture, murder, or public support of such brutal practices.

Both punishment and compensation run into difficulties as models for the correction of wrongdoing in collective cases, especially when significant periods of time and changes in group membership separate the present from the injustices of the past. These difficulties may well be resolvable, but my topic in this book is neither punishment nor compensation as such but atonement.

I have asked not what corrective responses might be compelled from wrong-doers but what they ought voluntarily to do in response to wrongs. And I have argued that the proper principle of atonement is distinct from both retribution and compensation.

In this chapter I argue that the combination of the reconciliation model of atonement with the assumption of collective responsibility for wrongdoing does not yield objectionable results.[6] Nonperpetrating members of wrong-doing groups are not treated unfairly under such a scheme. Demonstrating the compatibility of the reconciliation theory of atonement with the concept of collective responsibility for group wrongdoing increases the credibility of both moral ideas. Our moral objections to attributing responsibility to groups will be reduced if such attributions do not commit us to any unfair demands for atonement. Conversely, the appeal of the reconciliation theory of atonement will be increased if it permits us to attribute a meaningful sort of responsibility to groups.

By applying the reconciliation theory of atonement to the case of the Magdalen asylums, I argue that it deals well with collective wrongdoing. When we first discussed the case in chapter 1, we saw the destructive and degrading norms under which the "fallen women" of Ireland were made to atone for the sin of sex. The Magdalen case awakened us to the oppressive potential of an ethic of atonement. In this chapter we view the Magdalen system as an injustice committed by the religious orders that were in charge of the asylums and by the Catholic Church of Ireland as a whole, with the collusion of families and the Irish state. We ask how the church institutions, in particular, ought to respond to this history of injustice. I believe that the differences between the reconciliation theory's prescriptions for the church and the demands they previously placed on the women and girls in their care support my claim that an ethic of atonement need not be oppressive.

In sections 7.2 and 7.3 I defend my interpretation of the Magdalen case as involving collective wrongdoers and distinctively collective sorts of harms. Section 7.4 reviews the goals of atonement as identified by the reconciliation theory and argues that these goals continue to be appropriate in collective cases. In section 7.5 I recommend a number of particular methods of atonement that the orders should implement in response to the Magdalen case. I argue that these are not unfair even if we imagine that they are to be performed by group members who bear no personal guilt for the injustices of the Magdalen system. Section 7.6 answers the objection that, although reconciliation would certainly be desirable in this case, the present-day orders have no obligation to atone.

7.2   The Magdalen System as Collective Injustice

Over the course of two centuries, tens of thousands of women and girls were illegally imprisoned and forced into hard labor in the Magdalen laundries. They were robbed of their physical freedom, their labor, their self-respect, their moral autonomy, and often their babies.[7] Most had committed no crime. Some had not even violated the church's strict sexual rules but instead were merely presumed to be especially prone to sin or seen as tainted by the sexual sins of others.

The injustices committed against the Magdalen inmates were not the misdeeds of a few bad apples within the orders in charge—orders with cruelly ironic names such as the Sisters of Mercy, the Sisters of Our Lady of Charity of Refuge, and the Good Shepherd. There certainly were bad apples. Survivors relate stories of particularly violent nuns and sexual victimization by individual priests.[8] However, the systematically oppressive structure of the Magdalen asylums was the result of explicit rules and policies formulated and revised over decades by highly organized groups of nuns, priests, and lay volunteers, as well as less formal practices that were both well known and tacitly condoned within the orders (and perhaps more broadly). Even the particular abuses that were prohibited by the orders, such as sexual molestation, implicate the orders themselves. As Jean Harvey writes:

> If the prohibited wrong is one generally recognized in society as immoral, and yet there are a number of victims over a period of months or even years, then something is very wrong with the relationship between the powerful members of that institution and the victims. Either the victims protested and were ignored, or were summarily dismissed as liars, or suffered retaliation or harassment, or the victims were too intimidated to protest, or were trapped in an isolated and enclosed environment with no-one to protest to, or something else was terribly wrong.[9]

No one knows how frequent the sexual or the physical abuse of the Magdalen penitents was. However, Harvey's description of institutional environments that breed such abuses sounds as if it were written explicitly for the Magdalen asylums. As we know, some women and girls were locked away in the first place *because* they had been victimized.

The systematic wrongs perpetrated against the inmates were possible only because their abuser was a highly organized institution, not merely a collection of individual actors. The commonality of identity, purpose, and history and the prestige attributed to the orders are key causal factors in this story. Only because of their particular institutional identities were the orders given physical and emotional power over these women, allowed to operate unchecked by the state, and enabled to stifle any protest from their victims. As survivor Martha Cooney reports, "In Ireland, especially in them days ... the church was always right. You never criticized the priest. You never criticized them holy nuns. You did what they said without questioning the reason why."[10] Survivor Phyllis Valentine agrees: "You see, the nuns, they were gods to you; you didn't dare question them."[11]

This astounding degree of authority was available to the orders because of the standing in Ireland of the Roman Catholic Church as a whole. Other groups and institutional actors within the Church of Ireland supported the Magdalen asylums by encouraging families to send their wayward daughters there, sending some of their own wards from the orphanages straight to the asylums, and contracting with the asylums for their laundry services. More important, the larger institution had the right of oversight over the Magdalen asylums but never exercised it appropriately. So the Church of Ireland as a whole shares in the responsibility for the injustices done to the Magdalen inmates.

James M. Smith argues that the Magdalen asylum system also gained crucial support from the postindependence Irish state, the family, and Irish society in general. "No woman entered a Magdalen laundry without the knowing, if passive, complicity of a family member, an employer, a neighbor, or a friend in her disappearance from the community."[12] The social stigma attached to illegitimate births and nonmarital sex was so great that families abandoned their daughters to the Magdalen system and never returned for them. Even in cases of rape, the fear of scandal was allowed to overpower any loyalty to the victimized daughter, sister, niece, or cousin. Many women entered or were convinced to stay in the asylums because they believed they had nowhere else to go, and those beliefs were often justified.

The plight of the penitents within the laundries was an open secret even though the general pubic was probably largely ignorant of the details of life behind the walls.[13] Survivors of the asylums were ashamed to relate their experiences, and few others wanted to hear about them until recently. Nonetheless, the general public had some idea of what was going on. Girls were threatened into good behavior by the prospect of being sent to the laundries.[14] "We knew the girls that went in there didn't get out," recalls Philomena Collins, who was herself taken to the Gloucester Street asylum in Dublin for unruly behavior at age fourteen and was still there when the asylum closed fifty years later.[15] Family members and neighbors disappeared overnight, never to be heard from or spoken of again. People who lived near the asylums would see and hear the unhappy penitents and sometimes witness attempts to escape. A long-time neighbor of the Gloucester Street Convent recalls, "The girls would be coming over the wall and running for their life along Gerry's Lane out on to Railway Street, with their smocks blowing up in their faces as they ran, and the kids would be cheering them on, shouting 'Run, run, you'll make it!' "[16]

The state was supportive of the Magdalen institutions in a number of ways. Smith charges the state with complicity in the Magdalen system for having "long ignored the flagrant disregard for the Magdalen women's civil and constitutional rights: false imprisonment; the absence of due process; exploitative and dangerous work practices; the denial of educational and human developmental resources; and emotional, physical, and, in some cases, sexual abuse."[17]

Concerns about the nature and extent of state complicity with the asylums caught the Irish public's attention in 2003, when they belatedly learned of the following events.[18] In 1993 the High Park Convent had applied to exhume 133 bodies from the graveyard for Magdalen penitents in Drumcondra in order to sell the property. The convent was unable to provide legally required death certificates for 58 of the bodies, but the authorities issued the exhumation licenses anyway. When workers began the exhumations, they found 155 bodies altogether, something that would normally call for a police investigation. Instead, the paperwork required for the extra 22 exhumations was supplied, and the discovery of the extra bodies was kept from the public for ten years. Since the bodies were cremated, no one will ever know who those nameless women were, how they died, or how they came to be buried there.

The Irish state also provided more active support to the operations of the asylums over the years. Courts sent prostitutes, troublesome minors and even infanticides to confinement in the asylums.[19] There are reports that the police would return runaway penitents to the nuns.[20] An oft-reprinted photo reported to depict a group of Magdalen inmates taking part in a public parade shows a procession of women surrounded on both sides by lines of uniformed police officers. Whether the police are meant to protect or, as Smith suggests, to contain the women is unclear and was likely unclear to the women themselves.[21]

Smith argues that the institutional confinement of female sexuality exemplified by the Magdalen system was part of the nation-building project of the Irish Free State from the 1920s on.[22] Newly independent from Britain, the Irish state worked to represent itself as both distinctive from and morally superior to its former colonizer through its tight connections with the Catholic Church. To maintain the image of Ireland as a Catholic nation, evidence of single motherhood, rape, incest, and pedophilia had to be hidden away, and the Magdalen asylums helped perform that function.[23] Smith argues that the state permitted and protected the asylums as part of a joint effort with the church "effectively to criminalize sexual relations outside of marriage and thereby inscribe moral purity into the project of national identity formation."[24]

The injustices of the Magdalen asylums were systematic and structural. They were inflicted on the inmates through the regular functioning of institutions, both formal and informal. The direct wrongs of socially "disappearing" female sexual transgressors had indirect, repressive effects on Irish women and girls generally. These injustices resulted from the active and the passive participation of large groups of people. We cannot explain these wrongs simply by describing the actions of particular nuns, family members, policemen, or politicians. Just as importantly, we cannot begin to imagine how the inmates were harmed, insulted, and threatened unless we recognize that the most authoritative institutions in their society worked together to hide them away and make them suffer, leaving them with little or no recourse. The injustices of the Magdalen asylums were collective ones.

7.3 Attempts to Excuse the Wrongdoing Groups

Since the story of the Magdalen laundries has been brought to the public's attention (largely by the 1998 documentary *Sex in a Cold Climate*, Peter Mullan's 2002 feature film *The Magdalene Sisters*, the reports in 1993 and 2003 of the Drumcondra exhumations, and two controversial memoirs by Kathy O'Beirne in 2005 and 2006),[25] the church's response to the Magdalen case has been almost uniformly defensive. Only one of the orders has issued an apology.[26] The others have declined requests by groups of survivors to do so. Most of the orders have refused to release archival records to historians, especially those records covering the twentieth century.[27] To date, the Irish state has insisted that the abuses inside the Magdalen asylums were not its responsibility because they were under the control of the church.[28] In contrast, an official state apology and a reparations program has been set up for the survivors of other abusive institutions—orphanages, industrial and reformatory schools—that were also headed by religious orders.[29] The ostensible explanation for the distinction is that the state provided direct subsidies for the care of the children in these other institutions but not for the Magdalen penitents. There are no reparation programs for the surviving victims, no official investigations, and few memorials.[30]

In press reports and other accounts, one finds a number of strategies for morally excusing the institutions and institutional actors in question. For instance, a nun interviewed about the closing of the last laundry insists, "Many of the women didn't have a hope in hell without us. The alternative in many cases was to go on the streets. Girls have gone on the streets and been murdered. I've seen it happen. It might have happened to a lot more if it hadn't been for the convent."[31] Yet, the fact that other people might have treated these women and girls even worse does nothing to excuse the mistreatment they suffered at the hands of the sisters.

Elizabeth Butler Cullingford raises the possibility that the nuns running the Magdalen asylums were unable to recognize that their treatment of the penitents was wrongful:

> The penitents were cloistered, their labor was unpaid, they wore uniforms, their names were changed, their lives were an endlessly repeated alternation of work and prayer, they were expected to keep silence, and they were forbidden "particular friendships." They were nuns in all but name. Perhaps this explains why the real nuns were not ashamed of their actions: both they and the penitents were seeking salvation through mortification of the flesh.[32]

Still, as Cullingford herself responds, "The difference between a vocation and a punishment ... lies not in the strictness of the discipline but in the will to perform it."[33] The nuns' self-incarceration was (heralded to be) voluntary.[34] Both within the asylums and without, the nuns were clearly differentiated from the penitents through both power and prestige.

Of course, the nuns believed sex outside of marriage to be, "like murder, a mortal sin"[35] that would be punished by eternal suffering if left unatoned. As Mary Gordon points out, "If you really believed this, it could certainly be seen as an act of kindness to lock someone up, even for life, to subject her to humiliation and deprivation, if that would purge her sin and wash her as white as the sheets she scrubbed."[36] However, the church allegedly learned long ago that it is wrong to torture people for the sake of their souls, a lesson made clear in the shameful history of the Inquisition. The nuns may well have believed they were helping the penitents, but they should have known that the measures they took were unjustified.

"You can't judge those times by the standards of today," say the defenders of the asylums.[37] Suppose we grant that the particular women and men who designed and implemented the Magdalen asylums should be credited with good intentions, excused for limited understanding of the moral character of their actions, and even seen as victims of a culture that demonized sexuality.

What should we say about the institutions themselves, which seem to have closed down their laundries as a result of the economics of the home washing machine and a loosening of sexual mores in Irish society rather than a change in view about the wages of sin?[38] And how are we to vindicate the victims—those who survive and suffer today, as well as those buried in anonymous graves?

7.4 The Goals of Collective Atonement

I have argued that atonement should have as its goal the moral reconciliation of victims, wrongdoers, and involved communities. Wrongdoers must work to reestablish mutual respect for the equal dignity of all of the parties. They must remove the grounds their previous misdeeds provided for distrust and continued resentment. The overarching goal of moral reconciliation is to be pursued through the wrongdoer's moral improvement, respectful communication with victims and relevant communities, and the reparation of the harms caused by the wrongful actions.

I have argued that we cannot understand the Magdalen asylums unless we identify the institutions involved as wrongdoers. To attribute responsibility for wrongdoing is to endorse a call for atonement. Given the theory of atonement I support, this is a call to the institutions to work toward moral reconciliation, but are they the sorts of entities that can reconcile? Does it make sense to describe institutions as standing in relationships? While I grant that there are metaphysical issues worth worrying about here, it is a fact of modern life that we *do* regard institutions as standing in relationships with us.

Strawson, focusing on our attitudes toward other individuals, draws a distinction between the objective stance and the participant stance.[39] To regard someone from the objective stance is to see that person as a particularly complex object to be studied and manipulated. In contrast, when we take the participant stance toward another person, we regard that individual as a subject rather than an object—a free agent who will be guided by norms and act for reasons. We regard the other as a participant in ongoing relationships shaped by expectations of goodwill and regard.[40] When we take the objective stance to someone (say, a small child or a person with a serious mental disability), our intentions may be good. Our attitude may be one of pity or concern. "But," Strawson insists, "it cannot include the range of reactive attitudes which belong to involvement or participation with others in inter-personal human relationships; it cannot include resentment, gratitude, forgiveness, anger, or [love]."[41]

In interacting with institutions, I submit, we frequently take the participant stance. We experience reactive attitudes, such as resentment and gratitude, toward them because we expect our dealings with them to be shaped by basic standards of morality. Strawson labels such attitudes "reactive" because they are reactions to perceived attitudes in the other. We interpret institutions as expressing attitudes toward us. Their operations communicate messages of respect or disrespect, goodwill or hostility. Our reactive attitudes toward institutions are not always straightforward generalizations of those we hold toward agents of those institutions, either. For instance, we often sympathize with the hapless bank employee who is obliged to execute the maddening policies of his employer. We resent the bank, although we do not resent him.

Of course, it is possible that we are deeply mistaken in taking the participant stance and holding reactive attitudes toward institutions. We might be making a grave metaphysical error in assuming that we can stand in moral relationships to entities such as banks. However, we could also be making a similarly grave mistake by taking the participant stance toward other human beings. It is helpful to recall that Strawson draws the distinction between the participant and the objective stance as part of a discussion of the problem of free will. The plausibility of determinism might tempt us to take the objective stance toward one another all of the time. Nevertheless, Strawson presents two reasons for not doing so. First, he argues that we cannot limit ourselves to the objective stance continually. Our psychology forbids it. "The human commitment to participation in ordinary inter-personal relationships is, I think, too thoroughgoing and deeply rooted."[42] Second, even if we could manage to restrict ourselves to the objective stance, we should not because doing so would mean losing the benefits of relationship.[43] Our interactions would lack in moral meaning and our lives would thereby be significantly impoverished. We can extend Strawson's argument to the case of institutions as well. It is unlikely that we would be psychologically able always to maintain the objective stance toward institutions. Still, even if we could, we should not. When we regard institutions as standing in relationships to us and as subject to expectations of goodwill and regard, we are better off because our interactions with institutions will be imbued with meaning. When we regard institutions (including those in which we are members) as subject to moral expectations, they are more likely to meet those expectations.

We act as though we stand in moral relationships to institutions, and we have good reason to continue to do so. Our relationships with institutions are not identical to those with other people. While resentment can sensibly be held toward both individuals and institutions, love probably cannot.[44] Moral relationships to other individuals respect rights not also held by institutions.

It is wrong to steal from both individuals and institutions, but eliminating an institution is not obviously immoral in the way killing a person is. Such differences are interesting and important, but for our purposes the conclusion that institutions stand in moral relationships is enough to be getting on with.

If institutions do stand in moral relationships with others, then those connections will be damaged or threatened by wrongdoing. The injustices of the Magdalen system clearly damaged the relationships among the Church of Ireland, the direct victims, and the broader community, as well as within the church itself. By establishing and maintaining the Magdalen system, the church expressed a terrible disrespect for the inmates. By robbing them of their physical freedom, their labor, their autonomy, their self-respect, their names, their babies, and their connections with the outside world, the church treated them as something less than equally valuable moral agents. The Magdalen system encouraged these women and girls to regard themselves as lowly and dirty, and it encouraged the broader community to see them that way as well. The fact that women were incarcerated for nonmarital sex but men were not is an insult to all women. The exposure of the Magdalen system's injustices—one of a long line of scandals in the Church of Ireland since the 1990s—has left the Catholic faithful feeling betrayed by the institution that presented itself as their moral guide on earth. Current-day members of the orders, the great majority of whom surely joined these groups with a sense of moral purpose, have felt themselves tainted by association with this history. The general standing of the church in Irish society has plummeted since the revelation of this and other scandals, as have church attendance and the number of vocations.

Although damaged by institutional wrongdoing, these relationships can also be reconciled, and the pattern of atonement is the same as that found in cases of individual wrongdoing. The church needs to reestablish itself as a trustworthy member of the moral community.[45] It needs to show that it is dedicated to the dignity and equal moral status of all human beings. It must provide others and its own members with good reason to believe that it will abide by moral norms and the just laws of the state in the future by satisfying the legitimate claims against it. In order to regain its standing as morally trustworthy, the church must improve itself, communicate respectfully with the victims and the larger community, and repair the damage it caused insofar as that is possible. Its efforts cannot be limited to ensuring good behavior in the future because the past will continue to provide grounds for suspicion unless the matter is satisfactorily addressed. The church must acknowledge the past as wrongful and accept responsibility for it. It must approach its victims with respect, goodwill, and humility. It must also show itself willing to repair those forms of damage that lie within its sphere of influence.

7.5   The Means to Collective Atonement

I have argued that the goals of atonement identified by the reconciliation theory are fitting for both wrongdoing institutions and wrongdoing individuals. In this section I examine the specific means that the orders and the church as a whole could use in pursuit of these goals in the Magdalen case. Most of these closely parallel the sorts of atoning responses that individuals use to reestablish their moral trustworthiness and heal their relationships. However, I highlight some important differences. In the collective case, as in the individual, the wrongdoer should pay heed to the reasonable judgments of victims and involved communities regarding the desirability and proportionality of the various atoning responses.

For the orders to atone, individual members would have to perform the atoning responses. Yet, the entry of most of these individuals into the orders postdates the worst of the abuses in the Magdalen asylums. So we must ask whether, in demanding these forms of atonement from the church, we mistreat these nonperpetrating members.[46] I argue that the forms of atonement I recommend are fair and just, though other forms of atonement must be ruled out. Because the nonperpetrating member of the institution presents the most significant obstacle to my claim that institutions must atone for their wrongdoing, I imagine the following responses being made by those individuals, specifically by members of the orders whose membership began after the practices of confinement ended in the 1970s. More by way of atonement would be expected of perpetrators who are guilty of individual wrongdoing.[47] Earlier chapters have addressed what they owe in terms of atonement, so I do not address those responsibilities here.

7.5.1   EMOTIONS OF MORAL ASSESSMENT

In cases of individual wrongdoing, we insist upon guilty and repentant feelings because we require the moral judgments and attitudes that naturally give rise to these emotions. However, it would be odd to say the same in institutional cases because institutions simply do not seem to be the sorts of things that can feel. However, we are working under the assumption that their actions can be interpreted as expressing attitudes. The actions of an atoning institution should communicate those attitudes that underlie the emotions of guilt and repentance in individuals—judgments that the past was wrongful, that the victims deserved better, and that the wrongdoer justly bears responsibility for the harms, as well as the intention not to repeat the wrong in the future. An institution can communicate these stances through the various acts of amends that I discuss later—such as apology and reparations. Any declaration by prominent or representative group members of personal regret, shame, or grief will provide some measure of evidence that the character of the group is changing for the better. One sometimes hears statements that claim that an institution itself regrets a certain act. While such assertions are initially puzzling, they can communicate either an aggregation of individual group members' emotions or a joint commitment to endorse and cultivate feelings of regret among individual group members.[48]

It would be objectionable to require guilt, remorse, and repentance of nonperpetrating members of wrongdoing groups. Those emotions seem to rest on judgments of personal blameworthiness, and these people are not themselves culpable. There are other appropriate emotions, though, that do not imply any judgment of personal wrongdoing. Regret is surely fitting. However, it is an emotion that any morally sensitive person will feel with respect to a case of wrongdoing placed before his eyes, no matter how unconnected he is to the case. Because of their closer connection, it seems fair to expect something more than mere regret from members of wrongdoing groups even if they are not themselves perpetrators. Grief, the emotion associated with mourning what has been lost, seems proper. In cases of untimely deaths, all may feel a sense of regret, but only those connected to the departed will grieve. Similarly, everyone might feel regret over an injustice, but grief befits those who are more closely associated with it. Grief does not carry any judgment of individual responsibility but instead marks a sense of caring and personal involvement.

Shame, too, is an appropriate emotion for the nonperpetrating member. Shame is an emotion attached to a sense of being seen by an audience (whether real or imagined). To be a member of a wrongdoing group is to be placed in a context where one will be viewed in connection with wrongdoing. One will thus be looked upon with suspicion. In feeling shame and accepting rather than resisting or resenting it, nonperpetrating group members acknowledge the legitimacy of that point of view. This is proper. They are members of a group that is regarded with suspicion for good reason, not because of unfair prejudice but because of its own unaddressed history of injustice. Their moral relationships with others are thus damaged by their membership in this group. Institutions, like individuals, have characters that persist over time. The new member's voluntary participation in a wrongdoing institution raises the question of whether she shares in the patterns of belief, behavior, and character that led to the past injustices. She ought to acknowledge this question because it is neither unfair nor unreasonable. In feeling shame, she exhibits her respectful sensitivity to the legitimate suspicions of her group's victims and the broader community.[49] Hopefully, this sense of shame will spur her on to repair those relationships.

Empathy is a further emotional stance that is fitting in cases of institutional wrongdoing. The members of the institutions should remember that their groups violated not just abstract rules of morality but people. By actively cultivating empathy with the victims' point of view, the members of the institutions acknowledge both the moral significance of the past and its connection to the present and are better able to understand how they should act in the future.

Regret, grief, shame, and empathy with those who have suffered all bring a measure of pain, but this is not punishment. Thus, we do not treat nonperpetrating members of wrongdoing groups unfairly by expecting them to feel such emotions. Instead, we insist that they acknowledge the moral character of the past and the way the past and their membership in the wrongdoing group have shaped their own relationships to the victims and the community.

7.5.2 APOLOGY

Formal public apologies performed by prominent members on behalf of wrongdoing groups are crucial in cases of institutional wrongdoing such as the Magdalen case. With a formal apology, the institution officially acknowledges the wrongs of the past. The spokesperson symbolically withdraws the insult and the threat that the past issued against both the victims and those who resemble the victims in relevant ways. She declares a renewed respect for these people and promises that current members of the institution will accord this respect as well. The spokesperson should express a sense of regret, grief, or shame, both on her own part and on behalf of the other group members, to lend credibility to the claim that the institution fully recognizes and cares about the wrongfulness of the past.

Apologies that are coupled with excuses or counteraccusations do not encourage reconciliation. A nonperpetrating member of an institution understandably feels loyalty to her fellow members. She often wants to provide excuses for them, claim they had good intentions, and argue that monstrous practices can arise in the absence of individual monsters. Such impulses are fine in themselves so long as they do not become dishonest or condone wrongdoing. However, any mitigating excuses must not be allowed to distract from the message that the wrongs were wrongs and that the victims deserved better. It is probably best that such excuses on behalf of individual perpetrators be separated from formal apologies on behalf of institutions. Apologies are gestures of respect to victims, and victims deserve to have their own moral claims be the focus of the apology.[50]

Vague apologies are unsatisfactory. Those that mention merely "any wrongs that may or may not have taken place" suggest that the institution does not believe (or does not care to know) that injustice occurred. Instead of assuaging moral distrust, they actually provide continued reason for suspicion. If the spokespeople genuinely remain in doubt as to the facts of the past or the extent of the injustice, they would do better to apologize for the wrongs they know about and promise to investigate further.

Objectionable, too, are apologies that attempt to draw a line under the past or end discussion of it. An apology should be part of a dialogue, and a proper atonement must include listening. In the Magdalen case, the victims were silenced. An institutional apology is best thought of as a beginning stage of an atonement process, not the end.

7.5.3   TRUTH TELLING AND EXPLANATION

One of the cruelest features of the Magdalen case is that the penitents were presented as evil and low, whereas their abusers were regarded as saintly. No one would have believed the penitents' accusations of injustice, and resistance to the nuns would only have been taken as further evidence of moral corruption. In *Sex in a Cold Climate*, as survivor Christina Mulcahy tells her story, she repeats over and over again, "I'm not crazy." Mulcahy was not only abused but also pressured to accept the mistreatment as deserved and to believe that her own moral perceptions were deranged. Most survivors of the asylums kept a fearful silence about their experiences, and this surely increased their suffering. The victims need a public confirmation that they are telling the truth about what happened. They need to be reassured that their stories will be fairly heard and credited, should they choose to relate them.[51]

Toward this end, the orders should cooperate with efforts to uncover the truth and enable survivors to tell their stories. Understandably, victims and the public may not trust the orders to disclose the past faithfully. The Magdalen asylum system used secrecy to operate in the first place—with locked doors, high stone walls, and controlled communications with the outside world. Thus, the orders should open their records to responsible journalists or historians. Some have refused to do so in the name of protecting the victims' privacy. However, it is possible to conceal the names of victims while uncovering other facts. Because the orders have lost their credibility as defenders of their wards' interests, they should place decisions about the opening of their records in the trust of survivors' organizations or a neutral third party who will consider both the survivors' and the orders' concerns. This sort of openness to the truths of the past will help the orders rebuild their claim to trustworthiness.

7.5.4 MATERIAL REPARATIONS

Material reparations are defensible in the Magdalen case on two different grounds. First, material restitution is owed to the survivors as compensation for the labor they performed in the laundries. This labor went to the penitents' (meager) physical upkeep, but it also supported the nuns, only some of whom also worked in the laundries. The penitents' labor paid for the maintenance and expansion of properties and other forms of wealth still held by the Church of Ireland today. Nonperpetrating members of the institutions are recipients of stolen goods, and they must return them to their rightful owners. In acknowledging that they have come to benefit from these forms of wealth unjustly, nonperpetrating group members do not suggest that they are personally guilty. However, knowingly retaining those assets would both result in new guilt and serve as continuing evidence that the institutions have not faced up to the moral facts of their past.

As I noted with respect to the issue of restitution for slavery in the United States, difficulties sometimes arise in determining proper compensation for historical wrongs. The Magdalen case presents fewer practical obstacles, however. The main wrongdoing groups are easy to identify and have retained their institutional identities. Assuming record-keeping practices improved in the course of the twentieth century, most of the surviving victims should be identifiable. The value of a particular penitent's labor is calculable within a reasonable range of accuracy even if the other harms done to her are not. While a danger always exists that compensation will be misinterpreted as placing a monetary value on human dignity, that risk is greatly reduced when compensation is not presented as the whole or final response to the injustice but instead as part of a process of atonement. Still, victims and their survivors should be consulted before pursuing any plan for material reparation.

Second, material reparations beyond any due compensation would serve as a powerful symbol of regret, renewed respect, and concern for the victims and obviate the need for highly precise calculations of compensation. As noted earlier, the Irish state and the church have together offered material reparations to the victims of child abuse in the church-run orphanages and the industrial and reformatory schools. This highly public and widely praised response to a history that is similar in many ways to the Magdalen case sets a standard of earnestness for an atoning response. The church's failure to offer a similarly significant form of amends to the Magdalen penitents has been taken as a sign of disrespect.[52] It appears to draw a distinction between the "innocent" children and the "dirty" women. Given that the injustices committed against the Magdalen women and girls were rooted in a misplaced sense of moral entitlement to punish them for sexual sin, such an impression must be avoided.

If material reparations are offered to the former inmates, they should not be joined with confidentiality agreements of the sort sometimes seen between the church and survivors of sexual abuse in the United States.[53] Reparations must acknowledge wrongdoing and express respect for the victims. Confidentiality agreements turn reparations into hush money. Putting victims in the position of having to agree to continued silence in return for a just atonement is unfair, especially given that silencing was a fundamental element in the original victimization of these people.

While I have defended reparations for the victims of the Magdalen asylums, I have not addressed reparations for their heirs. There are reasonable grounds for wanting spouses, direct descendants, and intentionally designated heirs of deceased victims to inherit compensation or even symbolic reparations. Nonetheless, I am troubled by the prospect of members of the extended family being considered heirs for this purpose. After all, the birth families of the Magdalen women were usually complicit in their confinement.[54]

7.5.5   CARE WORK AND SERVICE

In the Magdalen case, care work and service have both practical and symbolic value as forms of atonement. Many of the survivors of the Magdalen asylums require significant forms of care. Many are now elderly, and some were so damaged by their extended institutionalization that they are incapable of living independently.[55] Service to them at this point would be a form of reparation for the past. Service to young women and girls who resemble the penitents of old—prostitutes, unwed mothers, and victims of sexual assault—could also be powerfully symbolic. However, in both of these scenarios it is crucial to avoid the mistakes of the past. The members of the orders must respect rather than degrade those they serve, nurture their moral autonomy rather than infantilize or domineer them, and help them to heal their relationships with others rather than isolate them. The asylum survivors must be allowed and even encouraged to talk about the past. Providing assistance to these populations in a way that supports renewed trust rather than continued suspicion will not be easy given the weight of the past, but it could be a powerful way for current-day members to help their victims and to reestablish the orders' reputations as caring institutions.

7.5.6 PROCEDURAL REFORMS

The likelihood and the desirability of service to the asylum survivors, as well as to other needy parties, highlight the necessity of procedural reforms within the orders. Policies must be designed and publicized that safeguard against future abuse. Transparency, oversight by organizations other than the church, and effective, accessible procedures that ensure a voice to the vulnerable are crucial to a renewal of trust.

7.5.7 FUTURE BEHAVIOR

A track record of actual, improved behavior on the part of the institution is another required component of atonement. Future injustices would tear away at any good the atoning responses mentioned earlier might achieve. Should any new abuse occur, whether it is collective in nature or due solely to the failings of an individual member, the institution must respond promptly and convincingly.

7.5.8 RITUALS

Given the religious context of the Magdalen case, ritual forms of atonement seem particularly appropriate. Masses should be held for the souls of the victims, so long as those masses honor the victims as victims. Memorials should be erected on the sites of the laundries and the graveyards of the Magdalen penitents. In the Drumcondra case, the bodies of the exhumed penitents were cremated in order to reduce the cost of reburial even though canon law "earnestly recommends that the pious custom of burial be retained."[56] Such an insult to the memory of the departed victims of the asylums, whose own forced labor added to the wealth the convents were so concerned to preserve, demands a ritual response. Rituals communicate renewed respect and a recommitment to shared norms in a solemn and public fashion. For the church, an institution thoroughly defined by ritual, a failure to issue such responses would cast doubt on the sincerity of any other responses it might make.

7.5.9 PUNISHMENT FOR PROHIBITED WRONGS

So far I have made no mention of punishment as a form of atonement. To call for the self-punishment of all of the members of a wrongdoing institution in response to a collective wrong would be unjust. Furthermore, my defense of reparations is not a defense of punishment, but only of compensation and the communication of regret and goodwill. Individual perpetrators may find that their own guilt justifies some form of self-punishment (though such judgments should be made with caution).

Regarding the institutional response to collective wrongdoing, one particular form of punishment is befitting and important, however. The institution must penalize any of its own members who committed wrongs prohibited by the institution's own legitimate rules. In the Magdalen asylums, many abuses were matters of official or tacit policy. The orders lack the proper authority to punish those of its members who carried out its policies, though it should encourage them to atone. However, the orders prohibited some of the maltreatment—such as the sexual abuse of inmates and (at least in some cases) physical violence.[57] The institutions should exercise their authority to punish those of its members who are known to be guilty of such violations. In those cases in which the rule violation was also a crime, the wrongdoer should be reported to the state.

I have dismissed the collective self-punishment of the church as a morally problematic form of atonement, one that is not necessary to the proper goals of atonement. However, one argument for insisting on a punitive collective atonement requires examination. The church should atone through some form of self-punishment, one might argue, because that is the standard of atonement that it has traditionally endorsed and also required of the asylum inmates. The church cannot choose the conciliatory path of atonement for itself and yet recommend retributive forms of atonement to the faithful.

The discrepancy between the forms of atonement demanded of the Magdalen penitents and the church's reactions to its own revealed sins is a scandal in itself. Young girls and women, many of whom were ignorant of even the basic facts about sex, were bullied into years and even lifetimes of remorse, confinement, and backbreaking penance for engaging in sexual activity. No care was taken to separate those "guilty of sin" from those who were "tainted" by the sins of others. Yet, when the church itself was revealed to have been guilty of wrongdoing in the case of the asylums, orphanages, and industrial schools, as well as in the cover-up of sexual abuse by priests, forgiveness was the order of the day. Sin was declared to be a matter between the abusers and their God, and other parties, even victims and local congregations, were treated as if they had no right to involve themselves. Reparations were rejected as an unfairly harsh penalty. Groups refused to apologize or acknowledge wrongdoing for fear that a few false accusations might be mixed up with the many true ones.[58] The hypocrisy in the church's double standards for atonement is an additional, devastating insult to the survivors of the asylums and a huge obstacle to reconciliation.

Tempting though it is to demand that "what goes around comes around," I cannot recommend that the orders apply to their own members the retributive, degrading forms of atonement they imposed upon their victims. However, the objection does lead me to add the following item to the list of means to atonement.

7.5.10 NORM CLARIFICATION

The church should publicly and explicitly address the application of its own view of atonement to the case of the Magdalen asylums. It ought to declare the extent to which the practices of the asylum violated or conformed to its own ideals of atonement. It should also clarify its norms for interpersonal and collective atonement. If the church is to have any hope of reestablishing its position as a trustworthy member of the moral community, let alone as an authority on moral matters, it must provide a reasonable defense of its own treatment of the past.

These recommended forms of atonement would, I believe, have a powerful, transformative effect on the relationships among the church, the victims of the Magdalen asylums, and Irish society as a whole. Even if we imagine that institutional actors whose membership postdates the abuses are to carry out these atoning actions, these responses are appropriate. None of them degrades the members of the orders or punishes the innocent for the crimes of the guilty. Many of the atoning responses discussed here are difficult, but they are not punitive (with the obvious exception of the punishment of individual rule breakers). Facing the wrongful past of one's group will likely be painful. But when that pain is a side effect of genuinely caring about victims, about one's moral relationships with others, and about the moral standing of one's group, it is not objectionable. The payment of compensation to the victims would lead to hardships, but the orders have no right to retain wealth that was wrongfully acquired.[59] The forms of atonement I defend here ask group members to dedicate themselves to something positive—to stand up for what is right and just, to rebuild respect and goodwill, and to redeem the reputations of the organizations to which they have dedicated their lives. The orders and the church as a whole have as much to gain from the work of atonement as the victims.

7.6 Collective Atonement as Obligatory

Few, I suspect, would disagree that it would be a good thing for the church to respond to the Magdalen case with the goals of expressing respect and working to rebuild normal relationships of trust. Reconciliation would surely be valuable in cases of institutional abuse generally. The controversial claim is that these efforts at reconciliation should be conceived as *atonement*, especially given the assumption that these groups are now largely made up of members who were not present at the time of the abuses. This raises the question of whether the group members are *obliged* to respond in conciliatory ways.

If institutions are guilty of wrongdoing, then they are obliged to atone. However, the nonperpetrating members of those institutions are not guilty of wrongdoing, so why should we conclude that *they* are obliged to atone? There are at least three reasons. First of all, especially in a voluntary and highly organized group such as a religious order, to become a member is to accept an obligation to help the group fulfill its obligations. So, although nonperpetrating members are not themselves guilty of wrongdoing, they have incurred an obligation to respond to the institution's guilt.

Second, while the nonperpetrating members of the orders are not themselves guilty of the wrongs, they are morally burdened by the wrongs in a significant way that can create an obligation to respond. They have voluntarily chosen to share an identity with a group of people guilty of wrongdoing. As we have repeatedly noted, wrongs have expressive power. The injustices of the Magdalen asylums sent the message that the inmates were less valuable than other people and that this inferiority gave the nuns (as well as the state and the inmates' own families) a right to coerce, confine, and torment them. These messages are both insulting and threatening because they provide the victims reason to expect continued disrespect, disregard, and harm in the future. Institutional and religious groups are marked by shared values. Thus, victims and the broader moral community are left to wonder how deeply the values expressed in the wrongful actions are shared within the group, whether they continue to be shared by the older group members, and whether new members agree with them. By joining the wrongdoing group, the new member has become an object of reasonable suspicion. If she does not declare her condemnation of the past and her commitment to better values, she allows herself to be associated with that past. Simply to insist that others should take her moral trustworthiness for granted is to deny the reasonableness of the doubts held by the victims and the broader community. It is also to deny their interpretation of the history of the group as wrongful and threatening and their perception of her as a member of that same group. So in refusing to respond to the past in a way that encourages reconciliation, the nonperpetrator allows herself to be implicated in the continuing harms, insults, and threats of the past. The new group member is not guilty for past injustices.

Nonetheless, if she refuses to distance herself from it in an appropriate way, then she incurs guilt of her own.[60] She is guilty of callous disregard for the victims and the community, and she is guilty of acting disrespectfully toward them. She becomes complicit in their continued suffering, shame, fear, and anger. The nonperpetrating group member is obliged to atone because a failure to atone would incur new guilt.

A third reason for requiring current group members to repair historical injustices is that they are the only ones who can do so. They have an unequaled ability to alter the continued meaning of the past because they can incorporate a past injustice into a narrative of redemption. Doing so would not merely redress the wrongs of the past but would also lead to a better future. As Elizabeth Kiss argues, collective responsibility "requires that people who identify with a group be honest and accept that the moral and political future of their community depends on the actions its members take today to shape it."[61]

7.7   Conclusion

Approaching collective injustice with the resources of the reconciliation theory of atonement yields results that are acceptable and give us hope. Were the orders to respond in the ways I have recommended, the victims, the community, and the wrongdoing groups themselves would be better off in significant ways. Because doing so does not make guilty feelings, punishment, or degradation a requirement of atonement, we can ask groups to atone without mistreating those group members who are not individually responsible for wrongdoing. Because the reconciliation theory proceeds by matching atoning responses to the particular insults, threats, and harms created by the wrong in question, it need not insist on forms of atonement that are inappropriate or incoherent in collective cases. The compatibility of an ethic of atonement with the concept of collective responsibility, I believe, makes both moral ideas more plausible.

In chapter 1 I used the example of the Magdalen asylums to give weight to the concern that norms of atonement might be oppressive. I hope that, in applying the reconciliation theory of atonement to the real wrongdoers in this case, I have shown that an ethic of atonement, when properly conceived and applied, can play a positive, constructive role in our lives. We must guard against the misuse of norms of atonement. However, so long as our conception of atonement is grounded in ideals of moral autonomy, equal respect, and human dignity, we have reason for optimism.

The scandals that have rocked the Catholic Church since the 1990s have been horrifying in part because of the church's unwillingness to atone. Yet if the penitential regime inflicted on the Magdalen inmates is any true indication of the church's views on the nature of atonement, then it is little wonder that the church is reluctant to atone now that it finds itself in the role of the wrongdoer. I take this as further evidence that retributive and satisfaction theories of atonement are unacceptable. However, internal repentance and reconciliation with God (the approaches to atonement that, under a charitable interpretation, might be supposed to underlie the church's defensive rejections of public scrutiny, recrimination, and demands for reparations in the aftermath of the scandals) are not satisfactory approaches to atonement, either. A theory of atonement must address the social nature of wrongdoing. In other words, it must repair the relationships among victims, wrongdoers, and communities. Atonement requires moral reconciliation.

NOTES

Chapter 1

1. Herbert Morris, "Guilt and Suffering," in *On Guilt and Innocence* (Berkeley: University of California Press, 1976), 96.

2. Thomas Hardy, *The Mayor of Casterbridge* (New York: Penguin, 1994). I return to this example later in the chapter.

3. *The Virginian* (dir. Victor Fleming, 1929). "The Virginian does ... what he 'has to do,' and in avenging his friend's death wipes out the stain on his own honor," writes critic Robert Warshow. "Yet his victory cannot be complete: no death can be paid for and no stain truly wiped out; the movie is still a tragedy, for though the hero escapes with his life, he has been forced to confront the ultimate limits of his moral ideas.... This mature sense of limitation and unavoidable guilt is what gives the Westerner a 'right' to his melancholy" (Warshow, "The Westerner," in *The Western Reader*, ed. Jim Kitses and Gregg Rickman [New York: Limelight Editions, 1998], 40).

4. *Sex, Lies, and Videotape* (dir. Steven Soderbergh, 1989). Graham is engaged in a project to make amends for having mistreated his ex-wife, Elizabeth. While he was once a pathological liar who used to terrorize the people close to him, he has become a gentle person, obsessed with truth telling and suffering from a self-imposed impotence (though he pursues sexual satisfaction by videotaping women talking frankly about sex). He has moved back to the town where Elizabeth lives but has not yet contacted her. Ann, who has been mistreated and lied to by her own husband and so represents a kind of moral authority on the issue, asks Graham whether he plans to approach Elizabeth and show her who he has become. Her voice dripping with disdain, Ann asks whether he intends to present his new self to Elizabeth "like it's some gift or something." On the whole, Graham's ideas of atonement are portrayed as pathetic and self-destructive. "Why are you doing this to yourself?" Ann asks. The last scene of the movie, which we are meant to greet with approval, suggests that he has given up his obsession with atonement and his plan to contact Elizabeth. No longer living in the past, he has entered into a promising new relationship with Ann.

5. *My Name Is Earl* (produced by Greg Garcia, 2005–2008). Earl Hickey is a ne'er-do-well who wins the lottery, is promptly hit by a car, and loses the ticket in the mishap. Concluding that karma is out to get him because of all the bad things he has done in his life, he decides to make amends in hopes of finally finding happiness. In this television show, what is mistakenly labeled "karma" is a magical force that instantly rewards or punishes Earl for his deeds. As soon as he commits himself to making amends, the wind miraculously carries the lottery ticket back to him ("Pilot," original airdate September 20, 2005).

6. *Magnificent Obsession* (dir. Douglas Sirk, 1954).

7. This book focuses solely on wrongdoing committed by an agent or a group against another agent or group. This leaves out the category of wrongs that one commits against oneself (should that turn out to be a genuine type of wrongdoing), failures to fulfill imperfect duties (which are cases of wrongdoing in which no one can be identified as a victim), and wrongs committed against nonhumans. While the concept of making amends may yet apply in meaningful ways to these other categories, I cannot explore that possibility here. My thanks go to Dale Jamieson for requiring me to clarify this point.

8. *Oxford English Dictionary*, s.v. "amends."

9. Chen-Bo Zhong and Katie Liljenquist, "Washing Away Your Sins: Threatened Morality and Physical Cleansing," *Science* 313 (Sept. 8, 2006): 1451–52. The study was reported in Benedict Carey, "Lady Macbeth Not Alone in Her Quest for Spotlessness," *New York Times*, Sept. 12, 2006, http://www.nytimes.com/2006/09/12/health/psychology/12macbeth.html.

10. Zhong and Liljenquist, "Washing Away Your Sins," 1452.

11. *Oxford English Dictionary*, s.v. "atonement."

12. Ibid.

13. Ibid., s.v. "redemption."

14. Josiah Royce, "Atonement," in *The Problem of Christianity* (Chicago: University of Chicago Press, 1968), 165–86.

15. Richard Swinburne, *Responsibility and Atonement* (New York: Oxford University Press, 1989), 84–88.

16. Interestingly, both Judaism and Islam teach that atonement to God must be accompanied or preceded by atonement to any human victims. So, in the theological literature there is precedence for an interpersonal conception of atonement. Cf. Jacob Neusner, "Repentance in Judaism," in Etzioni and Carney, *Repentance: A Comparative Perspective*, 66; and Mahmoud Ayoub, "Repentance in the Islamic Tradition," in ibid., 102.

17. Michael Wyschogrod, "Sin and Atonement in Judaism," in *The Human Condition in the Jewish and Christian Traditions*, ed. Frederick E. Greenspahn (Hoboken, N.J.: Ktav, 1986), 121.

18. Ibid., 121–22.

19. Josiah Royce, "Time and Guilt," in Royce, *Problem of Christianity*, 161.

20. Wyschogrod, "Sin and Atonement in Judaism," 122.

21. Ibid.

22. Hermann Cohen, *Religion of Reason out of the Sources of Judaism*, 2d ed., trans. Simon Kaplan (Atlanta: Scholars Press, 1995). Summarizing Cohen's view, Martin Yaffe writes that "Ethics is limited to setting forth the ideal, quite apart from individual

failures as such. The problem of ethical failure, or of what biblical religion calls 'sin,' is the distinctive problem of religion and religious atonement" (Yaffe, "Liturgy and Ethics: Hermann Cohen and Franz Rosenzweig on the Day of Atonement," *Journal of Religious Ethics* 7, no. 2 [1979]: 217).

23. Wyschogrod, "Sin and Atonement in Judaism," 122.

24. Ibid., 124.

25. Immanuel Kant, *Grounding of the Metaphysics of Morals*, 3d ed., trans. James W. Ellington (Indianapolis: Hackett, 1993), chap. 3.

26. Interestingly, Kant argues that atonement is possible only through God, but his reasons differ considerably from Wyschogrod's. I address Kant's view in chapter 3, section 3.2.

27. Jeffrie Murphy reports that his own newly mixed, though not fully negative, feelings about retribution are based on such grounds. See his *Getting Even: Forgiveness and Its Limits* (New York: Oxford University Press, 2003), 88–89.

28. Jacob Adler, *The Urgings of Conscience* (Philadelphia: Temple University Press, 1992), 14.

29. Ibid., 23.

30. Jon Elster, "Redemption for Wrongdoing: The Fate of Collaborators after 1945," *Journal of Conflict Resolution* 50, no. 3 (2006): 324–38.

31. Actions that did not involve significant personal risk strike Elster as especially irrelevant. For example, a number of French bankers decided at the eleventh hour simply to transfer large sums of money to the Resistance (ibid., 327n8).

32. Ibid., 336.

33. Ibid.

34. Ibid.

35. In the nineteenth century, Catholic and Protestant groups also established Magdalen asylums in England, Scotland, continental Europe, and the United States. However, the following discussion, like most of the available literature on the topic, focuses on Ireland and the asylums run by the Catholic Church.

36. Although the Irish asylums stopped taking new inmates in the 1970s, some of these women remained in residence until as late as 1996 (Frances Finnegan, *Do Penance or Perish: Magdalen Asylums in Ireland* [New York: Oxford University Press, 2004], ix; Gary Culliton, "Last Days of a Laundry," *Irish Times*, Sept. 25, 1996, 15).

37. Finnegan, *Do Penance or Perish*, 18, 24, 31–35. See also the documentary film *Sex in a Cold Climate* (dir. Steve Humphries, 1998) and James M. Smith, *Ireland's Magdalen Laundries and the Nation's Architecture of Containment* (Notre Dame, Ind.: University of Notre Dame Press, 2007).

38. Finnegan, *Do Penance or Perish*, 16. On the financial importance of the laundry see also Joanne Monk, "Cleansing Their Souls: Laundries in Institutions for Fallen Women," *Lillith* 9 (1996): 22.

39. Finnegan, *Do Penance or Perish*, 47–49.

40. Ibid., 17; *Sex in a Cold Climate*. Linda Mahood, writing about the Magdalen asylums of nineteenth-century Scotland, argues that " 'prostitute' was a label or censure, encompassing a constellation of women's behaviour which moral reformers found objectionable or threatening" and was apt to be extended not just to unwed mothers but also to "any woman found in the streets who could not give a satisfactory account of

how she earned her living" (Mahood, *The Magdalenes: Prostitution in the Nineteenth Century* [New York: Routledge, 1990], 68, 70).

41. Finnegan, *Do Penance or Perish*, 38–40; *Sex in a Cold Climate*; Smith, *Ireland's Magdalen Laundries*, 20.

42. Finnegan, *Do Penance or Perish*, 17.

43. Ibid., 73, 153, 236.

44. Ibid., 45, 73, 153, 236.

45. Ibid., 6–19. For similar statistics in Scotland see Mahood, *Magdalenes*, 95, 99.

46. Finnegan, *Do Penance or Perish*, 44–45. According to Smith, "With no official sentence, and thus no mandated release, some of these women lived and died behind the Magdalen's walls. In the vast majority of the cases there was no judge and no jury" (*Ireland's Magdalen Laundries*, 136).

47. *Sex in a Cold Climate*.

48. Finnegan, *Do Penance or Perish*, 44–45. In some places, penitents' heads were shaved "in order to suppress the desire to get out" (Mahood, *Magdalenes*, 80). See also Finnegan, *Do Penance or Perish*, 26.

49. According to Finnegan's study, inmates employed violence, foul language, and refusals to work in order to have themselves expelled. Some members of the hardened prostitute class became quite skilled at entering and leaving Magdalen asylums at will. Those inmates who harbored a desire to remain "good girls" were more vulnerable to the system.

50. Finnegan, *Do Penance or Perish*, 28. Because penitents were sometimes assigned new names (Finnegan, 26) and moved among institutions that kept poor records, we have reason to wonder whether families were able to find their daughters, sisters, and cousins when they went looking for them.

51. According to Finnegan's study only 5 percent of the penitents left the asylum for "a situation" (ibid., 74, 154, 237).

52. Ibid., 35–36, 170; *Sex in a Cold Climate*.

53. The figure of thirty thousand is given in *Sex in a Cold Climate*. Practices of confinement did not end until the 1970s, and the last Magdalen laundry in Ireland closed in 1996. See Maggie O'Kane, "Washing Away Their Sins," *Guardian* (Oct. 30, 1996), 2; and Elizabeth Butler Cullingford, "'Our Nuns Are *Not* a Nation': Politicizing the Convent in Irish Literature and Film," *Éire-Ireland* 41, no. 1–2 (2006): 12.

54. Sarah Hamilton, *The Practice of Penance, 900–1050* (Rochester, N.Y.: Royal Historical Society/Boydell Press, 2001), 1–2.

55. Finnegan, *Do Penance or Perish*, 243–44.

56. Elster, "Redemption for Wrongdoing," 331–33.

57. Ibid., 331.

58. R. Scott Appleby, "How the Church Has Learned to Say, 'I'm Sorry,'" *U.S. Catholic* 64, no. 3 (1999): 40.

59. Ibid.

60. Finnegan, *Do Penance or Perish*, 19.

61. Ibid., 41.

62. John Cottingham points out that the standard practice of sentencing second-time offenders to harsher sentences also conflicts with the claim that undergoing criminal punishment "settles accounts" or "wipes the slate clean." See his "Varieties of Retribution," *Philosophical Quarterly* 29 (1979): 244–45.

63. Joanne Carlson Brown and Rebecca Parker, "For God So Loved the World?" in *Christianity, Patriarchy, and Abuse: A Feminist Critique*, ed. Joanne Carlson Brown and Carole R. Bohn (New York: Pilgrim, 1989), 1–30.

64. But see Ariel Glucklich, *Sacred Pain: Hurting the Body for the Sake of the Soul* (New York: Oxford University Press, 2001).

65. Royce, "Time and Guilt," 162.

66. Unfortunately, such actions did not save Stanley "Tookie" Williams from execution. Williams was one of the founders of the Crips street gang. Convicted of four murders, he spent his time on death row working to discourage youths from violence and was nominated for a Nobel Peace Prize for his work. The adequacy and relevance of his atonement became a matter of heated debate. See, for example, Jenifer Warren and Maura Dolan, "Tookie Williams Is Executed," *Los Angeles Times*, Dec. 13, 2005, http://www.latimes.com/news/local/la-me-execution13dec13,0,799154. story?coll=la-home-headlines.

Chapter 2

1. John Cottingham shows how retributive and restitutive concepts are often blended in "Varieties of Retribution," *Philosophical Quarterly* 29 (1979): 238–46.

2. Anselm of Canterbury, "Why God Became Man," in *Anselm of Canterbury: The Major Works*, ed. Brian Davies and G. R. Evans (New York: Oxford University Press, 1998), 260–356. Other labels given to the view are "objective theory," "Latin theory," or simply "the Anselmian doctrine."

3. Ibid., 283.

4. Ibid.

5. Ibid., 303.

6. Gustaf Aulén, *Christus Victor: An Historical Study of the Three Main Types of the Idea of Atonement*, trans. A. G. Herbert (Eugene, Ore.: Wipf and Stock, 2003), 81–82.

7. Anselm, "Why God Became Man," 287. Swinburne also defends retribution as a form of restitution. In response to the objection that "there doesn't seem to be any natural good in hurt being attached to wrongdoing" (Richard Swinburne, *Responsibility and Atonement* [New York: Oxford University Press, 1989], 95), he responds, "A debt is a debt; and even if the creditor cannot use the only things the debtor has, such as his liberty and freedom from pain, he still has the right to take them" (Swinburne, 97). See also his discussion of criminal punishment (Swinburne, 93–109).

8. Anselm, "Why God Became Man," 282, 303. Philip Quinn emphasizes the role of honor in his reading of Anselm. See Quinn's "Christian Atonement and Kantian Justification," *Faith and Philosophy* 3 (1986): 440–62. On the importance of joining faith and repentance with satisfaction see also Eleonore Stump, "Atonement according to Aquinas," in *Philosophy and the Christian Faith*, ed. Thomas V. Morris, University of Notre Dame Studies in the Philosophy of Religion, no. 5 (Notre Dame, Ind.: University of Notre Dame Press, 1988), 71–73. In this article Stump distances Aquinas's version of satisfaction theory from Anselm's in various respects.

9. Aulén, *Christus Victor*, 86; Anselm, "Why God Became Man," 300–9.

10. The relevance of theories of this sort to a theory of interpersonal atonement is considered in chapter 3.

11. Anselm, "Why God Became Man," 284–86.

12. Aulén, *Christus Victor*, 89.

13. Ibid., 82.

14. Ibid.

15. There are many interesting debates about the details of satisfaction theory, but I cannot enter into them here. For example, theorists differ over how much merit Jesus provides to the sinner and whether it is enough to completely cover the sinner's debt or just that part attributable to original sin. In the latter case, it appears that sinners must contribute their own suffering or good works as well.

16. Aulén, *Christus Victor*, 128.

17. Timothy Gorringe, *God's Just Vengeance: Crime, Violence, and the Rhetoric of Salvation* (New York: Cambridge University Press, 1996), 107. Gorringe offers a fascinating exploration of the historical connections between religious theories of atonement and the development of the British penal system.

18. In *Reconciliatio et Pœnitentia*, John Paul II defines satisfaction in terms of suffering, characterizing it as "a joining of one's own *physical and spiritual mortification* to the passion of Jesus" (emphasis added; quoted in William H. Woestman, *Sacraments: Initiation, Penance, Anointing of the Sick: Commentary on Canons 840–1007*, 2d ed. [Ottawa: Faculty of Canon Law, Saint Paul University, 1996], 223).

19. In at least some versions of satisfaction theory, not only Jesus but also saints and even ordinary humans can transfer their merit to others. The pope of the Roman Catholic Church is believed to administer a "treasury of merit" that has been built up by Jesus and the saints, which he can distribute to the faithful (Woestman, *Sacraments*, 300–20). Catholic women sometimes offer up their labor pains for the benefit of souls in purgatory (Pamela E. Klassen, *Blessed Events: Religion and Home Birth in America* [Princeton, N.J.: Princeton University Press, 2001], 191).

20. John Hick, "Is the Doctrine of Atonement a Mistake?" in *Reason and the Christian Religion: Essays in Honor of Richard Swinburne*, ed. Alan G. Padgett (Oxford, UK: Clarendon, 1994), 253.

21. Quoted in Gorringe, *God's Just Vengeance*, 109.

22. Might God value Jesus's suffering merely as an instrumental rather than an intrinsic good, say as a deterrent or a means to the education of humanity? Such theories of the Atonement, as well as their implications for a theory of interpersonal atonement, are discussed in chapter 3. See also Aulén, *Christus Victor*, 133–42, and Hick, "Is the Doctrine of the Atonement a Mistake?" Satisfaction theorists generally reject such claims on the grounds that they do not adequately defend either the significance or the necessity of Jesus's death, given that the same goals could have been achieved through less drastic measures. Satisfaction theorists reject the idea that Jesus is merely a powerful example or a messenger who changes the hearts of sinners, insisting instead that his death secured an objective change in the relationship between humanity and God. See Aulén, *Christus Victor*, 1–7.

23. John W. Marshall made this point to me in conversation.

24. The Magdalen asylums run by the Roman Catholic Church are believed to have been more brutal than the Protestant-run homes (James M. Smith, *Ireland's Magdalen Laundries and the Nation's Architecture of Containment* [Notre Dame, Ind.: University of Notre Dame Press, 2007]; Frances Finnegan, *Do Penance or Perish: Magdalen Asylums in Ireland* [New York: Oxford University Press, 2004]). However, today the Roman Catholic Church places more emphasis on confession and contrition than on penance.

25. Joanne Carlson Brown and Rebecca Parker criticize the social influence of satisfaction theories of atonement in "For God So Loved the World?" in *Christianity, Patriarchy, and Abuse: A Feminist Critique*, ed. Joanne Carlson Brown and Carole R. Bohn (New York: Pilgrim, 1989), 1–30.

26. For a notable exception see Jacob Adler, *The Urgings of Conscience* (Philadelphia: Temple University Press, 1992).

27. Cottingham writes, "There could not be an atonement theory of punishment; atonement is something voluntarily undertaken, punishment something exacted" ("Varieties of Retribution," 238).

28. Cf. Herbert Morris, "Guilt and Suffering," in *On Guilt and Innocence* (Berkeley: University of California Press, 1976), 107.

29. Stanley I. Benn, "Punishment," in *The Encyclopedia of Philosophy*, ed. Paul Edwards (New York: Macmillan, 1967), 29.

30. Ibid.

31. John L. Mackie, "Morality and the Retributive Emotions," in *Persons and Values*, ed. Joan Mackie and Penelope Mackie (Oxford, UK: Clarendon, 1985), 206–19.

32. Michael S. Moore, "The Moral Worth of Retribution," in *Responsibility, Character, and the Moral Emotions: New Essays in Moral Psychology*, ed. Ferdinand Schoeman (New York: Cambridge University Press, 1987), 179–219. Another theorist who starts with notions of atonement is R. A. Duff, who moves from the judgment that penance is justified to a defense of criminal punishment as inspiring repentance. See Duff, *Trials and Punishments* (New York: Cambridge University Press, 1986). Duff's defense of self-punishment combines an expressionist version of retributivism (see section 2.3.5) with an ideal of repentance.

33. Jeffrie G. Murphy agrees: "There is, of course, an obvious connection between repentance and suffering. Repentant people feel *guilty*, and a part of feeling guilty is a sense that one ought to suffer punishment" (Murphy, *Getting Even: Forgiveness and Its Limits* [New York: Oxford University Press, 2003], 46).

34. Moore, "Moral Worth of Retribution," 212.

35. Ibid., 213.

36. For example, Joel Feinberg maintains that "a person's desert of X is always a reason for giving X to him, but not always a conclusive reason" and that "considerations irrelevant to his desert can have an overriding cogency in establishing how he ought to be treated on balance" (Feinberg, "Justice and Personal Desert," in Joel Feinberg, *Doing and Deserving: Essays in the Theory of Responsibility* [Princeton, N.J.: Princeton University Press, 1970], 60).

37. Moore, "Moral Worth of Retribution," 214.

38. For the moment I ignore the differences among guilt, regret, remorse, and shame since they do not affect the overall argument. I then return to them in chapters 3 and 4.

39. One might hope, with Duff, that punishment will inspire a change of attitudes. Nonetheless, Moore's position, unlike Duff's, does not appeal to such a forward-looking goal in order to defend punishment.

40. Jeffrie G. Murphy, "Forgiveness and Resentment," in *Forgiveness and Mercy*, ed. Jeffrie G. Murphy and Jean Hampton (New York: Cambridge University Press, 1988), 18. According to Royce, commitment to a norm is wrapped up in the very meaning of

one's life. "When a man becomes conscious of his own rule of life, of his own ideal of what makes his voluntary life worth while, he tends to arrange his ideas of right and wrong acts so that, for him at least, *some* acts ... appear to him to be acts such that they would involve for him a kind of moral suicide,—a deliberate wrecking of what makes life, for himself, morally worth while" (Josiah Royce, "Time and Guilt," in Josiah Royce, *The Problem of Christianity* [Chicago: University of Chicago Press, 1968], 154). Violating such ideals surely entails emotional consequences, although Royce refrains from naming them. "What the pungency of the odors, what the remorseful griefs, of the hell of the irrevocable may be, for a given individual, we need not attempt to determine" (Royce, "Time and Guilt," 163).

41. Rüdiger Bittner's claim that one can be committed to morality but not suffer over one's violation of it suggests an overly intellectualist understanding of commitment. See also Bittner's assertion that one can love another person romantically without being hurt by the lover's rejection ("Is It Reasonable to Regret Things One Did?" *Journal of Philosophy* 89, no. 5 [1992]: 272–73). Agreeing that certain actions are moral and others are immoral is not the same thing as being committed to morality, just as agreeing that a certain person is charming and attractive is not the same thing as being in love.

42. P. F. Strawson, "Freedom and Resentment," *Proceedings of the British Academy* 48 (1962): 187–211.

43. Morris addresses the link between caring and the vulnerability to suffering in "Guilt and Suffering."

44. Similarly, one can endorse the emotion of grief without taking a retributive stance to the grieving. We find something criticizable about a person who does not grieve over the death of her father not because we think that she deserves to suffer but because we suspect that she lacks attitudes toward her father that she ought to have.

45. Sigmund Freud, *Civilization and Its Discontents*, in *The Standard Edition of the Complete Psychological Works of Sigmund Freud*, vol. 21, trans. and ed. James Strachey and Anna Freud (London: Hogarth Press and the Institute of Psycho-Analysis, 1961), 64–145; Friedrich Nietzsche, *On the Genealogy of Morals*, trans. Walter Kaufmann and R. J. Hollingdale (New York: Vintage, 1967).

46. Moore's theory of punishment falls in this category. Just as guilt is justified by the fact of wrongdoing, so is resentment, he argues.

47. In the case of criminal punishment, I doubt whether the argument can establish even the *permissibility* of expressing resentment and indignation through punishment. In our moral lives as a whole, cases in which it is legitimate for a victim to express resentment (let alone for a third party to express indignation) in aggressive action are surely the exception rather than the rule. We usually react to one another's wrongdoings through social distancing or verbal expressions of our disapproval. My neighbor can earn my resentment in all sorts of ways, but it would be a rare situation indeed where my kicking her in the shins would be justified (or even excused). Aggression against another person must be grounded in something more than justified resentment in order to be permissible.

48. Immanuel Kant, *The Metaphysics of Morals*, trans. and ed. Mary Gregor (New York: Cambridge University Press, 1996), 104–9 (6: 331–37). Interestingly, Thomas E. Hill Jr. argues against the traditional interpretation of Kant as a pure retributivist in "Kant on Wrongdoing, Desert, and Punishment," *Law and Philosophy* 18 (1999): 407–41.

49. Kant, *Metaphysics of Morals*, 105–6 (6: 332).

50. "In [the criminal's] act, the act of a rational being, is involved a universal element, which by the act is set up as a law. This law he has recognized in his act, and has consented to be placed under it as under his right" (G. W. F. Hegel, *Philosophy of Right*, trans. S. W. Dyde [Amherst, N.Y.: Prometheus, 1996], 97, para. 100).

51. Immanuel Kant, *Religion within the Limits of Reason Alone*, trans. T. M. Greene and H. H. Hudson (New York: Harper and Row, 1960), 50–72. I discuss Kant's view of repentance in chapter 3.

52. Because it is a public act, criminal punishment offers victims a chance to experience some kind of satisfaction in seeing the wrongdoer punished. However, a self-punishing act will not necessarily become known to the victim.

53. Feinberg, "The Expressive Function of Punishment," in Feinberg, *Doing and Deserving*, 96.

54. Ibid., 101–5.

55. Ibid., 98.

56. Jean Hampton, "The Retributive Idea," in Murphy and Hampton, *Forgiveness and Mercy*, 141.

57. Jean Hampton, "Correcting Harms versus Righting Wrongs: The Goal of Retribution," *UCLA Law Review* 39 (1992): 1691–92; Feinberg, "Expressive Function of Punishment," 103–4. Feinberg also attributes this idea to Kant.

58. Feinberg, "Expressive Function of Punishment," 100.

59. Ibid., 116.

60. Ibid.

61. See Jean Hampton, "Forgiveness, Resentment, and Hatred" and "The Retributive Idea," both in Murphy and Hampton, *Forgiveness and Mercy*; "A New Theory of Retribution," in *Liability and Responsibility: Essays in Law and Morals*, ed. R. G. Frey and Christopher W. Morris (New York: Cambridge University Press, 1991), 377–414; "An Expressive Theory of Retribution," in *Retributivism and Its Critics*, ed. Wesley Cragg (Stuttgart: Franz Steiner, 1992), 1–25; and "Correcting Harms versus Righting Wrongs," *UCLA Law Review* 39 (1992): 1659–1702. By the end of this series of papers, Hampton has backed away from the claim that only punishment can correct wrongdoing. Instead, she makes the paradoxical claim that "retribution includes all sorts of responses to human beings, only some of which are punitive" ("Correcting Harms versus Righting Wrongs," 1685).

62. Hampton, "Forgiveness, Resentment, and Hatred," 52; "Correcting Harms versus Righting Wrongs," 1661–66.

63. Hampton, "Correcting Harms versus Righting Wrongs," 1672. One might object that wrongdoing is just as frequently a result of the wrongdoer's feelings of inferiority and self-hatred, as opposed to a feeling of superiority. But this objection misrepresents Hampton's claim. She finds an assertion of superiority in the semantic content of the action, not in the offender's mental state.

64. Hampton, "New Theory of Retribution," 401–2.

65. Ibid., 402.

66. Ibid.

67. Hampton, "Expressive Theory of Retribution," 13.

68. Hampton, "Retributive Idea," 134.

69. Ibid.

70. Heather J. Gert, Linda Radzik, and Michael Hand, "Hampton on the Expressive Power of Punishment," *Journal of Social Philosophy* 35 (2004): 79–90.

71. Daniel E. Farnham, "A Hegelian Theory of Retribution." *Journal of Social Philosophy,* forthcoming.

72. Ibid., manuscript p. 6.

73. Ibid., manuscript p. 12.

74. Hampton, "Retributive Idea," 142.

75. Criminologist John Braithwaite comments: "Liberal retributivists like to say that punishment is more dignified than rehabilitation. This view has long been disparaged by those who question how dignified it can be to have one's head shaved, [be] put in prison fatigues, [be] subjected to rectal searches for drugs, live in daily fear of bashings and rape and countless more subtle humiliations. Actual punishment practices seem more plausibly described in terms of communal lusts for afflicting indignity on the evil" ("Repentance Rituals and Restorative Justice," *Journal of Political Philosophy* 8, no. 1 [2000]: 116).

76. Failures to condemn might be excused or justified, of course. For example, victims might be either too damaged to express condemnation, or they might have other legitimate concerns or goals that outweigh the importance of condemnation in a particular case.

77. See, for example, Roger Wertheimer's characterization of condemnation in "Constraining Condemning," *Ethics* 108 (1998): 489–501. Duff claims that moral blame is retributive because it is painful and nonconsequentially justified (*Trials and Punishments*, chap. 2).

78. *Oxford English Dictionary*, s.v. "condemn."

79. Brown and Parker, "For God So Loved the World?" 19. Morris writes that "guilt is the price we pay for something in human life we are unprepared to sacrifice, a concerned involvement with others" ("Guilt and Suffering," 92).

80. Daniel Van Ness and Karen Strong review the ancient roots of justice schemes based on restitution in "Restitution to Rehabilitation: How and Why Victims Were Removed from the Criminal Justice Process," *Crime Victims Report* 4, no. 6 (January/February 2001): 81, 92–93.

81. Cottingham points out that 'retribution' comes from "*re+tribuo*, Latin, *to pay back*" ("Varieties of Retribution," 238).

82. Randy E. Barnett, "Restitution: A New Paradigm of Criminal Justice," *Ethics* 87, no. 4 (1977): 279–301; David B. Hershenov, "Restitution and Revenge," *Journal of Philosophy* 96, no. 2 (1999): 79–94; Margaret R. Holmgren, "Punishment as Restitution: The Rights of the Community," *Criminal Justice Ethics* 2 (1983): 36–49; and Joseph Ellin, "Restitutionism Defended," *Journal of Value Inquiry* 34 (2000): 299–317.

83. I adapt these terms from Barnett's discussion of restitutive theories of criminal justice ("Restitution," 288).

84. Ibid., 288–89.

85. In his defense of pure restitution in criminal law, Barnett allows for third-party repayment. Whether this third party then demands reimbursement from the wrongdoer or mercifully forgives the debt is morally up to that party (ibid., 291).

86. Cf. Gerry Johnstone, *Restorative Justice: Ideas, Values, Debates* (Portland, Ore.: Willan, 2002), 26–27. Barnett's lack of interest in the state of mind of the one who caused the harm is evident in both his suggestion that insanity defenses would be rejected

under his restitution-based theory of criminal justice and his claim that the crime/tort distinction would disappear. See Barnett, "Restitution," 299–300.

87. Barnett responds to the objection as follows: "The response is that we cannot have it both ways. If the fines would be high enough to bother the rich, then they would be so high that a project worker would have no chance of earning that much and would, therefore, have no incentive to work at all" (Barnett, "Restitution," 298). He rejects the idea of a sliding scale of penalties based on the wrongdoer's ability to pay as a reversion to retributivist ideas that wrongdoers should suffer. Instead, *"Equality of justice means equal treatment of victims,"* so there is no reason the victim of a wealthier person should receive higher restitution than the victim of a poorer person (Barnett, 298).

88. Both Holmgren ("Punishment as Restitution") and Hershenov ("Restitution and Revenge") talk about the loss of a sense of security as a kind of harm that must be compensated.

89. Barnett, "Restitution," 292.

90. Ibid., 295.

91. I do not intend this critique of restitution-based theories of atonement to undermine restitution in the law generally. While many of the critiques I offer here are also appropriate critiques of restitution as a basis of criminal law, restitution has a more secure place in tort law. In civil lawsuits, victims can only demand something of their abusers that the state can also compel. Monetary compensation can be compelled, but remorse or moral improvement cannot. Furthermore, if victims are willing to accept monetary compensation as restitution for their pain and suffering, however incommensurable those things may be, this decision is probably best left up to them.

92. Hershenov states that "The vindictive pleasures accompanying legal punishment can either increase the value of any other form of payment received, or, where the criminal is destitute, can actually take the place of receiving financial compensation" ("Restitution and Revenge," 80).

93. Herbert Morris, "Persons and Punishment," *Monist* 52 (1968): 475–501. Morris's theory is frequently categorized as retributivist rather than restitutive.

94. Interestingly, Morris does not convert his theory of punishment into a theory of atonement. In "Guilt and Suffering" he says that self-punishment is not necessary for a satisfactory response to guilt. Self-punishment can contribute to atonement for moral wrongdoing but Morris does not describe it as the relinquishment an unfair advantage. Instead, the value of self-punishment lies in its ability to communicate to the victim "how deeply hurt one has been by the damage [one created] and how deeply committed one is to the relationship" ("Guilt and Suffering," 106). In his account of atonement, Morris places the restoration of relationships—not compensation and not retribution—in the key role.

95. Mackie, "Morality and the Retributive Emotions," 211.

96. Hampton, "Retributive Idea," 115.

Chapter 3

1. Jeffrie Murphy combines the characteristic judgments and phenomenology in defining repentance as "the remorseful acceptance of responsibility for one's wrongful and harmful actions, the repudiation of the aspects of one's character that generated the

actions, the resolve to do one's best to extirpate those aspects of one's character, and the resolve to atone or make amends for the harm that one has done" (*Getting Even: Forgiveness and Its Limits* [New York: Oxford University Press, 2003], 41).

2. Such disagreements come to the fore in the symposia included with the two English editions of Simon Wiesenthal's memoir: *The Sunflower* (New York: Schocken Books, 1976) and *The Sunflower: On the Possibilities and Limits of Forgiveness*, rev. and exp. ed. Ed. Harry James Cargas and Bonny V. Fetterman (New York: Schocken, 1998).

3. Immanuel Kant, *Religion within the Limits of Reason Alone*, trans. T. M. Greene and H. H. Hudson (New York: Harper and Row, 1960), book II, section 1, p. 66; emphasis in original.

4. Ibid.

5. See John R. Silber's introductory essay, "The Ethical Significance of Kant's *Religion*," in ibid., cxxxii.

6. Kant, *Religion*, 67.

7. Silber, "Ethical Significance of Kant's *Religion*," cxxxii.

8. Kant, *Religion*, 65n.

9. Ibid.

10. Ibid., 63n.

11. Ibid., 64n.

12. Ibid.

13. Ibid., 70.

14. Ibid. Silber argues that this move does not sit well with the rest of Kant's views on justice. "Why should God or any righteous judge decide to qualify the requirements of the moral law or fail to hold the absolutely free being responsible for his exercise of freedom? Kant himself knew, I think, that he was in trouble" (Silber, "Ethical Significance of Kant's *Religion*," cxxxii). On this point see also Philip Quinn, "Christian Atonement and Kantian Justification," *Faith and Philosophy* 3 (1986): 440–62.

15. Alister E. McGrath, "The Moral Theory of the Atonement: An Historical and Theological Critique," *Scottish Journal of Theology* 38, no. 2 (1985): 213.

16. Kant, *Religion*, 68; second emphasis added.

17. An interesting issue (one that I cannot properly pursue here) arises with regard to the continuing role of punishment in Kant's account of atonement. He insists that some "satisfaction" must yet be made to God for past sins and that this satisfaction rightly takes the form of punishment. Kant finds the required element of pain in the transition that is made from the old self to the new self. This is apparently the pain of the emotion of repentance. However, he seems to say that the pain of repentance is something felt by the new person because of the sins of the old person. Yet this violates the very idea that motivates Kant's theory of atonement: that the punishment of one person cannot discharge the debt of another. See ibid., 67–68; Richard Swinburne, *Responsibility and Atonement* (New York: Oxford University Press, 1989), 89–90n; and Quinn, "Christian Atonement and Kantian Justification," 451–52.

18. Even these cases are complex, though. We might want to continue to regard the brain-injured person as morally continuous with the preaccident person in at least some ways. For instance, we approve of the retention of property rights, so that wealth and insurance policies held by the preaccident person may rightfully pay the bills of the severely injured person. However, we would disapprove of punishing the new person for

the wrongs of the old. Perhaps the new person should be seen as the heir of the old one, inheriting that person's money but not his guilt.

19. For Kant in *Religion*, it is not one's actions that are morally judged but one's entire moral disposition, "something supersensible" that "can only be thought of as an absolute unity" (Kant, *Religion*, 64n). This creates a problem, however, with regard to what we are to say about wrongful individual acts that do not reflect one's true disposition but are instead done "out of character" and about the victims who are harmed by those acts.

20. Meir Dan-Cohen, "Revising the Past: On the Metaphysics of Repentance, Forgiveness, and Pardon," in *Forgiveness, Mercy, and Clemency*, ed. Austin Sarat and Nasser Hussain (Stanford, Calif.: Stanford University Press, 2007), 117–37.

21. Ibid., 121–22.

22. Ibid., 122–23.

23. Josiah Royce, "Time and Guilt," in Josiah Royce, *The Problem of Christianity* (Chicago: University of Chicago Press, 1968), 160.

24. Josiah Royce, "Atonement," in Royce, *The Problem of Christianity*, 180–81.

25. Ibid., 180.

26. John E. Hare holds a similar view: "If the victim prefers the state of the world with my offence and my subsequent response to the state of the world with neither, then I have undone what I have done in the relevant sense" (*The Moral Gap: Kantian Ethics, Human Limits, and God's Assistance* [New York: Oxford University Press, 1996], 232).

27. Royce, "Atonement," 169.

28. Max Scheler, "Repentance and Rebirth," in *On the Eternal in Man*, trans. Bernard Noble (New York: Harper and Brothers, 1960), 39.

29. Ibid., 39–40.

30. Ibid., 40.

31. A similar view of repentance as changing the interpretation of the past is presented in Aryeh Botwinick, "In Defense of Teshuvah: A Modern Approach to an Ancient Concept," *Judaism* 26, no. 4 (1977): 475–80.

32. Scheler, "Repentance and Rebirth," 40–41.

33. Ibid., 42.

34. Ibid. Hermann Cohen, too, connects repentance with freedom: "Now, too, for the first time it becomes clear of what this new heart and this new spirit can and should consist: of the turning away from the previous way of life, and of the capacity to enter upon a new way of life. Only now does the man become the master of himself; no longer is he subject to fate. It was fate that would not allow man to abandon the way of sin. Man becomes free from this fate through the teaching that sin does not become a permanent offense for man, a permanent reason for stumbling" (*Religion of Reason out of the Sources of Judaism*, 2d ed., trans. Simon Kaplan [Atlanta: Scholars Press, 1995], 194).

35. Scheler, "Repentance and Rebirth," 54.

36. Ibid., 61.

37. Pamela Hieronymi argues that the meaning of the past is socially constructed and that this fact prevents wrongdoers from changing the meaning of the past through their own actions. See "Articulating an Uncompromising Forgiveness," *Philosophy and Phenomenological Research* 62, no. 3 (2001): 550. I examine Hieronymi's arguments on this point in chapter 5.

38. Scheler, "Repentance and Rebirth," 52.

39. *Unforgiven* (dir. Clint Eastwood, 1992).

40. Herbert Morris, "Guilt and Suffering," in *On Guilt and Innocence* (Berkeley: University of California Press, 1976), 108.

41. Cheshire Calhoun, "An Apology for Moral Shame," *Journal of Political Philosophy* 12, no. 2 (2004): 127–46; Gabriele Taylor, *Pride, Shame, and Guilt: Emotions of Self-Assessment* (New York: Oxford University Press, 1985), 53–84.

42. Lucien Jerphagnon, "Repentance," *Philosophy Today* 3 (1959): 176–82.

43. Rüdiger Bittner raises this objection in response to guilt and regret, but it seems equally appropriate to repentance ("Is It Reasonable to Regret Things One Did?" *Journal of Philosophy* 89, no. 5 [1992]: 262–73).

44. The last example is taken from Ian McEwan's novel *Atonement* (New York: Talese/Doubleday, 2001). After falsely accusing her sister's boyfriend of rape, the narrator writes an account of the events as a literary form of atonement.

45. In Judaism, believers are told that repentance will be met with God's forgiveness. But they are also told that, for sins committed against both human victims and God, they must approach their victims in an atoning fashion before approaching God. This interpersonal atonement is usually described in terms that emphasize reparation, as well as repentance. For example, in the days leading up to Yom Kippur, the Day of Atonement, people are directed to approach those whom they may have offended with apologies and, where necessary, offers of restitution. Only then can they ask God for forgiveness. See, for example, Jacob Neusner, "Repentance in Judaism," in Etzioni and Carney, *Repentance: A Comparative Perspective*, 60–75. Islam too combines repentance with other elements, including restitution for offenses against others, public confession for public wrongdoing, and punishment. See Mahmoud Ayoub, "Repentance in the Islamic Tradition," in Etzioni and Carney, *Repentance: A Comparative Perspective*, 96–121; and Fazlur Rahman, *Major Themes of the Qur'an* (Minneapolis: Bibliotheca Islamica, 1980).

46. The "subjective theory" and the "moral theory of the Atonement" are other common labels for this view. Abelard's critique of Anselm is often cited as the *locus classicus* and is discussed by Gustaf Aulén, *Christus Victor: An Historical Study of the Three Main Types of the Idea of Atonement*, trans. A. G. Herbert (Eugene, Ore.: Wipf and Stock, 2003), 95–98. On the development of this view during the Enlightenment period see Aulén, *Christus Victor*, 133–42. See also Auguste Sabatier, *The Doctrine of the Atonement and Its Historical Evolution* (London: Williams and Norgate, 1904), and, as a good introduction for the uninitiated, see John Hick, "Is the Doctrine of Atonement a Mistake?" in *Reason and the Christian Religion: Essays in Honor of Richard Swinburne*, ed. Alan G. Padgett (Oxford, UK: Clarendon, 1994), 247–63.

47. Hick, "Is the Doctrine of Atonement a Mistake?" 256.

48. J. R. Lucas sums up the major objection to this kind of account of the Atonement of Christ as follows: "It is held to be too subjective, and not to register the objective difference that the crucifixion effected.... If I do something for real, it may indeed be a good example to others, but if I do it only to set an example, I am just play-acting" ("Reflections on the Atonement," in Padgett, *Reason and the Christian Religion*, 268).

49. Aulén, *Christus Victor*, 95–98, 133–42.

50. Hick, "Is the Doctrine of Atonement a Mistake?" 252–53.

51. In Judaism and Islam, too, redemption is not earned but granted by a merciful God. Cf. Neusner, "Repentance in Judaism"; and Ayoub, "Repentance in the Islamic Tradition."

52. Anselm of Canterbury, "Why God Became Man," in *Anselm of Canterbury: The Major Works*, ed. Brian Davies and G. R. Evans (New York: Oxford University Press, 1998), 284–86; Aulén, *Christus Victor*, 89.

53. See Oscar D. Watkins, *A History of Penance* (New York: Burt Franklin, 1961).

54. The exception is the consequentialist reading of the transformation of the past action, which, as we saw, in concentrating on the general good, places too little emphasis on the wrongdoer.

Chapter 4

1. Jeffrie G. Murphy, "Forgiveness and Resentment," in Murphy and Hampton, *Forgiveness and Mercy*, 14–34; and Jean Hampton, "Forgiveness, Resentment, and Hatred," in Murphy and Hampton, *Forgiveness and Mercy*, 35–87.

2. Murphy, "Forgiveness and Resentment," 25.

3. Hampton, "Forgiveness, Resentment, and Hatred," 44.

4. Murphy, "Forgiveness and Resentment," 16; Hampton, "Forgiveness, Resentment, and Hatred," 54–55; and Pamela Hieronymi, "Articulating an Uncompromising Forgiveness," *Philosophy and Phenomenological Research* 62, no. 3 (2001): 546.

5. See, for example, Murphy, "Forgiveness and Resentment," 16; and Hieronymi, "Articulating an Uncompromising Forgiveness," 531.

6. Daniel E. Farnham, "A Hegelian Theory of Retribution," *Journal of Social Philosophy*, forthcoming.

7. Jean Hampton, "Correcting Harms versus Righting Wrongs: The Goal of Retribution," *UCLA Law Review* 39 (1992): 1659, 1687.

8. Hieronymi, "Articulating an Uncompromising Forgiveness," 546.

9. Trudy Govier and Wilhelm Verwoerd, "Forgiveness: The Victim's Prerogative," *South African Journal of Philosophy* 21 (2002): 99–100.

10. Ibid., 100.

11. Hieronymi, "Articulating an Uncompromising Forgiveness," 546; emphasis removed.

12. Hampton, "Forgiveness, Resentment, and Hatred," 51; Howard Zehr, *Changing Lenses: A New Focus for Crime and Justice* (Scottsdale, Penn.: Herald, 1990), chap. 2.

13. Hampton, "Forgiveness, Resentment, and Hatred."

14. Christine M. Korsgaard, *The Sources of Normativity* (New York: Cambridge University Press, 1996), chap. 3–4.

15. Ian McEwan's novel *Atonement* (New York: Talese/Doubleday, 2001) provides a powerful image of this experience of guilt. The main character, Briony, writes and rewrites her confession over the course of fifty-nine years.

16. Norvin Richards, "Forgiveness," *Ethics* 99 (1988): 79.

17. This is a very common feature of victimhood. It is also a morally perilous one. Fears may generalize in ways that are either reasonable or unreasonable, fair or bigoted. In atoning, wrongdoers must respond to the epistemically and morally reasonable fears of their victims but not to those that are unreasonable. I discuss this issue in "Collective Responsibility and Duties to Respond," *Social Theory and Practice* 27, no. 3 (2001): 455–71.

18. *Oxford English Dictionary*, s.v. "atonement."

19. I find suggestions of the view that atonement is a matter of reconciliation in a number of sources, some more explicit than others. See Herbert Morris, "Guilt and Suffering," in *On Guilt and Innocence* (Berkeley: University of California Press, 1976), 89–110; Jean Harvey, "The Emerging Practice of Institutional Apologies," *International Journal of Applied Philosophy* 9, no. 2 (1995): 57–66; Richard Swinburne, *Responsibility and Atonement* (New York: Oxford University Press, 1989), chap. 5; John E. Hare, *The Moral Gap: Kantian Ethics, Human Limits, and God's Assistance* (New York: Oxford University Press, 1996), chap. 9; Margaret R. Holmgren, "Self-forgiveness and Responsible Moral Agency," *Journal of Value Inquiry* 32 (1998): 75–91; Elazar Barkan, *The Guilt of Nations: Restitution and Negotiating Historical Injustices* (Baltimore: Johns Hopkins University Press, 2000); Christopher Bennett, "Varieties of Retributive Experience," *Philosophical Quarterly* 52 (2002): 145–64; Kathleen A. Gill, "The Moral Functions of an Apology," in *Injustice and Rectification*, ed. Rodney C. Roberts (New York: Peter Lang, 2002), 111–23; Janna Thompson, *Taking Responsibility for the Past: Reparation and Historical Injustice* (Malden, Mass.: Polity, 2002); Aaron Lazare, *On Apology* (New York: Oxford University Press, 2004); Roy L. Brooks, *Atonement and Forgiveness: A New Model for Black Reparations* (Berkeley: University of California Press, 2004); Margaret Urban Walker, *Moral Repair: Reconstructing Moral Relations after Wrongdoing* (New York: Cambridge University Press, 2006); Charles L. Griswold, *Forgiveness: A Philosophical Exploration* (New York: Cambridge University Press, 2007); and many of the writers in the restorative justice literature, whom I discuss in chapter 6.

20. But see Michael L. Hadley, *The Spiritual Roots of Restorative Justice* (Albany, SUNY: State University of New York Press, 2001).

21. Chapter 5 addresses the question of whether reconciliation could be not just merited but also deserved.

22. Cf. Herbert Morris, "A Paternalistic Theory of Punishment," *American Philosophical Quarterly* 18 (1981): 265.

23. Compare Stephen Darwall's distinction between recognition respect and appraisal respect in "Two Kinds of Respect," *Ethics* 88 (1977): 36–49.

24. Christopher Bennett, "Personal and Redemptive Forgiveness," *European Journal of Philosophy* 11 (2003): 133. Bennett also associates the relationship among members of the moral community with trust. "The agent we recognise as a fellow member is an agent we trust (at least in the absence of evidence that we ought not to trust) in various forms of social cooperation. We trust such agents, for example, in the sense that we leave our interests vulnerable to them" (132).

25. Hampton, "Forgiveness, Resentment, and Hatred," 37.

26. Hampton uses this image to characterize forgiveness in ibid., 36–43.

27. Aurel Kolnai, "Forgiveness," *Proceedings of the Aristotelian Society* 74 (1974): 101.

28. Moral reconciliation and forgiveness are not precisely the same thing, but the differences do not matter here. They become relevant in chapter 5, where I ask whether victims might have a duty to reconcile with or forgive wrongdoers.

29. This principle is included in the handbook of Alcoholics Anonymous, *Twelve Steps and Twelve Traditions* (New York: Alcoholics Anonymous World Services, 1981), 83–87.

30. Not every action says something profound about our characters. Sometimes we genuinely act out of character. However, we still have a task to do. One might recognize

what made one act out of character (e.g., too much drink), or one might simply reflect on the action and the possibility of one's character evolving in that direction and resolve to be on guard against any such development.

31. My favorite example of a creative form of reparation comes from the television series *My Name Is Earl*. A few years back, Earl let a friend go to jail for two years for a crime he himself had committed. While the friend mercifully accepts an apology as grounds for forgiveness, his elderly mother demands that Earl give her back the two years she lost with her son. Earl attempts to do just that by helping her quit smoking, thereby increasing her life expectancy. (Unfortunately, Earl kidnaps the mother in order to compel her cooperation in his plan.) ("Quit Smoking," *My Name Is Earl*, original airdate Sept. 27, 2005.)

32. Gabriele Taylor, *Pride, Shame, and Guilt: Emotions of Self-assessment* (New York: Oxford University Press, 1985), 57.

33. Ibid. Here, for "status" we may substitute "status or standing," as I have been using those terms.

34. Bernard Williams argues that shame is a valuable emotion because it controls the excesses of moral autonomy. Shame signals to us that we may have overlooked or undervalued legitimate moral points of view. "Without it, the convictions of autonomous self-legislation may become hard to distinguish from an insensate degree of moral egoism" (Williams, *Shame and Necessity* [Berkeley: University of California Press, 1993], 100). In "An Apology for Moral Shame" (*Journal of Political Philosophy* 12, no. 2 [2004]: 127–46), Cheshire Calhoun emphasizes that, when representative members of a group evaluate us as shameful, we are defined as shameful within that group. Our ability to function within the shared moral practice of that group will be shaped by the shameful identity we have been assigned. Sensitivity to the character of other people's definitions of one's own moral identity is not a sign of moral immaturity, Calhoun argues. Rather, it is a valuable skill of a *practitioner* of morality, one who must live and function with others within social practices that one will not always fully endorse.

35. The actual gaze of real social others is not necessary for shame. We often feel shame because we imagine what our families or friends would think of us if only they knew the facts. We might also feel shame under the imagined gaze of a fictional community, one we wish for but have not actually found in the real world. See Williams, *Shame and Necessity*, 82.

36. Ibid., 94.

37. Margaret Holmgren seems to have this worry not just about shame but about guilt as well ("Self-forgiveness and Responsible Moral Agency"). I address Holmgren's arguments in detail in chapter 5.

38. Cf. Robin S. Dillon, "How to Lose Your Self-respect," *Ethics* 29 (1992): 126–27.

39. Cf. P. F. Strawson, "Freedom and Resentment," *Proceedings of the British Academy* 48 (1962): 1–25.

40. Michelle Mason, "Contempt as a Moral Attitude," *Ethics* 113 (2003): 241.

41. Michelle Mason notes the globalizing scope of contempt for others (ibid., 258–60). She does not specify whether this is also an aspect of self-contempt that might distinguish it from shame, which is an emotion that frequently comes and goes with changes of context and audience. To illustrate the globalizing scope of contempt for others, Mason offers us the example of Paul, who offers sexual access to his wife,

Camille, in return for professional advancement but who also volunteers regularly in a soup kitchen (ibid., 259). His volunteer work does not give Camille reason to limit her disapprobation to only parts of Paul's character. Instead, the fact that Paul is morally sensitive to the needs and dignity of strangers but not to his wife increases her contempt for him.

42. Aurel Kolnai, "The Standard Modes of Aversion: Fear, Disgust, and Hatred," *Mind* 107 (1998): 581–95.

43. Robin Dillon writes, "For self-respect to respect our human reality, it must include the ability to accept oneself despite failure, even when there isn't much to feel good about oneself" ("How to Lose Your Self-respect," 128).

44. Cf. Morris, "A Paternalistic Theory of Punishment," 265; William Neblett, "The Ethics of Guilt," *Journal of Philosophy* 71 (1974): 661–62.

45. Do all victims of wrongs suffer? They do not all suffer physical pain or material loss, but they all suffer insults. All victims of wrongdoing suffer demeaning treatment. Sometimes people are wronged without realizing that they have been victimized. Even though these people do not experience the pain of being demeaned, a wrongdoer who wishes to atone for such a wrongful act will still feel pained. Some victims may not know that they have been demeaned, but the wrongdoers know it. In empathizing with a victim's situation, the wrongdoer will feel the pain of the insult.

46. Thanks to Shaun Longstreet for raising this objection.

47. Some writers allow for the category of apology to cover more than pointedly communicative acts. However, they usually expand the category of "apology" to include what I am referring to as "atonement" or "amends" generally. See, for example, Lazare, *On Apology*; and Glen Pettigrove, "Apology, Reparations, and the Question of Inherited Guilt," *Public Affairs Quarterly* 17, no. 4 (2003): 319–48.

48. Louis F. Kort, "What Is an Apology?" in *Injustice and Rectification*, ed. Rodney C. Roberts (New York: Peter Lang, 2002), 109–10.

49. Ibid., 109.

50. The kind of wrongdoing in question need not be moral wrongdoing. I might apologize for legal wrongdoing that was not also morally wrong or apologize to my teammates for striking out.

51. Lazare, *On Apology*, 25.

52. Erving Goffman, *Relations in Public* (New York: Harper Colophon Books, 1972), 109–13.

53. Lazare, in *On Apology*, documents many such cases.

54. Ibid., 204–27.

55. Thanks to Scott Forschler for pointing out this feature of apology to me.

56. Gill, "Moral Functions of an Apology," 116.

57. Goffman, *Relations in Public*, 118 (emphasis removed) and 118n, respectively.

58. See, for example, Brooks, *Atonement and Forgiveness*, 144.

59. This points out another way in which making amends with other people differs from making amends with God. In asking for reconciliation with another human being, one is asking that person to accept a particular kind of risk. One is asking for trust, yet that trust might be violated in a way that could cause further harm. However, in asking God for forgiveness and reconciliation, one is not asking for something that would put God or anyone else at risk.

60. Swinburne, *Responsibility and Atonement*, 81, 84; Brooks, *Atonement and Forgiveness*, 142.

61. Lazare records several such examples in *On Apology*.

62. Howard Zehr, *Changing Lenses: A New Focus for Crime and Justice* (Scottsdale, Penn.: Herald, 1990), 19–32.

63. See, for example, Robert I. Rotberg and Dennis Thompson, eds., *Truth v. Justice: The Morality of Truth Commissions* (Princeton, N.J.: Princeton University Press, 2000).

64. Neblett, "Ethics of Guilt," 656.

65. Marcel Mauss, *The Gift: The Form and Reason for Exchange in Archaic Societies*, trans. W. D. Halls (New York: Norton, 1990).

66. *Gandhi* (dir. Richard Attenborough, 1982).

67. A depiction of just such an atonement gone wrong is included in the Disney remake of *The Hunchback of Notre Dame* (dir. Gary Trousdale and Kurt Wise, 1996). In this version of the story, the infant Quasimodo comes under the care of the nefarious Frollo because a priest tells Frollo that the only way he can sufficiently atone for causing the death of Quasimodo's mother is to care for her child. However, Frollo views Quasimodo as an inferior kind of creature and torments the child. In Victor Hugo's original story, Frollo adopts Quasimodo in a very different gesture of atonement, one that is motivated by satisfaction theology. Frollo performs the act of charity with the intention of donating its merit to his brother Jehan "in case the young rogue should someday run short of that kind of currency that is the only one accepted at the tollgate of Paradise" (Hugo, *The Hunchback of Notre-Dame*, trans. Catherine Liu [New York: Modern Library, 2002], 136).

68. In the case of fasting, as in other examples, it may not be clear whether suffering is in fact a goal of the action. Some people who fast cite an interest in an altered state of mind rather than suffering per se.

69. Morris, "Guilt and Suffering," 106.

70. Ibid.

71. Immanuel Kant, *Grounding of the Metaphysics of Morals*, 3d ed., trans. James W. Ellington (Indianapolis: Hackett, 1993), chap. II.

72. Whether imposing punishment on others for the sake of their own improvement can be made consistent with this moral requirement is another issue, which raises further questions about respect for autonomy. See Jean Hampton, "The Moral Education Theory of Punishment," *Philosophy and Public Affairs* 13 (1984): 208–38.

73. Cf. chap. 2 of this work and Heather J. Gert, Linda Radzik, and Michael Hand, "Hampton on the Expressive Power of Punishment," *Journal of Social Philosophy* 35 (2004): 79–90.

74. Marc Lacey, "Atrocity Victims in Uganda Choose to Forgive," *New York Times*, Apr. 18, 2005, http://www.nytimes.com/2005/04/18/international/africa/18uganda.html, 1.

75. In order to concentrate on other aspects of the case, I must put aside important questions about the moral permissibility of the sexual behaviors in question, such as prostitution or nonmarital intercourse. I must also gloss over the fact that some of these women and girls, including those with a mental disability and those who were victims of sexual abuse, were not guilty of wrongdoing even by the church's own strict standards.

Chapter 5

1. At this point, the communities I have in mind are not states but smaller groups such as families, groups of coworkers, and circles of friends. Questions about atonement and the state are addressed in chapter 6.

2. Karen Jones, "Trust as an Affective Attitude," *Ethics* 107 (1996): 4.

3. Cf. Trudy Govier and Wilhelm Verwoerd on what they refer to as the "temporal element" of forgiveness in "Forgiveness: The Victim's Prerogative," *South African Journal of Philosophy* 21 (2002): 99–100.

4. Ibid.

5. Because they are interested primarily in forgiveness, Govier and Verwoerd talk about victims "*giving up* the moral claim against the perpetrator as a result of his or her wrongdoing" (ibid., 99; emphasis added). However, the wrongdoer could also become released by *satisfying* the claim.

6. For example, Uma Narayan, "Forgiveness, Moral Reassessment, and Reconciliation," in *Explorations of Value*, ed. Thomas Magnell (Atlanta: Rodopi, 1997), 175–76.

7. Jean Hampton uses the image of abandoning the roles of 'victim' and 'wrongdoer' and reestablishing civil relations ("Forgiveness, Resentment, and Hatred," in Murphy and Hampton, *Forgiveness and Mercy*, 35–87). Aurel Kolnai talks about forgiveness as a kind of reacceptance and normalization of relations ("Forgiveness," *Proceedings of the Aristotelian Society* 74 [1974]: 91–106).

8. Christopher Bennett disagrees in "Personal and Redemptive Forgiveness," *European Journal of Philosophy* 11 [2003]: 143.

9. Joseph Butler, *Fifteen Sermons* (Charlottesville, Va.: Lincoln-Rembrandt, 1993), sermons VIII and IX. See also Jeffrie G. Murphy, "Forgiveness and Resentment," in Murphy and Hampton, *Forgiveness and Mercy*, 15. In "Forgiveness" (*Ethics* 99 [1988]: 77–97), Norvin Richards extends the characterization of forgiveness to include resentment as well as the other negative emotions listed earlier.

10. Murphy "Forgiveness and Resentment," 23–24.

11. Ibid., 23.

12. In this debate one issue that might seem pressing for my topic is this: Shall we label as forgiveness the overcoming or foreswearing of resentment against a person who has made sincere and proportional amends? Cheshire Calhoun is reluctant to do so, labeling this attitude merely "minimal forgiveness." See her "Changing One's Heart," *Ethics* 103 (1992): 76–96. Calhoun's argument is that abandoning resentment in response to a proper offer of amends is a matter of giving the wrongdoer his due, whereas genuine forgiveness is more like a gift freely given (77–80). I provide an argument against this claim in section 5.6.

13. The example is drawn from Daniel Kehlmann's novel *Die Vermessung der Welt* (Reinbeck bei Hamburg: Rowohlt, 2005). Kehlmann presents a fictionalized account of Alexander von Humboldt and Aimé Bonpland's 1799–1804 exploration of South America. Bonpland continually puts his life in Humboldt's hands as they climb mountains, tromp through jungles, and descend into caves. He counts on Humboldt to handle their equipment properly, keep a skillful eye out for dangers of all sorts, and stay by his side when he becomes ill or injured. Bonpland's attitude is not mere reliance but genuine trust. He knows that, although Humboldt is morally flawed in other ways that are profoundly

damaging to their relationship, in these respects Humboldt is both highly competent and committed to him. At the same time, Bonpland deeply resents Humboldt for having taken advantage of his naiveté in talking him into this expedition in the first place, as well as for continually deciding to venture into ever more dangerous terrain. Bonpland both trusts Humboldt with his life and resents him for endangering it many times over.

14. Govier and Verwoerd, "Forgiveness." See also Richard Swinburne, *Responsibility and Atonement* (New York: Oxford University Press, 1989), 87–88.

15. Jean Harvey, "Forgiveness as an Obligation of the Moral Life," *International Journal of Moral and Social Studies* 8 (1993): 215 (emphasis removed).

16. This, by the way, is one reason some theologians reject the satisfaction theory of atonement. If atonement is merely the paying off of a debt to God, then, when God forgives the debt, this forgiveness does not display God's merciful and loving nature in any significant way. Forgiveness and redemption become something transactional rather than the culmination of God's loving relationship with human beings. See John Hick, "Is the Doctrine of Atonement a Mistake?" in Padgett, *Reason and the Christian Religion*, 247–63.

17. Interestingly, it would be unseemly for the reverse to happen—for Joe to refuse an offer of a public apology and ask instead for a gift. This can be explained without denying victim authority. Instead, the explanation has to do with the nature of a gift. A gift demanded is no longer a gift at all. Instead, it would become a form of restitution, and to demand material restitution in return for an insult is to put a dollar value on one's honor. For that reason, demanding a gift rather than a public apology would display a vice. Material reparation for libel in civil court, however, is not usually unseemly because in these cases the offender is apparently unwilling to atone, because the intention is as much to deter or condemn the offender as to compensate the victim, and because material payment is one of the few things a court can compel from a wrongdoer. Plaintiffs generally can demand material reparations without compromising their dignity.

18. Margaret Urban Walker argues that taking responsibility for one's wrongful actions

> requires accepting the power and the right of others, especially the victims of wrong but also the morally authoritative community, to give their own accounts of the damage and insult done and to express their anger, despair, fear, and grief in response to it. This entails that wrongdoers relinquish a good deal of control over accounts of what has happened, especially reckonings of what harm they have done to others and what they have revealed about themselves in so acting. No wrongdoer is required to be a scapegoat for falsely or unfairly attributed harm. Yet if he or she is indeed implicated in serious wrong, too legalistic a defense (at least outside a courtroom, and even sometimes in one) is likely to appear as denial or evasion and to add the proverbial insult to injury. (*Moral Repair: Reconstructing Moral Relations after Wrongdoing* [New York: Cambridge University Press, 2006], 200)

19. Cf. Govier and Verwoerd, "Forgiveness," 105.

20. Zoltán Balázs seems to be making this point in the following:

> Imagine someone who repents (carries out an act of repentance), but tells the victim that he "does [not] need her forgiveness, because he owes repentance to the moral order, not to her." It is surely right to acknowledge that his act was a

transgression of the moral order, but it seems to be a proud, arrogant, even cruel attitude toward the victim (in a similar vein, religious morality can mislead the believer to repent "before God," but not before the victim). ("Forgiveness and Repentance," *Public Affairs Quarterly* 14, no. 2 [2000]: 123)

For this reason Balázs concludes that repentance is real only when it is aimed at the restoration of relevant relationships.

21. Pamela Hieronymi, "Articulating an Uncompromising Forgiveness," *Philosophy and Phenomenological Research* 62, no. 3 (2001): 529–55; Kolnai, "Forgiveness."

22. Hieronymi, "Articulating an Uncompromising Forgiveness," 550.

23. Ibid.

24. Ibid.

25. Ibid.

26. Ibid., 551n39.

27. Cf. Richards, "Forgiveness," 86: "In short, not to forgive minor misbehavior to which one is oneself prone exhibits either a general intolerance of human frailty or an unwarranted exaltation of oneself. It is wrong to enact either trait, for both are flaws of character."

28. If the original rapist does not allow the rape of his family member, then this is a case of wrongful punishment rather than a wrongful demand for atonement. Nicholas Kristof has reported on this sort of use of rape for the *New York Times*, especially in regard to the case of a Pakistani woman named Mukhtaran Bibi, who fought back against her rapists. See, for example, Kristof, "Sentenced to Be Raped," *New York Times*, Sept. 29, 2004, http://www.nytimes.com/2004/09/29/opinion/29kris.html.

29. We might appeal to community standards and the community's view of the wrong in order to determine whether the victim is laboring under some sort of vice or self-deception. However, as the case of Joe and Jennifer suggests, this should leave room for individual variation in victims' judgments of what atonement requires.

30. But see Marcel Mauss, *The Gift: The Form and Reason for Exchange in Archaic Societies*, trans. W. D. Halls (New York: Norton, 1990).

31. Cf. Kolnai, "Forgiveness"; Murphy, "Forgiveness and Resentment."

32. Charles Griswold discusses the virtue of "forgivingness" in *Forgiveness: A Philosophical Exploration* (New York: Cambridge University Press, 2007), 17–18. Is there also a virtue associated with the wrongdoer? Griswold argues that there is and suggests the label "integrity" for it (Griswold, 18). As I see it, the virtue would include both a willingness to atone for one's wrongful acts and the skill of atoning properly.

33. Richards, "Forgiveness," 96.

34. Annette Baier, "Trust and Antitrust," *Ethics* 96, no. 2 (1986): 235. Recall also Jones's definition of trust as "an attitude of optimism that the goodwill and competence of another will extend to cover the domain of our interaction with her, together with the expectation that the one trusted will be directly and favorably moved by the thought that we are counting on her" ("Trust as an Affective Attitude," 4).

35. Baier, "Trust and Antitrust," 242.

36. Bennett, "Personal and Redemptive Forgiveness," 132.

37. An analogy with epistemic justification might be helpful here. Some epistemologists claim that one's simple perceptual beliefs about the external world (e.g., "the cat is on the mat") are justified prima facie. Believers do not need to be able

to produce an indubitable set of reasons in defense of their beliefs (such as those that Descartes sought). Instead, the perceptual belief that "the cat is on the mat" is justified in the absence of unanswered evidence to the contrary, such as the belief that "I am currently standing in the holograph laboratory at the university, where the researchers are capable of producing visual images that are indistinguishable from reality." In the presence of such counterevidence, I do not now need to produce a full Cartesian defense of my belief that "the cat is on the mat" in order to become justified in believing it. Instead, it is enough that I rebut the particular counterevidence, for example, by petting the cat and thereby confirming that it is not a holograph. See John L. Pollock and Joseph Cruz, *Contemporary Theories of Knowledge*, 2d ed. (Boulder, Colo.: Rowman and Littlefield, 1999).

38. Baier, "Trust and Antitrust," 238.

39. Harvey, "Forgiveness as an Obligation of the Moral Life," 219.

40. Ibid., 219–20.

41. Ibid., 218–20. Harvey constructs her argument in terms of an obligation to forgive. However, her conception of "wide forgiveness" is much closer to my concept of moral reconciliation than it is to the definition of forgiveness I am assuming here.

42. Ibid., 220.

43. Ibid.

44. I examine this argument in the context of a criminal justice system in "Do Wrongdoers Have a Right to Make Amends?" (*Social Theory and Practice* 29, no. 2 [2003]: 325–41).

45. Jeffrie G. Murphy, *Getting Even: Forgiveness and Its Limits* (New York: Oxford University Press, 2003), 84.

46. Govier and Verwoerd, "Forgiveness," 102.

47. John L. Mackie, "Morality and the Retributive Emotions," in *Persons and Values*, ed. Joan Mackie and Penelope Mackie (Oxford, UK: Clarendon, 1985), 206–19.

48. Walker writes that "moral repair is always at the same time a communal responsibility" because "the task of reproducing standards of responsibility and senses of responsibility is the basic shared task of every community, including those very amorphous communities that are called ... 'society'" (*Moral Repair*, 29).

49. Wrongdoers will not have incurred moral debts to mere bystanders (though they might have to secondary victims). Thus the forms of amends that are appropriate here properly focus on respectful communication and moral improvement.

50. Govier and Verwoerd, "Forgiveness," 102–6.

51. Govier and Verwoerd present a case that constitutes an exception. It is one in which the indirect harms are more significant than the direct harms. While a homeowner loses only material goods to a robber, her elderly mother, who lives in the house, suffers more from the loss of her sense of security (ibid., 106).

52. Robin S. Dillon speaks eloquently to these sorts of dangers in "Self-forgiveness and Self-respect," *Ethics* 112 (2001): 53–83. See also Barbara Flanagan, *Forgiving Yourself: A Step-by-Step Guide to Making Peace with Your Mistakes and Getting On with Your Life* (New York: Macmillan, 1996).

53. Murphy, *Getting Even*, 65.

54. I add the word "fully" here because the processes by which one atones and reconciles with others are frequently drawn out in time. It seems appropriate that the wrongdoer's negative self-assessment and sense of self-alienation will gradually diminish as his relations with his victim and community improve. The important point is that the

actual or reasonably predicted reactions of the victim (and sometimes of the community as well) guide the wrongdoer's self-directed attitudes.

55. Flanagan, *Forgiving Yourself*; Robert D. Enright and the Human Development Study Group, "Counseling within the Forgiveness Triad: On Forgiving, Receiving Forgiveness, and Self-forgiveness," *Counseling and Values* 40 (1996): 107–27.

56. Margaret R. Holmgren, "Self-forgiveness and Responsible Moral Agency," *Journal of Value Inquiry* 32 (1998): 85.

57. Victims, too, are permitted to forgive only after going through a process in which they deal appropriately with the wrong. See Margaret R. Holmgren, "Forgiveness and the Intrinsic Value of Persons," *American Philosophical Quarterly* 30, no. 4 (1993): 341–52.

58. Holmgren, "Self-forgiveness and Responsible Moral Agency," 76–78.

59. Ibid., 76.

60. As I read Holmgren, the only other real obstacle to acceptable self-forgiveness is failing to have the proper view of one's victim. But, one cannot have the proper view of oneself without also having a proper view of one's victim. The former, according to Holmgren, includes the recognition that one's status as a moral agent accounts for one's intrinsic, equal, and unchangeable moral value. That is a status one shares with one's victim.

61. Holmgren, "Self-forgiveness and Responsible Moral Agency," 82.

62. See Holmgren's account of interpersonal forgiveness in "Forgiveness and the Intrinsic Value of Persons."

63. Holmgren, "Self-forgiveness and Responsible Moral Agency," 77.

64. Ibid.

65. Robin Dillon makes this point about Holmgren's argument as well in "Self-forgiveness and Self-respect."

66. Stephen Darwall, "Two Kinds of Respect," *Ethics* 88 (1977): 36–49.

67. Ibid.

68. This line of reasoning mirrors the argument writers in the Kantian tradition often make in defense of blaming and punishing others. Punishment does not deny moral status, they argue; rather, it presupposes it. See, for example, Bennett, "Personal and Redemptive Forgiveness."

69. Hampton, in "Forgiveness, Resentment, and Hatred," distinguishes several forms of hatred and argues that some of them are compatible with a Kantian theory of human value. Michelle Mason argues that contempt is compatible with recognition-respect in "Contempt as a Moral Attitude," *Ethics* 113 (2003): 234–72.

70. Holmgren, "Self-forgiveness and Responsible Moral Agency," 82.

71. However, I agree with Holmgren when she writes that "As an autonomous moral agent, [the wrongdoer] is fully responsible for developing her own attitudes. If she simply reacts to her victim's decision and allows his attitudes to determine her own, she fails in this responsibility" (ibid.). As I argue in section 5.4, a victim's forgiveness is not sufficient for redemption because it may be given before the wrongdoer deserves it. Moreover, a victim's forgiveness is not sufficient for self-forgiveness.

72. Ibid., 83.

73. Ibid.

74. Ibid., 85.

75. Ibid., 83.

76. The dying Nazi's assumption that he could receive forgiveness from just any Jew displays a continuing tendency to see the Jewish people merely as a group and not also as

individuals with dignity and value of their own. Furthermore, as Eva Fleishner points out in her essay in *The Sunflower*, the soldier probably placed Wiesenthal in increased danger by confessing to him (*The Sunflower: On the Possibilities and Limits of Forgiveness*, rev. and exp. ed., ed. Harry James Cargas and Bonny V. Fetterman [New York: Schocken, 1998], 142–43). Had another Nazi overheard this interaction, it is likely that he or she would have simply killed Wiesenthal on the spot in order to prevent Wiesenthal from feeling any satisfaction at the confession (which he did not) or to stop his telling others about it (which he did almost immediately).

77. Because Holmgren insists that 'ought' implies 'can' in the case of the atonement (a claim I discuss later) and is willing to allow the other aspects of the atonement process to fail to be fulfilled as long as the wrongdoer comes to a proper Kantian view of the value of moral agents, she sees even this soldier as a real candidate for permissible self-forgiveness.

78. In fairness to Holmgren, I do not think her view of the nature of wrongdoing is so simplistic.

79. Holmgren, "Self-forgiveness and Responsible Moral Agency," 84.

80. Hieronymi, "Articulating an Uncompromising Forgiveness," 549.

81. See, for example, Holmgren, "Self-forgiveness and Responsible Moral Agency"; Nancy Snow, "Self-forgiveness," *Journal of Value Inquiry* 27 (1993): 75–80; and Dillon "Self-forgiveness and Self-respect."

82. Robin S. Dillon, "How to Lose Your Self-respect," *Ethics* 29 (1992): 128 ff.

83. Ibid., 128.

84. In this way I try to thread the needle so as to recognize that moral standing is by its very nature a social relation even though social groups do not always properly accord standing to their members.

85. Holmgren, "Self-forgiveness and Responsible Moral Agency," 81.

86. Murphy, *Getting Even*, 70.

Chapter 6

1. The similarities between restorative justice, as I have represented it here, and the moral theory of atonement I have defended are not at all coincidental. My attention was first drawn to the moral concept of making amends by reading the restorative justice literature, and I have been heavily influenced by what I found there. However, my particular construction of restorative justice is contentious. While I give a broadly Kantian reading of the justification for restorative justice practices, those same approaches have been defended from other theoretical perspectives as well. In fact, I have seen restorative justice linked more and less explicitly with utilitarianism, libertarianism, communitarianism, a feminist ethic of care, and virtue theory. Such a theoretical hodgepodge might lead one to wonder whether restorative justice should be considered a theory of justice at all rather than a social movement or perhaps a set of practices. Others would argue that the fact that a wide array of theories that are otherwise opposed to one another can defend restorative justice is a point of strength and a sign that it calls upon core intuitions about justice (see Gerry Johnstone and Daniel W. Van Ness, "The Meaning of Restorative Justice," in Johnstone and Van Ness, *Handbook of Restorative Justice*, 5–23).

2. Kathleen Daly and Russ Immarigeon, "The Past, Present, and Future of Restorative Justice: Some Critical Reflections," *Contemporary Justice Review*, 1 (1999): 29.

3. Cf. Mary Achilles and Howard Zehr, "Restorative Justice for Crime Victims: The Promise and the Challenge," in Bazemore and Schiff, *Restorative Community Justice*, 87–99.

4. When sentences are determined by plea bargaining, offenders are sometimes left unaware of what they have been sentenced to and why or even whether they have been sentenced at all. The chapter of the ACLU in my community regularly receives letters from prisoners complaining that they have been imprisoned without trial. These letters come from people who were sentenced through plea-bargaining processes so obscure to them that they did not understand that they forfeited their right to a trial (Dawn Arney, personal communication).

5. Howard Zehr, *Changing Lenses: A New Focus for Crime and Justice* (Scottsdale, Penn.: Herald, 1990), 35.

6. John Braithwaite, "Repentance Rituals and Restorative Justice," *Journal of Political Philosophy* 8, no. 1 (2000): 116–17. This phenomenon underwrites Braithwaite's opposition to punishment and leads him to charge the state with complicity in recidivist crime (Braithwaite, 116–17).

7. Daly and Immarigeon, "Past, Present, and Future of Restorative Justice," 22; Michael Braswell, John Fuller, and Bo Lozoff, *Corrections, Peacemaking, and Restorative Justice: Transforming Individuals and Institutions* (Cincinnati: Anderson, 2001), 141–43; John Braithwaite and Declan Roche, "Responsibility and Restorative Justice," in Bazemore and Schiff, *Restorative Community Justice*, 63; Daniel W. Van Ness and Mara Schiff, "Satisfaction Guaranteed? The Meaning of Satisfaction in Restorative Justice," in Bazemore and Schiff, *Restorative Community Justice*, 47; Braithwaite, "Repentance Rituals and Restorative Justice," 115.

8. Braithwaite, "Repentance Rituals and Restorative Justice," 115.

9. Tony Marshall, quoted in ibid.

10. I rely primarily on Braithwaite's description of sentencing conferences in "Repentance Rituals and Restorative Justice." Theories of restorative justice have been offered in support of a number of different kinds of victim-offender mediation and conferencing programs. See Gordon Bazemore and Mark Umbreit, "A Comparison of Four Restorative Conferencing Models," in Johnstone, *Restorative Justice Reader*, 225–43.

11. Braithwaite, "Repentance Rituals and Restorative Justice," 123.

12. Achilles and Zehr, "Restorative Justice for Crime Victims," 88–89; Zehr, *Changing Lenses*, 19–32.

13. Braithwaite, "Repentance Rituals and Restorative Justice," 123–24; Braithwaite and Roche, "Responsibility and Restorative Justice," 68. A surprising tendency toward victim forgiveness was also witnessed in the hearings of South Africa's restorative justice–inspired Truth and Reconciliation Commission, even though victims played no role in determining sentences and offenders were granted full amnesty. See Elizabeth Kiss, "Moral Ambition within and beyond Political Constraints: Reflections on Restorative Justice," in *Truth v. Justice: The Morality of Truth Commissions*, ed. Robert I. Rotberg and Dennis Thompson (Princeton, N.J.: Princeton University Press, 2000), 72.

14. Braithwaite, "Repentance Rituals and Restorative Justice," 123.

15. Braswell, Fuller, and Lozoff, *Corrections, Peacemaking, and Restorative Justice*, 79.

16. Ibid., 39–40; Zehr, *Changing Lenses*, 35–40.

17. Braswell, Fuller, and Lozoff, *Corrections, Peacemaking, and Restorative Justice*, especially chap. 8; Gordon Bazemore and Michael Dooley, "Restorative Justice and the

Offender: The Challenge of Reintegration," in Bazemore and Schiff, *Restorative Community Justice*, 111.

18. Braithwaite, "Repentance Rituals and Restorative Justice," 120.

19. The examples are drawn from Braithwaite and Roche, "Responsibility and Restorative Justice," 70–71.

20. Braithwaite, "Repentance Rituals and Restorative Justice," 119; Daly and Immarigeon, "Past, Present, and Future of Restorative Justice," 25–26. It is frequently claimed that the inspiration for restorative justice is drawn from the traditions of these cultures.

21. Gerry Johnstone, *Restorative Justice: Ideas, Values, Debates* (Portland, Ore.: Willan, 2002), 28.

22. Ibid., 22.

23. Victim participation must be voluntary. Some victims find facing their offenders counterproductive to their own healing.

24. Zehr, *Changing Lenses*, 51–52.

25. Ibid., 35.

26. Linda Radzik, "Do Wrongdoers Have a Right to Make Amends?" *Social Theory and Practice* 29, no. 2 (2003): 325–41. One might object that the current criminal justice system indeed allows offenders the opportunity to make amends. Criminal offenders can do so simply by submitting themselves to punishment at the hands of the state. While I have granted that submission to punishment can be a legitimate form of amends in some circumstances, its usefulness with regard to the overall goal of reconciliation is severely limited.

27. I cannot here consider the many other equally important practical and theoretical challenges to restorative justice. For example, I worry whether restorative justice practices are compatible with a defendant's right to a vigorous defense. Innocent suspects may agree to plead guilty and participate in restorative justice procedures given the horrifying risk of imprisonment. In practice, restorative processes often skip over the guilt-determination phase and become part of the plea-bargaining process. It is also unclear whether a theory of restorative justice can defend the continuing, parallel operation of the punitive justice system, which both motivates offender participation in restorative practices and provides an alternative for offenders and victims who either do not want to participate in restorative sentencing or find that they cannot come to an agreement.

28. Stephen P. Garvey, "Punishment as Atonement," *UCLA Law Review* 46 (1999): 1849–50.

29. Richard Delgado, "Prosecuting Violence: A Colloquy on Race, Community, and Justice: Goodbye to Hammurabi: Analyzing the Atavistic Appeal of Restorative Justice," *Stanford Law Review* 52 (2000): 751–75.

30. Timothy Garton Ash, "True Confessions," *New York Review of Books*, July 17, 1997, 37. In this essay Ash is specifically addressing the appeal to the values of reconciliation and restorative justice in defense of South Africa's Truth and Reconciliation Commission (TRC), which saw as its charge the reconciliation of the entire South African state in the aftermath of apartheid. For more on the debates surrounding the TRC and its vision of restorative justice see Rotberg and Thompson, *Truth v. Justice*.

31. Amy Gutmann and Dennis Thompson, "The Moral Foundations of Truth Commissions," in Rotberg and Thompson, *Truth v. Justice*, 33–34.

32. John Rawls, *Political Liberalism* (New York: Columbia University Press, 1993).

33. Garvey addresses this worry as well in "Punishment as Atonement," 1855–58.

34. Braithwaite and Roche, "Responsibility and Restorative Justice," 74.

35. See, for example, Jeffrie G. Murphy, "Retributivism, Moral Education, and the Liberal State," *Criminal Justice Ethics* 4 (1985): 3–11.

36. Jean Hampton, "The Common Faith of Liberalism," *Pacific Philosophical Quarterly* 75 (1994): 186–216. Of course, as Hampton points out, particular defenders of the liberal state disagree about exactly what freedom and equality involve.

37. Jean Hampton, "The Moral Education Theory of Punishment," *Philosophy and Public Affairs* 13 (1984): 208–38. Hampton's advocacy of moral education theory predates her defense of retributivism, which chapter 2 discusses at length.

38. Ash, "True Confessions."

39. Kiss, "Moral Ambition within and beyond Political Constraints," 84.

40. Colleen Murphy explores different conceptions of reconciliation that have been associated with the restoration of relationships among fellow citizens. See "The Nature and Importance of Political Reconciliation," PhD diss., University of North Carolina at Chapel Hill, 2004.

41. John Braithwaite, "Thinking Harder about Democratising Social Control," in *Family Conferencing and Juvenile Justice: The Way Forward or Misplaced Optimism?* ed. Christine Alder and Joy Wundersitz (Canberra: Australian Institute of Criminology, 1994), 199–216.

42. Cf. Zehr, *Changing Lenses*, 31–32.

43. Johnstone, *Restorative Justice*, 30–31.

44. See, for example, Braithwaite, "Thinking Harder about Democratising Social Control."

45. Nils Christie, "Conflicts as Property," *British Journal of Criminology* 17 (1977): 1–26.

46. Ibid., 7–8.

47. Ibid.

48. Ibid., 9.

49. Ibid.

50. Ibid., 7.

51. John Locke, *The Second Treatise on Civil Government* (Buffalo, N.Y.: Prometheus, 1986); Robert Nozick, *Anarchy, State, and Utopia* (New York: Basic, 1974).

52. According to the Lockean model these are negative rights, that is, rights to noninterference, rather than rights to positive support.

53. Jennifer Gerarda Brown, "The Use of Mediation to Resolve Criminal Cases: A Critique," *Emory Law Journal* 43 (1994): 1247–1309; Andrew Ashworth, "Responsibilities, Rights, and Restorative Justice," *British Journal of Criminology* 42 (2002): 578–95; and Delgado, "Prosecuting Violence."

54. Cf. Johnstone, *Restorative Justice*, 29–30.

55. Joel Feinberg, "The Expressive Function of Punishment," in Feinberg, *Doing and Deserving*, 95–118; Jean Hampton, "Correcting Harms versus Righting Wrongs: The Goal of Retribution," *UCLA Law Review* 39 (1992): 1659–1702.

56. Restorative justice advocates may justifiably retort that the standard punitive system is not immune from such prejudicial influences, either.

57. See, for example, Martha C. Nussbaum, "Adaptive Preferences and Women's Options," *Economics and Philosophy* 17 (2001): 67–88. Thanks to Colleen Murphy for bringing this literature to my attention.

58. To argue for equivalent state condemnation for equivalent crimes is not to revert to a retributive system since the moral message of condemnation can be carried out through other, more constructive means than retributive punishment.

59. Some of the models described by Gordon Bazemore and Mark Umbreit in "A Comparison of Four Restorative Conferencing Models" include a larger role for officials (in Johnstone, *Restorative Justice Reader*, 225–43).

Chapter 7

1. Restitution and compensation are kinds of material transfers that might be justified under a variety of moral principles. Here I consider material transfers that are justified in terms of the restitutive moral principle, which claims that victims deserve compensation.

2. Roy L. Brooks, *Atonement and Forgiveness: A New Model for Black Reparations* (Berkeley: University of California Press, 2004), 98–140.

3. See, for example, Jeremy Waldron, "Superseding Historic Injustice," *Ethics* 103, no. 1 (1992): 4–28; and Samuel C. Wheeler III, "Reparations Reconsidered," *American Philosophical Quarterly* 34, no. 3 (1997): 301–18.

4. Janna Thompson offers this diagnosis of some critics of compensation for historical injustices: "It is seen as visiting the sins of forebears on their children, as something similar to, and almost as objectionable as, punishing people for crimes they did not commit" (Thompson, *Taking Responsibility for the Past: Reparation and Historical Injustice* [Malden, Mass.: Polity, 2002], 25).

5. See Brooks, *Atonement and Forgiveness*, 135.

6. In this way my project shares many affinities with Brooks's *Atonement and Forgiveness*. He argues that the proper response to the history of slavery and Jim Crow laws in the United States should be conceived in terms of atonement, which he characterizes as apology and reparation (ibid., 144).

7. The children who were taken either through coercion or outright force from single mothers might be considered a secondary group of victims in the Magdalen affair. Many of these children landed in orphanages and industrial schools, which were themselves sites of terrible abuse (see Mary Raftery and Eoin O'Sullivan, *Suffer the Little Children: The Inside Story of Ireland's Industrial Schools* [Dublin: New Island, 1999]). Others were put up for adoption, often illegally, to Catholic families in the United States (Maggie O'Kane, "Washing Away Their Sins," *Guardian*, Oct. 30, 1996, 2). The adoptees were the lucky ones, although some still long for their lost birth mothers and histories (O'Kane, "Washing Away Their Sins"; see also the Adoption Ireland website, www.adoptionireland.com). Since most of these removals took place in institutions other than the Magdalen asylums themselves, though, I do not pursue the issue here.

8. *Sex in a Cold Climate* (dir. Steve Humphries, 1998).

9. Jean Harvey, "The Emerging Practice of Institutional Apologies," *International Journal of Applied Philosophy* 9, no. 2 (1995): 64.

10. *Sex in a Cold Climate*.

11. Ibid.

12. James M. Smith, *Ireland's Magdalen Laundries and the Nation's Architecture of Containment* (Notre Dame, Ind.: University of Notre Dame Press, 2007), 144. See also Mary Gordon, "How Ireland Hid Its Own Dirty Laundry," *New York Times*, Aug. 3, 2003, http://www.nytimes.com, 34.

13. Gordon, "How Ireland Hid Its Own Dirty Laundry."

14. Ibid.

15. O'Kane, "Washing Away Their Sins," 2. Collins did leave the asylum at one point: "I took a wild turn in 1950. I wanted to see what it was like on the outside, but I got very lonely for the other girls and I wanted to go back. I was an orphan, I didn't have a mother. The nuns were my mother" (quoted in ibid.).

16. Mick O'Brien, quoted in ibid.

17. Smith, *Ireland's Magdalen Laundries*, 185. Frances Finnegan describes how the Magdalen laundries were exempted from legislation designed to protect workers (*Do Penance or Perish: Magdalen Asylums in Ireland* [New York: Oxford University Press, 2004], 223–25).

18. The following incident is reported by Mary Raftery in "Restoring Dignity to the Magdalens," *Irish Times*, Aug. 21, 2003, 14.

19. Finnegan, *Do Penance or Perish*, 6–19. Smith discusses the state's practice of sending women charged with the deaths of newborns to the asylums in *Ireland's Magdalen Laundries*, 54–66. The women were considered to have been temporarily insane and requiring "not punishment but protection" (ibid., 54).

20. Gordon, "How Ireland Hid Its Own Dirty Laundry."

21. Smith, *Ireland's Magdalen Laundries*, 146–48.

22. Ibid., 1–20.

23. Ibid., 17.

24. Ibid., 4.

25. Kathy O'Beirne published two memoirs describing her childhood in a Magdalen asylum the veracity of which have been questioned: *Kathy's Story: A Childhood Hell inside Ireland's Magdalen Laundries* (Edinburgh: Mainstream Publishing, 2005); and *Don't Ever Tell: Kathy's Story: A True Tale of a Childhood Destroyed by Neglect and Fear* (Edinburgh: Mainstream Publishing, 2006). The controversy is described in Natalie Clarke, "Brutal Abuse of the Truth?" *Daily Mail* (London), Sept. 23, 2006, 36.

26. The apology came from the Sisters of Mercy of the Americas (Smith, *Ireland's Magdalen Laundries*, 238n6; Chris Kaltenbach, "Nuns' Order Apologizes for Abusive Conditions of Workers," *Detroit News*, Aug. 10, 2003). The Irish Sisters of Mercy have presented a significant apology for the abuse of children in their industrial and reformatory schools but left out mention of their Magdalen asylums (Smith, *Ireland's Magdalen Laundries*, 185–86; Mary Raftery, "Sisters of Mercy Break Ranks," *Irish Times*, May 6, 2004, 16; and Maeve Connolly, "Magdalene Laundries Women 'Ignored,'" *Irish News*, May 17, 2004, 3).

27. Smith, *Ireland's Magdalen Laundries*, 24.

28. Ibid., 46.

29. See Henry McDonald, "Dail and Church Agree Euros 1.3bn Payout to Child Abuse Victims," *London Observer*, Jan. 1, 2006, 3. Of the 1.3 billion Euros, the church will contribute only 128 million Euros and be protected from further claims as part of an agreement with the government (ibid.).

30. Smith, *Ireland's Magdalen Laundries*, 183–84. Smith describes the few existing memorials on pages 134–35 and 159–82.

31. Gary Culliton, "Last Days of a Laundry," *Irish Times*, Sept. 25, 1996, 15.

32. Elizabeth Butler Cullingford, "'Our Nuns Are *Not* a Nation': Politicizing the Convent in Irish Literature and Film," *Éire-Ireland* 41, no. 1–2 (2006): 20.

33. Ibid., 21.

34. There is some question as to how voluntary the choice to enter a convent was for Irish women over the centuries. Some may well have been coerced by family members or by a lack of acceptable alternatives. See ibid. on this issue.

35. *Sex in a Cold Climate*.

36. Gordon, "How Ireland Hid Its Own Dirty Laundry," 34.

37. An unidentified nun in the Gloucester Street Convent, quoted in Culliton, "Last Days of a Laundry," 15.

38. For an argument that an institution can be guilty of wrongdoing even if all of the constituent actors are excused, see David Copp, "On the Agency of Certain Collective Entities: An Argument from 'Normative Authority,'" *Midwest Studies in Philosophy* 30, no. 1 (2006): 194–221.

39. Strawson, "Freedom and Resentment," *Proceedings of the British Academy* 48 (1962): 1–25.

40. Ibid., 191–92, 194.

41. Ibid., 194–95.

42. Ibid., 197.

43. Ibid., 198–99.

44. Individuals feel something akin to love, though, in regard to certain institutions. Consider the affection and commitment alumni often extend to their alma mater or sports fans to their local teams.

45. However, the church should not even attempt to reclaim the blind, nonautonomous trust with which it was once regarded and that those with bad and good intentions alike misused and exploited.

46. By "nonperpetrating member" I refer to those members who did not play a causal role in designing, implementing, or preserving the abusive practices.

47. Between the categories of perpetrating and nonperpetrating members, we should include the categories of complicity and wrongdoing by omission. I am unable to address such cases adequately here, but see my "Collective Responsibility and Duties to Respond," *Social Theory and Practice* 27, no. 3 (2001): 455–71.

48. See Margaret Gilbert, "Collective Remorse," in *War Crimes and Collective Wrongdoing: A Reader*, ed. Aleksandar Jokić (Malden, Mass.: Blackwell, 2001), 216–35.

49. Shame can be mixed with pride. Feeling shame due to some aspects of the group's history does not preclude feeling pride due to others.

50. Harvey, "Emerging Practice of Institutional Apologies."

51. For this reason, a falsified memoir about victimization in the Magdalen asylums would also count as a wrong against the real victims. On the O'Beirne controversy see note 25.

52. Connolly, "Magdalene Laundries Women 'Ignored.'"

53. CNN.com, "Cardinal Apologizes for Sex Abuse by Priests," July 16, 2002, http://archives.cnn.com/2002/US/03/26/church.abuse/index.html.

54. O'Kane relates a story of one of the last Magdalen penitents whose family delayed informing her of her own mother's death so that she could not attend the funeral ("Washing Away Their Sins"). The issue of atonement in families lies beyond the scope of this work, but this incident points to the moral significance of the issue.

55. Some of these women are indeed being cared for by the orders that once confined them. See Finnegan, *Do Penance or Perish*, 241; O'Kane, "Washing Away Their Sins."

56. Canon 1176, quoted in Raftery, "Restoring Dignity to the Magdalens," 14.

57. Finnegan reports that "The Religious of the Good Shepherd were forbidden to strike the penitents" (*Do Penance or Perish*, 69). It is unclear whether that was the rule at all of the asylums or whether it was followed in practice. Survivors interviewed in *Sex in a Cold Climate* report regular practices of corporal punishment.

58. Patsy McGarry, "Abuse Victims Welcome Apology by Nuns: Sisters of Mercy Say Sorry for the Suffering," *Irish Times*, May 6, 2004, 6.

59. An obligation to make amends can be trumped by other moral considerations. Among these, it seems, is a right to continued existence. Sometimes wrongdoing institutions resist the call to atonement by claiming that the required reparations would lead to financial ruin. Nonetheless, the right of an institution to continued existence is far from obvious. Nations have such a right; businesses do not. I do not pursue the issue here since, while it is probable that the cost of compensation would bankrupt the particular orders that ran the asylums, these orders are part of a much larger and wealthier institution that shares in the responsibility for the past injustices.

60. Larry May, *Sharing Responsibility* (Chicago: University of Chicago Press, 1992), chap. 8. See also Radzik, "Collective Responsibility and Duties to Respond."

61. Elizabeth Kiss, "Saying We're Sorry: Liberal Democracy and the Rhetoric of Collective Identity," *Constellations* 4, no. 3 (1998): 392.

BIBLIOGRAPHY

Achilles, Mary, and Howard Zehr. "Restorative Justice for Crime Victims: The Promise and the Challenge." In Bazemore and Schiff, *Restorative Community Justice*, 87–99.

Adler, Jacob. *The Urgings of Conscience*. Philadelphia: Temple University Press, 1992.

Anselm of Canterbury. "Why God Became Man." In *Anselm of Canterbury: The Major Works*, ed. Brian Davies and G. R. Evans, 260–356. New York: Oxford University Press, 1998.

Appleby, R. Scott. "How the Church Has Learned to Say, 'I'm Sorry.'" *U.S. Catholic* 64, no. 3 (1999): 40–41.

Ash, Timothy Garton. "True Confessions." *New York Review of Books*, July 17, 1997, 33–38.

Ashworth, Andrew. "Responsibilities, Rights, and Restorative Justice." *British Journal of Criminology* 42 (2002): 578–95.

Aulén, Gustaf. *Christus Victor: An Historical Study of the Three Main Types of the Idea of Atonement*. Trans. A. G. Herbert. Eugene, Ore.: Wipf and Stock, 2003.

Ayoub, Mahmoud. "Repentance in the Islamic Tradition." In Etzioni and Carney, *Repentance: A Comparative Perspective*, 96–121.

Baier, Annette. "Trust and Antitrust." *Ethics* 96, no. 2 (1986): 231–60.

Balázs, Zoltán. "Forgiveness and Repentance." *Public Affairs Quarterly* 14, no. 2 (2000): 105–27.

Barkan, Elazar. *The Guilt of Nations: Restitution and Negotiating Historical Injustices*. Baltimore: Johns Hopkins University Press, 2000.

Barnett, Randy E. "Restitution: A New Paradigm of Criminal Justice." *Ethics* 87, no. 4 (1977): 279–301.

Bazemore, Gordon, and Michael Dooley. "Restorative Justice and the Offender: The Challenge of Reintegration." In Bazemore and Schiff, *Restorative Community Justice*, 101–26.

Bazemore, Gordon, and Mara Schiff, eds. *Restorative Community Justice: Repairing Harm and Transforming Community*. Cincinnati: Anderson, 2001.

Bazemore, Gordon, and Mark Umbreit. "A Comparison of Four Restorative Conferencing Models." In Johnstone, *Restorative Justice Reader*, 225–43.

Benn, Stanley I. "Punishment." In *The Encyclopedia of Philosophy*, ed. Paul Edwards, 29–36. New York: Macmillan, 1967.

Bennett, Christopher. "Personal and Redemptive Forgiveness." *European Journal of Philosophy* 11 (2003): 127–44.

———. "Varieties of Retributive Experience." *Philosophical Quarterly* 52 (2002): 145–64.

Bittner, Rüdiger. "Is It Reasonable to Regret Things One Did?" *Journal of Philosophy* 89, no. 5 (1992): 262–73.

Botwinick, Aryeh. "In Defense of Teshuvah: A Modern Approach to an Ancient Concept." *Judaism* 26, no. 4 (1977): 475–80.

Braithwaite, John. "Repentance Rituals and Restorative Justice." *Journal of Political Philosophy* 8, no. 1 (2000): 115–31.

———. "Thinking Harder about Democratising Social Control." In *Family Conferencing and Juvenile Justice: The Way Forward or Misplaced Optimism?* ed. Christine Alder and Joy Wundersitz, 199–216. Canberra: Australian Institute of Criminology, 1994.

Braithwaite, John, and Declan Roche. "Responsibility and Restorative Justice." In Bazemore and Schiff, *Restorative Community Justice*, 63–84.

Braswell, Michael, John Fuller, and Bo Lozoff. *Corrections, Peacemaking, and Restorative Justice: Transforming Individuals and Institutions*. Cincinnati: Anderson, 2001.

Brooks, Roy L. *Atonement and Forgiveness: A New Model for Black Reparations*. Berkeley: University of California Press, 2004.

Brown, Jennifer Gerarda. "The Use of Mediation to Resolve Criminal Cases: A Critique." *Emory Law Journal* 43 (1994): 1247–1309.

Brown, Joanne Carlson, and Rebecca Parker. "For God So Loved the World?" In *Christianity, Patriarchy, and Abuse: A Feminist Critique*, ed. Joanne Carlson Brown and Carole R. Bohn, 1–30. New York: Pilgrim, 1989.

Butler, Joseph. *Fifteen Sermons*. Charlottesville, Va.: Lincoln-Rembrandt, 1993.

Calhoun, Cheshire. "An Apology for Moral Shame." *Journal of Political Philosophy* 12, no. 2 (2004): 127–46.

———. "Changing One's Heart." *Ethics* 103 (1992): 76–96.

Carey, Benedict. "Lady Macbeth Not Alone in Her Quest for Spotlessness." *New York Times*, September 12, 2006. http://www.nytimes.com/2006/09/12/health/psychology/12macbeth.html (accessed July 7, 2008).

Christie, Nils. "Conflicts as Property." *British Journal of Criminology* 17 (1977): 1–26.

Clarke, Natalie. "Brutal Abuse of the Truth?" *Daily Mail* (London), Sept. 23, 2006, 36.

CNN.com. "Cardinal Apologizes for Sex Abuse by Priests." July 16, 2002. http://archives.cnn.com/2002/US/03/26/church.abuse/index.html (accessed July 7, 2008).

Cohen, Hermann. *Religion of Reason out of the Sources of Judaism*, 2d ed. Trans. Simon Kaplan. Atlanta: Scholars Press, 1995.

Connolly, Maeve. "Magdalene Laundries Women 'Ignored.'" *Irish News*, May 17, 2004, 3.

Conrad, Joseph. *Lord Jim*. New York: Penguin, 1986.

Copp, David. "On the Agency of Certain Collective Entities: An Argument from 'Normative Authority.'" *Midwest Studies in Philosophy* 30, no. 1 (2006): 194–221.

Cottingham, John. "Varieties of Retribution." *Philosophical Quarterly* 29 (1979): 238–46.

Cullingford, Elizabeth Butler. "'Our Nuns Are *Not* a Nation': Politicizing the Convent in Irish Literature and Film." *Éire-Ireland* 41, no. 1–2 (2006): 9–39.

Culliton, Gary. "Last Days of a Laundry." *Irish Times*, September 25, 1996, 15.

Daly, Kathleen, and Russ Immarigeon. "The Past, Present, and Future of Restorative Justice: Some Critical Reflections." *Contemporary Justice Review*, 1 (1999): 21–45.

Dan-Cohen, Meir. "Revising the Past: On the Metaphysics of Repentance, Forgiveness, and Pardon." In *Forgiveness, Mercy, and Clemency*, ed. Austin Sarat and Nasser Hussain, 117–37. Stanford, Calif.: Stanford University Press, 2007.

Darwall, Stephen. "Two Kinds of Respect." *Ethics* 88 (1977): 36–49.

Delgado, Richard. "Prosecuting Violence: A Colloquy on Race, Community, and Justice. Goodbye to Hammurabi: Analyzing the Atavistic Appeal of Restorative Justice." *Stanford Law Review* 52 (2000): 751–75.

Dillon, Robin S. "How to Lose Your Self-respect." *Ethics* 29 (1992): 125–39.

———. "Self-forgiveness and Self-respect." *Ethics* 112 (2001): 53–83.

Duff, R. A. *Trials and Punishments*. New York: Cambridge University Press, 1986.

Ellin, Joseph. "Restitutionism Defended." *Journal of Value Inquiry* 34 (2000): 299–317.

Elster, Jon. "Redemption for Wrongdoing: The Fate of Collaborators after 1945." *Journal of Conflict Resolution* 50, no. 3 (2006): 324–38.

Enright, Robert D., and the Human Development Study Group. "Counseling within the Forgiveness Triad: On Forgiving, Receiving Forgiveness, and Self-forgiveness." *Counseling and Values* 40 (1996): 107–27.

Etzioni, Amitai, and David E. Carney, eds. *Repentance: A Comparative Perspective*. Lanham, Md.: Rowman and Littlefield, 1997.

Farnham, Daniel E. "A Hegelian Theory of Retribution." *Journal of Social Philosophy*, forthcoming.

Feinberg, Joel. *Doing and Deserving: Essays in the Theory of Responsibility*. Princeton, N.J.: Princeton University Press, 1970.

———. "The Expressive Function of Punishment." In Feinberg, *Doing and Deserving*, 95–118.

———. "Justice and Personal Desert." In Feinberg, *Doing and Deserving*, 55–94.

Finnegan, Frances. *Do Penance or Perish: Magdalen Asylums in Ireland*. New York: Oxford University Press, 2004.

Flanagan, Barbara. *Forgiving Yourself: A Step-by-Step Guide to Making Peace with Your Mistakes and Getting On with Your Life*. New York: Macmillan, 1996.

Freud, Sigmund. *Civilization and Its Discontents*. In *The Standard Edition of the Complete Psychological Works of Sigmund Freud*, vol. 21. Trans. and ed. James Strachey and Anna Freud, 64–145. London: Hogarth Press and the Institute of Psycho-Analysis, 1961.

Gandhi. Dir. Richard Attenborough, 1982.

Garvey, Stephen P. "Punishment as Atonement." *UCLA Law Review* 46 (1999): 1801–58.

Gert, Heather J., Linda Radzik, and Michael Hand. "Hampton on the Expressive Power of Punishment." *Journal of Social Philosophy* 35 (2004): 79–90.

Gilbert, Margaret. "Collective Remorse." In *War Crimes and Collective Wrongdoing: A Reader*, ed. Aleksandar Jokić, 216–35. Malden, Mass.: Blackwell, 2001.

Gill, Kathleen A. "The Moral Functions of an Apology." In *Injustice and Rectification*, ed. Rodney C. Roberts, 111–23. New York: Peter Lang, 2002.

Glucklich, Ariel. *Sacred Pain: Hurting the Body for the Sake of the Soul*. New York: Oxford University Press, 2001.

Goffman, Erving. *Relations in Public*. New York: Harper Colophon, 1972.

Gordon, Mary. "How Ireland Hid Its Own Dirty Laundry." *New York Times*, August 3, 2003. http://www.nytimes.com (accessed July 7, 2008).

Gorringe, Timothy. *God's Just Vengeance: Crime, Violence, and the Rhetoric of Salvation*. New York: Cambridge University Press, 1996.

Govier, Trudy, and Wilhelm Verwoerd. "Forgiveness: The Victim's Prerogative." *South African Journal of Philosophy* 21 (2002): 97–111.

Griswold, Charles L. *Forgiveness: A Philosophical Exploration*. New York: Cambridge University Press, 2007.

Gutmann, Amy, and Dennis Thompson. "The Moral Foundations of Truth Commissions." In Rotberg and Thompson, *Truth v. Justice*, 22–44.

Hadley, Michael L. *The Spiritual Roots of Restorative Justice*. Albany: State University of New York Press, 2001.

Hamilton, Sarah. *The Practice of Penance, 900–1050*. Rochester, N.Y.: Royal Historical Society/Boydell Press, 2001.

Hampton, Jean. "The Common Faith of Liberalism." *Pacific Philosophical Quarterly* 75 (1994): 186–216.

———. "Correcting Harms versus Righting Wrongs: The Goal of Retribution." *UCLA Law Review* 39 (1992): 1659–1702.

———. "An Expressive Theory of Retribution." In *Retributivism and Its Critics*, ed. Wesley Cragg, 1–25. Stuttgart: Franz Steiner, 1992.

———. "Forgiveness, Resentment, and Hatred." In Murphy and Hampton, *Forgiveness and Mercy*, 35–87.

———. "The Moral Education Theory of Punishment." *Philosophy and Public Affairs* 13 (1984): 208–38.

———. "A New Theory of Retribution." In *Liability and Responsibility: Essays in Law and Morals*, ed. R. G. Frey and Christopher W. Morris, 377–414. New York: Cambridge University Press, 1991.

———. "The Retributive Idea." In Murphy and Hampton, *Forgiveness and Mercy*, 111–61.

Hardy, Thomas. *The Mayor of Casterbridge*. New York: Penguin, 1994.

Hare, John E. *The Moral Gap: Kantian Ethics, Human Limits, and God's Assistance*. New York: Oxford University Press, 1996.

Harvey, Jean. "The Emerging Practice of Institutional Apologies." *International Journal of Applied Philosophy* 9, no. 2 (1995): 57–66.

———. "Forgiveness as an Obligation of the Moral Life." *International Journal of Moral and Social Studies* 8 (1993): 211–21.

Hegel, G. W. F. *Philosophy of Right*. Trans. S. W. Dyde. Amherst, N.Y.: Prometheus, 1996.

Hershenov, David B. "Restitution and Revenge." *Journal of Philosophy* 96, no. 2 (1999): 79–94.

Hick, John. "Is the Doctrine of Atonement a Mistake?" In Padgett, *Reason and the Christian Religion*, 247–63.

Hieronymi, Pamela. "Articulating an Uncompromising Forgiveness." *Philosophy and Phenomenological Research* 62, no. 3 (2001): 529–55.

Hill, Thomas E., Jr. "Kant on Wrongdoing, Desert, and Punishment." *Law and Philosophy* 18 (1999): 407–41.

Holmgren, Margaret R. "Forgiveness and the Intrinsic Value of Persons." *American Philosophical Quarterly* 30, no. 4 (1993): 341–52.

———. "Punishment as Restitution: The Rights of the Community." *Criminal Justice Ethics* 2 (1983): 36–49.

———. "Self-forgiveness and Responsible Moral Agency." *Journal of Value Inquiry* 32 (1998): 75–91.

Hugo, Victor. *The Hunchback of Notre-Dame.* Trans. Catherine Liu. New York: Modern Library, 2002.

Hunchback of Notre Dame, The. Dir. Gary Trousdale and Kurt Wise, 1996.

Jerphagnon, Lucien. "Repentance." *Philosophy Today* 3 (1959): 176–82.

Johnstone, Gerry, *Restorative Justice: Ideas, Values, Debates.* Portland, Ore.: Willan, 2002.

———, ed. *A Restorative Justice Reader: Texts, Sources, Context.* Portland, Ore.: Willan, 2003.

Johnstone, Gerry, and Daniel W. Van Ness, eds. *The Handbook of Restorative Justice.* Portland, Ore.: Willan, 2007.

———. "The Meaning of Restorative Justice." In Johnstone and Van Ness, *Handbook of Restorative Justice,* 5–23.

Jones, Karen. "Trust as an Affective Attitude." *Ethics* 107 (1996): 4–25.

Kaltenbach, Chris. "Nuns' Order Apologizes for Abusive Conditions of Workers." *Detroit News,* August 10, 2003.

Kant, Immanuel. *Grounding of the Metaphysics of Morals,* 3d ed. Trans. James W. Ellington. Indianapolis: Hackett, 1993.

———. *The Metaphysics of Morals.* Trans. and ed. Mary Gregor. New York: Cambridge University Press, 1996.

———. *Religion within the Limits of Reason Alone.* Trans. T. M. Greene and H. H. Hudson. New York: Harper and Row, 1960.

Kehlmann, Daniel. *Die Vermessung der Welt.* Reinbeck bei Hamburg: Rowohlt, 2005.

Kiss, Elizabeth. "Moral Ambition within and beyond Political Constraints: Reflections on Restorative Justice." In Rotberg and Thompson, *Truth v. Justice,* 68–98.

———. "Saying We're Sorry: Liberal Democracy and the Rhetoric of Collective Identity." *Constellations* 4, no. 3 (1998): 387–98.

Klassen, Pamela E. *Blessed Events: Religion and Home Birth in America.* Princeton, N.J.: Princeton University Press, 2001.

Kolnai, Aurel. "Forgiveness." *Proceedings of the Aristotelian Society* 74 (1974): 91–106.

———. "The Standard Modes of Aversion: Fear, Disgust, and Hatred." *Mind* 107 (1998): 581–95.

Korsgaard, Christine M. *The Sources of Normativity.* New York: Cambridge University Press, 1996.

Kort, Louis F. "What Is an Apology?" In *Injustice and Rectification,* ed. Rodney C. Roberts, 105–10. New York: Peter Lang, 2002.

Kristof, Nicholas D. "Sentenced to Be Raped." *New York Times,* September 29, 2004. http://www.nytimes.com/2004/09/29/opinion/29kris.html (accessed July 8, 2008).

Lacey, Marc. "Atrocity Victims in Uganda Choose to Forgive." *New York Times,* April 18, 2005. http://www.nytimes.com/2005/04/18/international/africa/18uganda.html (accessed July 8, 2008).

Lazare, Aaron. *On Apology*. New York: Oxford University Press, 2004.

Locke, John. *The Second Treatise on Civil Government*. Buffalo, N.Y.: Prometheus, 1986.

Lucas, J. R. "Reflections on the Atonement." In Padgett, *Reason and the Christian Religion*, 265–75.

Mackie, John L. "Morality and the Retributive Emotions." In *Persons and Values*, ed. Joan Mackie and Penelope Mackie, 206–19. Oxford, UK: Clarendon, 1985.

Magdalene Sisters, The. Dir. Peter Mullan, 2002.

Magnificent Obsession. Dir. Douglas Sirk, 1954.

Mahood, Linda. *The Magdalenes: Prostitution in the Nineteenth Century*. New York: Routledge, 1990.

Mason, Michelle. "Contempt as a Moral Attitude." *Ethics* 113 (2003): 234–72.

Mauss, Marcel. *The Gift: The Form and Reason for Exchange in Archaic Societies*. Trans. W. D. Halls. New York: Norton, 1990.

May, Larry. *Sharing Responsibility*. Chicago: University of Chicago Press, 1992.

McDonald, Henry. "Dail and Church Agree Euros 1.3bn Payout to Child Abuse Victims." *London Observer*, January 1, 2006, 3.

McEwan, Ian. *Atonement: A Novel*. New York: Talese/Doubleday, 2001.

McGarry, Patsy. "Abuse Victims Welcome Apology by Nuns: Sisters of Mercy Say Sorry for the Suffering." *Irish Times*, May 6, 2004, 6.

McGrath, Alister E. "The Moral Theory of the Atonement: An Historical and Theological Critique." *Scottish Journal of Theology* 38, no. 2 (1985): 205–20.

Monk, Joanne. "Cleansing Their Souls: Laundries in Institutions for Fallen Women." *Lillith* 9 (1996): 21–32.

Moore, Michael S. "The Moral Worth of Retribution." In *Responsibility, Character, and the Moral Emotions: New Essays in Moral Psychology*, ed. Ferdinand Schoeman, 179–219. New York: Cambridge University Press, 1987.

Morris, Herbert. "Guilt and Suffering." In *On Guilt and Innocence*, 89–110. Berkeley: University of California Press, 1976.

———. "A Paternalistic Theory of Punishment." *American Philosophical Quarterly* 18 (1981): 263–71.

———. "Persons and Punishment." *Monist* 52 (1968): 475–501.

Murphy, Colleen. "The Nature and Importance of Political Reconciliation." PhD diss., University of North Carolina at Chapel Hill, 2004.

Murphy, Jeffrie G. "Forgiveness and Resentment." In Murphy and Hampton, *Forgiveness and Mercy*, 14–34.

———. *Getting Even: Forgiveness and Its Limits*. New York: Oxford University Press, 2003.

———. "Retributivism, Moral Education, and the Liberal State." *Criminal Justice Ethics* 4 (1985): 3–11.

———, and Jean Hampton, eds. *Forgiveness and Mercy*. New York: Cambridge University Press, 1988.

My Name Is Earl. Greg Garcia, 2005–2008.

Narayan, Uma. "Forgiveness, Moral Reassessment, and Reconciliation." In *Explorations of Value*, ed. Thomas Magnell, 169–78. Atlanta: Rodopi, 1997.

Neblett, William. "The Ethics of Guilt." *Journal of Philosophy* 71 (1974): 652–63.

Neusner, Jacob. "Repentance in Judaism." In Etzioni and Carney, *Repentance: A Comparative Perspective*, 60–75.

Nietzsche, Friedrich. *On the Genealogy of Morals*. Trans. Walter Kaufmann and R. J. Hollingdale. New York: Vintage, 1967.

Nozick, Robert. *Anarchy, State, and Utopia*. New York: Basic, 1974.

Nussbaum, Martha C. "Adaptive Preferences and Women's Options." *Economics and Philosophy* 17 (2001): 67–88.

O'Beirne, Kathy. *Kathy's Story: A Childhood Hell inside Ireland's Magdalen Laundries*. Edinburgh: Mainstream Publishing, 2005.

———. *Don't Ever Tell: Kathy's Story: A True Tale of a Childhood Destroyed by Neglect and Fear*. Edinburgh: Mainstream Publishing, 2006.

O'Kane, Maggie. "Washing Away Their Sins." *Guardian*, October 30, 1996, 2.

Padgett, Alan G., ed. *Reason and the Christian Religion: Essays in Honour of Richard Swinburne*. New York: Oxford University Press, 1994.

Pettigrove, Glen. "Apology, Reparations, and the Question of Inherited Guilt." *Public Affairs Quarterly* 17, no. 4 (2003): 319–48.

Pollock, John L., and Joseph Cruz. *Contemporary Theories of Knowledge*, 2d ed. Boulder, Colo.: Rowman and Littlefield, 1999.

Quinn, Philip. "Christian Atonement and Kantian Justification." *Faith and Philosophy* 3 (1986): 440–62.

Radzik, Linda. "Collective Responsibility and Duties to Respond." *Social Theory and Practice* 27, no. 3 (2001): 455–71.

———. "Do Wrongdoers Have a Right to Make Amends?" *Social Theory and Practice* 29, no. 2 (2003): 325–41.

———. "Making Amends." *American Philosophical Quarterly* 41, no. 2, (2004): 141–54.

———. "Offenders, the Making of Amends and the State." In Johnstone and Van Ness, *Handbook of Restorative Justice*, 192–207.

Raftery, Mary. "Restoring Dignity to the Magdalens." *Irish Times*, August 21, 2003, 14.

———. "Sisters of Mercy Break Ranks." *Irish Times*, May 6, 2004, 16.

———, and Eoin O'Sullivan. *Suffer the Little Children: The Inside Story of Ireland's Industrial Schools*. Dublin: New Island, 1999.

Rahman, Fazlur. *Major Themes of the Qur'an*. Minneapolis: Bibliotheca Islamica, 1980.

Rawls, John. *Political Liberalism*. New York: Columbia University Press, 1993.

Richards, Norvin. "Forgiveness." *Ethics* 99 (1988): 77–97.

Rotberg, Robert I., and Dennis Thompson, eds. *Truth v. Justice: The Morality of Truth Commissions*. Princeton, N.J.: Princeton University Press, 2000.

Royce, Josiah. "Atonement." In Royce, *Problem of Christianity*, 165–86.

———. *The Problem of Christianity*. Chicago: University of Chicago Press, 1968.

———. "Time and Guilt." In Royce, *Problem of Christianity*, 143–63.

Sabatier, Auguste. *The Doctrine of the Atonement and Its Historical Evolution*. London: Williams and Norgate, 1904.

Scheler, Max. "Repentance and Rebirth." In *On the Eternal in Man*, trans. Bernard Noble, 35–65. New York: Harper and Brothers, 1960.

Sex in a Cold Climate. Dir. Steve Humphries, 1998.

Sex, Lies, and Videotape. Dir. Steven Soderbergh, 1989.

Silber, John R. "The Ethical Significance of Kant's *Religion*." In *Religion within the Limits of Reason Alone*, trans. T. M Greene and H. H. Hudson, lxxix–cxxxiv. New York: Harper and Row, 1960.

Smith, James M. *Ireland's Magdalen Laundries and the Nation's Architecture of Containment*. Notre Dame, Ind.: University of Notre Dame Press, 2007.

———. "*The Magdalene Sisters*: Evidence, Testimony... Action?" *Signs: Journal of Women in Culture and Society* 32, no. 2 (2007): 431–58.

Snow, Nancy. "Self-forgiveness." *Journal of Value Inquiry* 27 (1993): 75–80.

Strawson, P. F. "Freedom and Resentment." *Proceedings of the British Academy* 48 (1962): 187–211.

Stump, Eleonore. "Atonement according to Aquinas." In *Philosophy and the Christian Faith*, ed. Thomas V. Morris. University of Notre Dame Studies in the Philosophy of Religion, no. 5, 61–91. Notre Dame, Ind.: University of Notre Dame Press, 1988.

Swinburne, Richard. *Responsibility and Atonement*. New York: Oxford University Press, 1989.

Taylor, Gabriele. *Pride, Shame, and Guilt: Emotions of Self-assessment*. New York: Oxford University Press, 1985.

Thompson, Janna. *Taking Responsibility for the Past: Reparation and Historical Injustice*. Malden, Mass.: Polity, 2002.

Twelve Steps and Twelve Traditions. New York: Alcoholics Anonymous World Services, 1981.

Unforgiven. Dir. Clint Eastwood, 1992.

Van Ness, Daniel W., and Mara Schiff. "Satisfaction Guaranteed? The Meaning of Satisfaction in Restorative Justice." In Bazemore and Schiff, *Restorative Community Justice*, 47–62.

Van Ness, Daniel, and Karen Strong. "Restitution to Rehabilitation: How and Why Victims Were Removed from the Criminal Justice Process." *Crime Victims Report* 4, no. 6 (January/February 2001): 81, 92–93.

Virginian, The. Dir. Victor Fleming, 1929.

Waldron, Jeremy. "Superseding Historic Injustice." *Ethics* 103, no. 1 (1992): 4–28.

Walker, Margaret Urban. *Moral Repair: Reconstructing Moral Relations after Wrongdoing*. New York: Cambridge University Press, 2006.

Warren, Jenifer, and Maura Dolan. "Tookie Williams Is Executed." *Los Angeles Times*, December 13, 2005. http://www.latimes.com/news/local/la-me-execution13dec13,0,799154.story?coll=la-home-headlines (accessed July 8, 2008).

Warshow, Robert. "The Westerner." In *The Western Reader*, ed. Jim Kitses and Gregg Rickman, 35–47. New York: Limelight Editions, 1998.

Watkins, Oscar D. *A History of Penance*. New York: Burt Franklin, 1961.

Wertheimer, Roger. "Constraining Condemning." *Ethics* 108 (1998): 489–501.

Wheeler, Samuel C., III. "Reparations Reconsidered." *American Philosophical Quarterly* 34, no. 3 (1997): 301–18.

Wiesenthal, Simon. *The Sunflower*. New York: Schocken, 1976.

———. *The Sunflower: On the Possibilities and Limits of Forgiveness*, rev. and exp. ed. Ed. Harry James Cargas and Bonny V. Fetterman. New York: Schocken, 1998.

Williams, Bernard. *Shame and Necessity*. Berkeley: University of California Press, 1993.

Woestman, William H. *Sacraments: Initiation, Penance, Anointing of the Sick: Commentary on Canons 840–1007*, 2d ed. Ottawa: Faculty of Canon Law, Saint Paul University, 1996.

Wyschogrod, Michael. "Sin and Atonement in Judaism." In *The Human Condition in the Jewish and Christian Traditions*, ed. Frederick E. Greenspahn, 103–28. Hoboken, N.J.: Ktav, 1986.

Yaffe, Martin D. "Liturgy and Ethics: Hermann Cohen and Franz Rosenzweig on the Day of Atonement." *Journal of Religious Ethics* 7, no. 2 (1979): 215–28.

Zehr, Howard. *Changing Lenses: A New Focus for Crime and Justice.* Scottsdale, Penn.: Herald, 1990.

Zhong, Chen-Bo, and Katie Liljenquist. "Washing Away Your Sins: Threatened Morality and Physical Cleansing." *Science* 313 (September 8, 2006): 1451–52.

self-punishment
    concept, 30–33
    by groups, 192–194
    and guilty feelings, 32–38
    as means to reconciliation, 101–103
    as restitution, 26, 50–54
    as retribution, 28–30, 33–44
self-respect
    and forgiveness, 72, 127–128
    and self-forgiveness, 141–144
    of victim, 76, 78, 95, 118, 155–156
sentencing conference, 156–159
Sex in a Cold Climate (documentary film),
    181, 189
Sex, Lies, and Videotape (film), 4, 199*n*4
shame
    and collective wrongdoing, 187–188
    defined, 67
    as non-retributive emotion, 35–37
    and reconciliation, 88–90, 143–144
    as retributive emotion, 32
Silber, John, 210*n*14
Sirk, Douglas, 4
slavery, 176
Smith, James M., 179–181, 212*n*46
Strawson, P. F., 35, 183–184
Stump, Eleonore, 203*n*8
Swinburne, Richard, 203*n*7

Taylor, Gabriele, 88
Thompson, Dennis, 161

Thompson, Janna, 227*n*4
trust
    defined, 114
    not part of theological atonement,
        216*n*59
    as prima facie justified, 129–132
    and reconciliation, 82–85,
        111–118, 123
Truth and Reconciliation Commission,
    120, 164, 224*n*13, 225*n*30
twelve-step programs, 115–116, 134–135

Unforgiven (film), 66

Valentine, Phyllis, 179
Van Ness, Daniel W., 208*n*80, 223*n*1
Verwoerd, Wilhelm, 77, 115, 130, 138
Virginian, The (film), 4, 199*n*3

Walker, Margaret Urban, 219*n*18, 221*n*48
Warshow, Robert, 199*n*3
Wertheimer, Roger, 208*n*77
Wiesenthal, Simon, 146–147
Williams, Bernard, 89, 215*n*34
Williams, Stanley (Tookie), 203*n*66
wrongdoing
    as debt, 25–26, 54
    as threatening relationships, 75–80
Wyschogrod, Michael, 10–11

Yaffe, Martin D., 200–201*n*22

CPSIA information can be obtained at www.ICGtesting.com
Printed in the USA
BVOW02s1353150315

391719BV00003B/19/P

9 780199 767250